Writing Skills for Social Work Students

www.thestudyspace.com – the leading study skills website

Study Skills

Academic Success
Academic Writing Skills for International Students
Ace Your Exam
Becoming a Critical Thinker
Be Well, Learn Well
Brilliant Essays
The Business Student's Phrase Book
Cite Them Right (11th edn)
Critical Thinking and Persuasive Writing for
   Postgraduates
Critical Thinking for Nursing, Health and Social Care
Critical Thinking Skills (3rd edn)
Dissertations and Project Reports
Doing Projects and Reports in Engineering
The Employability Journal
Essentials of Essay Writing
The Exam Skills Handbook (2nd edn)
Get Sorted
The Graduate Career Guidebook (2nd edn)
Great Ways to Learn Anatomy and Physiology
   (2nd edn)
How to Use Your Reading in Your Essays (3rd edn)
How to Write Better Essays (4th edn)
How to Write Your Literature Review
How to Write Your Undergraduate Dissertation
   (3rd edn)
Improve Your Grammar (2nd edn)
The Bloomsbury Student Planner
Mindfulness for Students
Presentation Skills for Students (3rd edn)
The Principles of Writing in Psychology
Professional Writing (4th edn)
Reading at University
Reflective Writing for Nursing, Health and Social
   Work
Simplify Your Study
Skills for Business and Management
Skills for Success (4th edn)
Smart Thinking
Stand Out from the Crowd
The Student Phrase Book (2nd edn)
The Student's Guide to Writing (3rd edn)
Studying in English; Studying Law (4th edn)
Study Skills for International Postgraduates
The Study Skills Handbook
The Study Success Journal
Success in Academic Writing
Teaching Study Skills and Supporting Learning
The Undergraduate Research Handbook (2nd edn)
The Work-Based Learning Student Handbook
   (3rd edn)
Writing for Biomedical Sciences Students
Writing for Engineers (4th edn)
Writing for Nursing and Midwifery Students
   (3rd edn)
Write it Right (2nd edn)

Writing for Science Students
Writing Skills for Education Students
Writing Skills for Social Work Students
You2Uni: Decide, Prepare, Apply

Pocket Study Skills

14 Days to Exam Success (2nd edn)
Analyzing a Case Study
Brilliant Writing Tips for Students
Completing Your PhD
Doing Research (2nd edn)
Getting Critical (2nd edn)
How to Analyze Data
Managing Stress
Planning Your Dissertation (2nd edn)
Planning Your Essay (3rd edn)
Planning Your PhD
Posters and Presentations
Reading and Making Notes (2nd edn)
Referencing and Understanding Plagiarism
   (2nd edn)
Reflective Writing (2nd edn)
Report Writing (2nd edn)
Science Study Skills
Studying with Dyslexia (2nd edn)
Success in Groupwork
Successful Applications
Time Management
Using Feedback to Boost Your Grades
Where's Your Argument?
Where's Your Evidence?
Writing for University (2nd edn)

50 Ways

50 Ways to Boost Your Grades
50 Ways to Boost Your Employability
50 Ways to Excel at Writing
50 Ways to Manage Stress
50 Ways to Manage Time Effectively
50 Ways to Succeed as an International Student

Research Skills

Authoring a PhD
The Foundations of Research (3rd edn)
Getting Published
Getting to Grips with Doctoral Research
The Good Supervisor (2nd edn)
The Lean PhD
Maximizing the Impacts of Academic Research
PhD by Published Work
The PhD Viva
The PhD Writing Handbook
Planning Your Postgraduate Research
The Postgraduate Research Handbook (2nd edn)
The Postgraduate's Guide to Research Ethics
The Professional Doctorate
Structuring Your Research Thesis

For a complete listing of all our titles in this area please visit
https://www.bloomsbury.com/uk/academic/study-skills/

Writing Skills for Social Work Students

Bella Ross

BLOOMSBURY ACADEMIC
LONDON • NEW YORK • OXFORD • NEW DELHI • SYDNEY

BLOOMSBURY ACADEMIC
Bloomsbury Publishing Plc, 50 Bedford Square, London, WC1B 3DP, UK
Bloomsbury Publishing Inc, 1385 Broadway, New York, NY 10018, USA
Bloomsbury Publishing Ireland, 29 Earlsfort Terrace, Dublin 2, D02 AY28, Ireland

BLOOMSBURY, BLOOMSBURY ACADEMIC and the Diana logo
are trademarks of Bloomsbury Publishing Plc

First published 2021 by RED GLOBE PRESS
Reprinted by Bloomsbury Academic, 2022, 2025

A catalogue record for this book is available from the British Library.

A catalogue record for this book is available from the Library of Congress.

ISBN: PB: 978-1-3520-1222-4
ePDF: 978-1-3520-1223-1

Printed and bound in Great Britain

For product safety related questions contact productsafety@bloomsbury.com.

To find out more about our authors and books visit www.bloomsbury.com
and sign up for our newsletters.

Publisher: Helen Caunce
Associate Commissioning Editor: Rosie Maher
Assistant Editor: Verity Rimmer
Cover Designer: Laura de Grasse
Production Editor: Elizabeth Holmes
Senior Marketing Manager: Amanda Woolf

Contents

PART II Key Types of Assessment

Acknowledgements

The authors would like to acknowledge:
Lova Bromander
Catherine Cook
Justin Devlin
Andela Hrovat
Gabby Lamb
Philip Mendes
Hiroko Nakashima
Carmela Otarra
Corey-Logan Robb
Steven Roche
Sussi Ross

Key Skills and How to Navigate Stages of the Writing Process

Understanding and Planning the Task

In this chapter you will learn:

- How to interpret the writing task
- Approaches to brainstorming
- How to plan a writing task
- How to identify the audience and a writing task
- How to use a marking rubric
- Approaches to structuring and organising a text
- How to identify and understand the main components of a written text

---

Understanding the task

The first step to producing a good written assignment is understanding what you are required to do. Often, assessment descriptions are worded in a way that may be a little confusing to understand.

Begin by reading the question and highlighting any terms you are unsure of. Once you have looked up the meanings and definitions of these terms, read the question again. Does it make sense? Do you understand what it is asking you to do?

The following terms (also called question, directive or process words) are commonly found in writing task instructions.

TABLE 1.1	UNDERSTANDING WHAT QUESTION WORDS ACTUALLY MEAN
Analyse	Break the topic into parts and evaluate each one. Identify strengths and weaknesses. Use evidence to support your ideas. Adopt a position/reach a conclusion.
Argue	Provide reasons for, or cite evidence in support of, an idea, action, intervention or theory. Keep in mind that the aim is to persuade the reader of your view.
Assess	Evaluate. Weigh something up using evidence/theory and outlining strengths or weaknesses and opposing views. Provide a persuasive argument.
Compare and contrast	Identify similar and different characteristics of something.
Critique/critically assess/critically evaluate	Analyse and provide an assessment or evaluation based on evidence. Show questioning of sources and good choice of sources. Justify your conclusion. Demonstrate deep understanding of the strengths and limitations of something, leading to well evaluated and logical conclusions. This does not mean only identifying negative aspects.
Define	State the properties of the term in question. Be clear and concise yet include necessary detail.
Demonstrate	Illustrate or explain something using examples.
Describe	Recount according to the facts. This does not mean adding your own interpretation.
Discuss	Analyse critically and include a conclusion. This includes outlining the advantages or disadvantages/strengths and limitations of the topic in question.
Draw on (something)	Use (something) to assist you in your analysis, discussion, etc.
Evaluate	To appraise systematically in order to determine or judge the worth, applicability or significance of something. Assess and provide your viewpoint. Use evidence to support your ideas. Consider opposing viewpoints.
Examine	Look at something in close detail. Identify the key issues and facts of a topic using evidence.
Explore	Use a questioning approach to a topic. Consider opposing viewpoints if relevant.
Highlight	Outline the key issues. This involves making a judgement of what is important.
Justify	Develop a case using evidence to support ideas and viewpoints. Consider opposing viewpoints if relevant before reaching a conclusion.
Outline	Provide the key points. Do not include details.
Review	Outline and critically evaluate a range of similar items (e.g. studies, interventions, approaches). Consider strengths and limitations.
State	Present the facts clearly and concisely. Do not add your own or others' interpretation.
Summarise	State the main points in a short and concise way.

Analysing question words (Suggested solutions on p. 12)

Some of the words in the previous table include elements of being critical while others are mainly focused on being descriptive. Can you identify which ones may include an element of critical analysis?

The following are two examples of a task description.

Writing task example 1: Case study analysis

Read the case study and answer the following questions:

1. Describe the ethical dilemma presented in the case and identify who is affected by the ethical decision.
2. Identify and discuss the issue in relation to human rights, legislation, the social work code of ethics, social work values and ethical theories.
3. Describe your proposed course of action. Identify the advantages and disadvantages of your chosen approach. Justify your approach using ethical decision-making principles.

Writing task example 2: Policy analysis essay

Analyse recent policy debates in an area of social policy (e.g. homelessness, poverty, child abuse, family violence, abortion, youth suicide, etc.) using the social policy literature. Essays must include the following:

1. A description of the present policy.
2. The arguments for and against the policy.
3. A critical assessment of the policy itself, including its impacts on service users – the key arguments for and against the policy. Use the views of opposition parties, lobby groups and academic literature.
4. Recommendations for change – listing a set of proposals for policy change and reform reflecting the views of opposition parties, lobby groups and academic literature.

Understanding the task and interpreting the question (Suggested solutions on p. 12)

- Read the two writing task descriptions again.
- Underline the question words.
- Which task requires critical analysis?
- Which task asks the student to be descriptive?
- Which task asks the student to develop an argument?

Brainstorming

Brainstorming on paper or on screen is a good way to gain an overview of the many thoughts you may have on a topic. You do not need a whiteboard or large piece of paper for the task – a simple notepad and pencil or Word document will do the trick. Write down all the topics, readings, arguments, ideas, themes and topics that you can identify as relevant to the task. Make a note of which of these you need to conduct research into. Do not worry at this stage that the ideas do not link up or seem coherent, just focus on noting down as many relevant thoughts as possible.
These may include:

- Ideas
- Questions
- Thoughts
- Arguments/positions
- Social work values and ethics
- Research/literature

Once you have done this, take a step back and try to identify if any of the thoughts connect or contrast. You can add lines, arrows or circles to help you make sense of these thoughts, as illustrated in the following example:

Essay topic: Discuss the connection between social work, human rights and social justice

- Discuss the connection between:

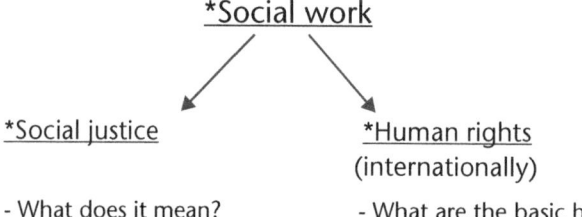

*Social work

*Social justice

- What does it mean?
- Who defines it?
- Link to social work?

*Human rights
(internationally)

- What are the basic human rights?
- Who decides?
- What is the history?
- Link to social work

*UN Universal Declaration of Human Rights

*History of connection between
- Social justice
- Human rights and
- Social work

*Link to laws
(internationally)?

*How can/do social workers promote
social justice and human rights?

If you identified any areas that you need to conduct further research on, this is a good time to do so. Understanding more about the topic will help you to organise your ideas and structure and plan the task.

If you have been given an argumentative or analytical task, you will need to identify what your argument or overall conclusion is. This may require extensive reading and thinking on the topic. Write this in a coherent sentence or two at the top of your notes.

LIMIT THE TASK

It can be tempting to include a range of topics, but one of the most important steps in planning your text is to limit what you will include. This may mean that you need to make some tough decisions. If it helps, create a second document for your backup ideas. You may revisit these during the writing stage or if you realise that you need to expand the content of your writing task.

Writing for the audience and using marking rubrics

At university, you are generally writing for your tutor, who will be assessing and marking your work (though the learning involved is of course to benefit yourself). Keep this in mind when you are working on an assignment. In addition to the task criteria, make sure you read the marking rubric carefully if you have been provided with one. You want to consult the rubric both before you start planning your outline and after you have completed a draft.

The purpose of a marking rubric is to provide clarity and transparency for both the student and the assessor in regard to assessment, and in particular marks. A rubric ensures consistency and validity in marking. It sets out details for each component of the writing task and what is required in order to receive a certain mark for each of those components. An excerpt of a rubric for a literature review task is provided below.

	Does not meet standards	Meets standards	Meets standards exceptionally
Review and evaluation of five published research papers (80%)	• Insufficient research literature identified (i.e. quantity, quality, relevance) • No rationale for choice of studies provided • Relevant description of findings is lacking	• At least three pieces of relevant literature are identified • Some rationale is provided for choice of material • Studies are described with too little or too much detail	• Five pieces of substantive literature are identified • The rationale for choice of material is clearly and succinctly outlined • Studies are accurately described • Findings are comprehensively yet concisely evaluated

	Does not meet standards	Meets standards	Meets standards exceptionally
	• Evaluation of studies and findings is not presented • The organising principle for presenting the literature is lacking or illogical • Trends and/or gaps in knowledge are not identified	• Some evaluation of findings presented • The presentation of the literature is organised logically • Some comparison of findings to inform discussion of trends and gaps in knowledge	• The presentation of the literature uses a logical and effective organisation • Insightful comparison of the findings to inform a thoughtful discussion of the evident trends and gaps in current knowledge
Communicating ideas (20%)	• Poor/inappropriate structure • Academic language and literacy are limited • No use of APA referencing • Limited or no proofreading and editing evident with typographical errors on many pages	• Appropriately organised and structured presentation • Clear literacy and use of academic language • APA referencing used, with minimal errors • Some typographical errors, but generally well proofread	• Well-organised and well-structured paper, which allows the argument to be clearly presented • Excellent literacy skills, with clear and appropriate use of academic language • Accurate use of APA referencing to support the paper's argument • Proofreading and editing are evident, with no typographical errors

In this example, most of the mark is awarded for content and a smaller percentage is awarded for how these ideas are communicated (e.g. structure, editing, referencing). There are six components for the review and evaluation of literature and four components for communicating the ideas.

Note that, in terms of content, most of the mark is awarded for describing and evaluating the articles in a succinct, insightful way with a focus on critical thinking (e.g. evaluation, ability to identify gaps and trends – see pp. 28–36 for more on this) and an ability to use good organising principles (see p. 45). Sometimes a criterion contains a prescribed number of elements that must be included in order to meet the standard of work (e.g. five pieces of substantive literature).

Using a rubric (Suggested solutions on p. 12)

- Read through the rubric on pp. 7–8 and highlight any descriptions that seem unclear.
- Identify any adjectives or adverbs.
- Identify any other qualifying words or phrases.
- Identify any quantitative rather than qualitative criteria.

Once you have completed a writing task, try to evaluate it objectively using the rubric. Take time to read each criterion and be honest with yourself. This process should highlight areas that you need to work on more and give you a good idea of the standard of your writing.

Planning the writing task

Once you have a good understanding of what the task requires and possible ideas of what to write about, the next step is to plan how you will organise and structure your text. In order to do this, you need to have a general idea of the various components of the writing task.

An essay, for example, will contain an introduction, a body and a conclusion. The body typically contains the following components: background, description, analysis, evidence and discussion. How these are arranged within the body, however, can be a key challenge when organising, structuring and writing a text.

The various ways of structuring and organising a social work text will be covered in the following sections. See Chapters 7–12 for advice specific to certain common social work texts.

Structuring a text

When you feel you have understood what the task is asking and you have brainstormed ideas and researched the topic, it is time to start planning your structure. Start by identifying what sort of structure is expected for the written task you are working on. An essay, for example, will have a different structure to a case study analysis or a literature review. Again, on a notepad or in a Word document, you may want to outline the overall structure.

Once you have done this, take a look at your brainstorming notes and see where the different thoughts fit in your outline – both with your argument or conclusion (if relevant to the task) and with the structure. At this stage, you may realise that there are extra components you want to include (for example, you may want to discuss a certain aspect relevant to the background of a topic that you had not thought of before). The following illustrates a possible essay structure outline including the argument:

Essay topic: Discuss the connection between social work, human rights and social justice

Argument:

Social work is closely connected to social justice and human rights internationally.

Introduction:

- Outline topic
- Brief background
    - Social work
    - Social justice
    - Human rights
- Argument
- Structure of paper

Body:

- **Social justice**
    - What does it mean?
    - What defines it?
- **Human rights**
    - What are the basic human rights?
    - Who decides?
    - History?
- **Historical connections** between social work, social justice and human rights internationally
- **Chronological outline** demonstrating close links
- Discuss the ways that social workers today promote social justice

Conclusion:

- Summarise main points
- Flag exceptions where social work is not closely linked to social justice and human rights

   This is the point where you will want to tidy up your thoughts and structure a bit. You may remove things that no longer fit. Remember that each paragraph should contain one main idea. Identify the main idea in each paragraph and how these ideas fit with your assignment. The following activity tests your ability to identify the components of a text and how these components are organised.

ACTIVITY 1.4

Identifying structural components and organising principles (Suggested solutions on p. 13)

- Identify the essay components provided in the example below.
- Identify the organising pattern that could be used in this writing task. Justify your choice. (See p. 45 for more on organising principles.)

Sample essay excerpt: Individual casework vs. community-based interventions

In social work, individual casework intervention focuses on the treatment of individual and/or family problems (Pentland 2009) and originates from individualistic and psychodynamic frameworks (Healy 2012). Individual casework interventions can assist individuals to learn coping skills and adapt to their existing social systems. In contrast, community-based interventions focus on addressing structural issues by accomplishing collective actions (Mendes 2008, p. 24). This essay will outline potential benefits of both casework and community-based interventions for the case study of Kifah. Analysis of these interventions will highlight the strengths and weaknesses of the proposed interventions and identify how they may assist in Kifah's case.

CONSIDERATIONS WHEN STRUCTURING A TEXT

- Considering the word count given for the task; how many paragraphs will you include?
- How many words per paragraph? (There is no hard rule, but generally a paragraph is 100–200 words.)
- Will you be able to explore in enough detail all of your ideas?
- Do you have enough to write about?
- Do your ideas link and follow logically?
- Do all of your paragraphs address the purpose of the writing task?
- Check your plan/structure against the rubric. Does your plan cover all of the requirements of the rubric?

Key points from this chapter

- You need to understand what the task requires, conduct research and plan your writing.
- Read the task description and rubric carefully both before you start and after you have written your draft.
- Carefully consider the structure and organisation of your planned text.

Suggested solutions

ACTIVITY 1.1

Analysing question words

Analyse, argue, assess, critique/critically assess/critically evaluate, discuss, evaluate, examine, explore, highlight, justify, review

ACTIVITY 1.2

Understanding the task and interpreting the question

Note that Example 1 uses the verbs 'describe', 'identify', 'discuss' and 'justify' whereas Example 2 uses the nouns 'analysis', 'description', 'arguments', 'critical assessment' and 'recommendation'.

Although they are worded quite differently, both examples ask the student to begin with a description and build on this with a discussion/critical analysis.

Both tasks require students to develop an argument (i.e. give reasons for, or cite evidence in support of, an idea, action, intervention or theory).

ACTIVITY 1.3

Using a rubric

Adjectives or adverbs:

- Accurate(ly), basic, clear(ly), competent, comprehensively, effective, excellent, (il)logical(ly), inappropriate, insightful, insufficient, lacking, limited, minimal, poor, relevant, simple, substantive, succinctly, thoughtful, well

Other qualifying words or descriptions:

- Too little or too much
- Some
- No

Quantitative criteria:

- At least three/four/five pieces of relevant literature are identified

ACTIVITY 1.4

Identifying structural components and organising principles

This is an excerpt from an introduction section.

This is evident as the topic is briefly outlined followed by the focus and structure of the essay.

An organising principle that could be used for this essay is the advantages and disadvantages pattern to examine the benefits and disadvantages of individual casework vs. community-based interventions. The compare and contrast pattern could be used to highlight the differences between these two approaches. Ideally, a combination of these two organising principles would be used.

Further reading

Bailey, S. (2018). *Academic writing: A handbook for international students.* 5th edition. London: New York: Routledge.

Brick, J., Herke, M. & Wong, D. (2020). *Academic culture: A student's guide to studying at university.* 4th edition. London: Red Globe Press (Available only in ANZ).

Brick, J., Wilson, N., Herke, M. & Wong, D. (2019). *Academic success: A student's guide to studying at university.*. London: Red Globe Press (Available for readers outside ANZ).

Creme, P. & Lea, M. (2008). *Writing at university: A guide for students.* 3rd edition. Maidenhead: Open University Press.

Godwin, J. (2019). *Planning your essay.* 3rd edition. London: Red Globe Press.

Greetham, B. (2018). *How to write better essays.* 4th edition. London: Red Globe Press.

Jordan, R. R. (2003). *Academic writing course: Study skills in English.* Harlow: Pearson Education.

Reading and Note-Making

> **In this chapter you will learn:**
> - How to strategically and efficiently approach reading
> - The difference between reading for the bigger picture and reading for detail
> - The importance of aligning and limiting reading with the assessment task
> - How to make effective notes that are helpful for your study purposes

Reading to understand the topic

When you start reading about a topic, it is always helpful to get a general idea about it before you start digging deeper into the details and complexities. In other words, start with the bigger picture and work your way down to the details.

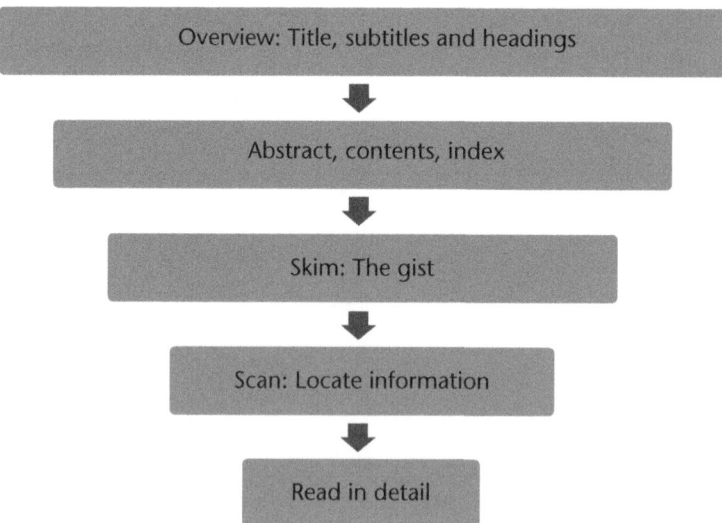

The types of resources you initially use to get an overall understanding of a topic generally differ from the types of resources you will use to understand the details, evidence and arguments within that topic.

When you begin researching a new topic, it is a good idea to start with a general online search of the topic or to consult a textbook. When you feel you know what the main issues are, you can then start researching those in detail and applying your critical thinking skills as you read (see pp. 28–36 for more on critical evaluation and thinking).

The types of resources you can use to understand the nuanced details of a topic are generally journal articles, reports (government or industry) and targeted textbooks.

ACTIVITY 2.1

Evaluating resources (Suggested solutions on p. 22)

Consider the following sample assignment question:

Discuss how social work education in the UK has integrated knowledge of international social work practice and approaches.

Evaluate how you might use the following types of resources to address the question above. Identify the benefits or disadvantages of these resource types.

- Textbook
- Government department report
- Journal article
- Social work association document
- Website

ACTIVITY 2.2

Researching the history of social work (Suggested solutions on p. 23)

Try using the following approach to gain an understanding of the history of social work. Start with an online search of its beginnings worldwide and then narrow down your search to your local context. Consider the following guiding questions.

- Which resource is most helpful to gain an overview?
- Is your initial choice a generic search engine (such as Google) or your university library search engine?
- Was the Wikipedia entry the top entry?
- Does a library search of journal articles help you more with the general history, or are you able to find more detailed articles about your local context?
- Which type of search gives you unexpected results or resources on topics that are related but not entirely on topic?
- Are these unexpected results helpful for your writing task?

Focusing your reading

Often when we start doing research and get involved and immersed in a topic, we might find ourselves a little lost. Sometimes, we get so interested in a topic that we just want to read everything we can. This can lead to a lot of time spent reading. Other times, we might find it difficult to identify what is actually useful to read and what is superfluous to the task at hand.

If you are like most students, you will not have endless time to read before writing an essay. This means that you will need to be targeted in your reading. You will need to set boundaries and identify when something is and is not relevant to your writing task.

You should continually go back to your task criteria, your notes and your writing plan as you read. Ask yourself whether that particular book chapter or journal article is truly helpful for addressing your writing task. You might need to be ruthless and place some resources on the 'maybe to read' list. You can always think of these resources as something you may come back to later if that helps.

Finding key points

When you are faced with a long text, you need to be able to quickly identify the key points. Knowing where to look for key information makes the reading task easier. Use the structure of the text to help you locate the key information that is relevant to your reading purposes. The parts of a text that are particularly useful for this include abstracts, headings and sub-headings, content lists, topic sentences and conclusion sections.

If you are reading a journal article or report, use the abstract or the executive summary to understand the key points or findings, the methodology and sample, and the overall conclusion. These sections are intended as a succinct summary of the main points and are therefore an excellent place to start your reading. Look for signposting words to locate information, e.g. 'The methodology used in this study...' or 'The main finding shows that...'.

The introduction sets out the argument of the text and generally outlines the structure. The conclusion contains a short summary of the key points. Each paragraph typically focuses on one main issue or point which is generally identified in the topic sentence.

Once you have determined that the text is relevant to your purposes, read on using the headings or sub-headings to guide you. If you are still uncertain of whether the text is useful to you, you may want to read the introduction followed by the conclusion. This will provide further context and details. The detail and complexity is found within the text but is often outlined in the concluding section.

Bear in mind that well-written texts are generally structured to contain one main point per paragraph. This main point is often stated in the topic sentence which typically starts the paragraph.

Reading critically is an essential component of any degree, and this will be covered in detail in Chapter 3.

The following annotated example of a journal article illustrates how to identify the different components of a research paper: the research aim, methodology, findings and authors' conclusions. The signposting words are underlined and assist you to locate these components quickly.

Example: Identifying key points in a research article using the abstract

Title: Institutional responsibilities: Providing placement for international students	The title of the article is descriptive of the study.
Abstract: Recent years have seen a rapid increase in the number of international students studying health professional degrees such as social work in Australia and internationally. Research indicates that placement educators perceive that extra time and effort is required to support international students on placement due to, for example, language barriers and cultural and educational differences. <u>This paper reports on</u> findings from a nationwide study investigating the experiences and support needs of placement educators who supervise international social work students. <u>The data consist of</u> 15 in-depth interviews and 66 survey responses from placement educators across Australia. <u>Findings reveal that</u> placement educators feel pressure from education providers to supervise international students, yet they also feel they lack support from the education provider to do so adequately. Placement educators cite a need to increase contact and coordination between agencies and education providers, including clarity around the education providers' expectations of their supervision. Placement educators want closer working relationships between agencies and education providers to ensure rewarding and enriching experiences for both students and placement educators. <u>Such findings suggest that</u> increased institutional support for, and collaboration with, placement educators is required to sustainably maintain quality placements for international students. (Ross, Ta & Oliaro 2020)	The abstract begins with the general context of the study.

The research aim is stated clearly in the sentence: 'This paper reports on findings…'. The methodology is outlined in the sentence starting: 'The data consists of…'. Findings are found in the three sentences starting with: 'Findings reveal that…'.

The authors' conclusion regarding the implications of this study are stated in the sentence starting: 'Such findings suggest that…'. |

ACTIVITY 2.3

Identifying key points (Suggested solutions on p. 23)

Read the abstract below and identify the following key points:

- Relevant background
- Research aim
- Study methodology
- Key findings

Title: The challenges in developing cross-national social work curricula

Abstract: Increasing expectations that social work education incorporate international perspectives and prepare graduates to work in cross-national contexts is resulting in schools of social work in different countries collaborating in curriculum development. This article reports on one such collaboration involving four Australian and four European schools of social work which struggled to develop elements of curriculum that could be used by all partners, and identifies issues that international collaborations need to take account of in the planning and implementing of shared curriculum. (Crisp 2017)

Making notes

There are many reasons for taking notes. While reading widely is helpful for gaining a thorough understanding of a topic, it is always a good idea to take notes as you read. It can be very frustrating when you want to reference that great idea or study that you read about but cannot remember which one it is.

Note-making is not simply about recording information – it is about increasing your knowledge and understanding of a topic. Taking notes allows you to identify what material you have or have not understood, and allows you to highlight the most important points. The main reasons for note-making are:

- To assist you in understanding a text
- To prepare for written assessments or exams
- To help you remember key points
- To avoid plagiarism

Take notes in your own words. This is a way for you to check that you actually understand what you are reading. You will also be able to use these notes in your draft and avoid unintentional plagiarism this way. If you are taking digital notes, it can be tempting to cut and paste, but for the reasons given above, it is best to resist this temptation.

It is generally a good idea to avoid taking too many notes or notes that are very detailed. This will not help you in your writing task, but will instead add confusion. There are exceptions to this, however, as the level of detail needed depends on the writing task. For example, a critique of a journal article will typically require more detailed notes than those required if reading 4–5 journal articles for an essay.

Example: A well-written note

Notes from: Ross, Ta & Oliaro 2020, Institutional responsibilities, Social Work Education	The resource is identified with key citation details provided – This will make it possible for the student to locate the resource again.
Background (pp. 666–667): • Quality placement experiences important for sw education • Quality supervision not always provided • Placement shortages found internationally • International students & EAL speakers disadvantaged in placement provision Findings: Key challenges for supervisors (pp. 671–673): • International & EAL students require additional time and support • Institutions provide inadequate support to supervisors	Sub-headings are used to highlight what the notes refer to: Background, Findings Page ranges are given, allowing the student to return to where the information is located. Good use of bullet points to list issues. Words are omitted to keep notes brief and to the point: are, is. Use of abbreviations and symbols: sw (social work), &, EAL (English as an additional language) These notes have been paraphrased using the student's own words and can therefore be used in the assessment task. Sentences are short and direct.

READING AND NOTE-MAKING ON SCREEN VS. PAPER

Note-making can be done on paper or screen. There are some great functions for notetaking on pdfs for example, or you can collect all your notes in a Word document. Some prefer to take notes by hand, and there is some evidence to suggest that note-taking by hand may be more effective than typing notes on a keyboard (Mangen et al. 2015; Mueller and Oppenheimer 2014) and may lead to better and more original work (Wrigley 2017).

You may also want to consider whether reading on a screen or on paper suits you best, as this may affect your comprehension and recall (Ross et al. 2017).

It can be a good idea to group your notes according to themes, questions, your understanding of how various elements link up, or the organisation or structure of your planned writing task. Consider using a non-linear or visual approach to note-making if that suits you (sometimes also called pattern notes – see Greetham 2018). For example, use the space on the paper or screen to show the relationships between ideas. You may want to start notes in the middle focusing on a central topic, essay question or text and work your way outwards. The following provides an illustration of what a visual approach to note-making for an article may look like:

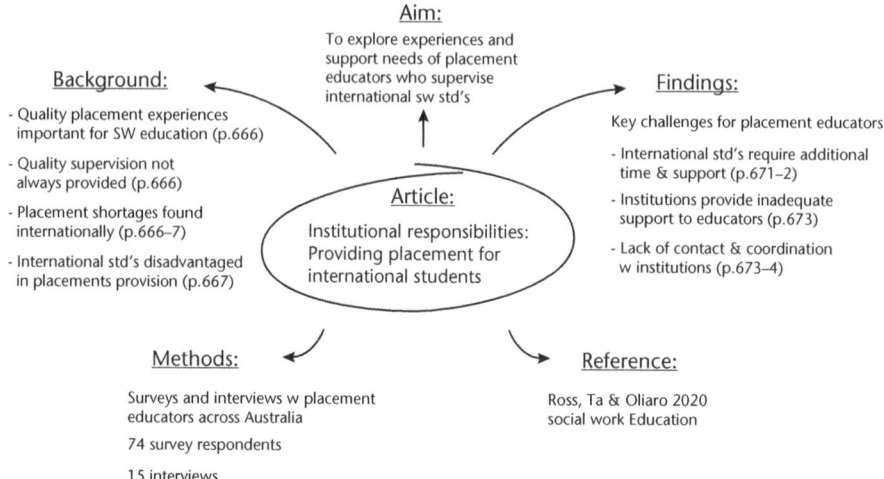

Aim:

To explore experiences and support needs of placement educators who supervise international sw std's

Background:

- Quality placement experiences important for SW education (p.666)
- Quality supervision not always provided (p.666)
- Placement shortages found internationally (p.666–7)
- International std's disadvantaged in placements provision (p.667)

Article:

Institutional responsibilities: Providing placement for international students

Findings:

Key challenges for placement educators:
- International std's require additional time & support (p.671–2)
- Institutions provide inadequate support to educators (p.673)
- Lack of contact & coordination w institutions (p.673–4)

Methods:

Surveys and interviews w placement educators across Australia

74 survey respondents

15 interviews

Reference:

Ross, Ta & Oliaro 2020 social work Education

TIPS: MAKING NOTES

- Be selective – only note what is relevant to your writing task.
- Do not include too much detail – keep notes simple and to the point.
- Paraphrase the key point(s) in your own words.
- Include any important thoughts you have at the time (e.g. critical analyses, identification of author bias).
- Use abbreviations for commonly used words (e.g. sw for social work).
- Use symbols where appropriate (+, =, >).
- Omit unnecessary words such as articles (a/the) or prepositions (in, of).
- Always include the reference (and the page).

Example: Evaluating notes

The example below illustrates how you might make notes for a journal article:

Crisp, B. R. (2017). The challenges in developing cross-national social work curricula. *International Social Work*, 60(1), 6–18.

The annotations highlight which notes are helpful and which may need further information.

This article is useful for my paper as it describes the challenges associated with the internationalisation of social work education. This has increasingly become a focus in higher education institutions in recent decades. See p. 8 in particular. Ref: Crisp 2017 The challenges in developing cross-national social work curricula. International Social Work, 60(1) 6–18.	Unnecessary to state that "the article is useful." Good paraphrasing of the overall point – that there is an increasing focus on the internationalisation of social work education. Inclusion of reference details including page number for future reference.

"Growing expectations of an international curriculum in social work have coincided in recent decades with increasing internationalisation of higher education more generally. Internationalisation is now at least an explicit aspiration, if not a key performance indicator, of many prestigious providers of higher education (Obst and Kuder, 2009). Hence, in recent decades, many universities have developed study tours or exchange programmes which aim to broaden the student experience through living and studying in another country and at the same time gaining credit for study abroad at their home institution." – Crisp	The use of a block quote is not ideal for note-making. It would be better to summarise and paraphrase the information. This reduces the length of the note and the risk of unintentional plagiarism. The reference provided: 'Crisp' will be difficult to identify at a later point in time.
Internationalisation of social work education is difficult but has benefits (Crisp 2017).	The information here is limited and vague. There is not enough detail provided for later use – e.g. what are the difficulties and what are the benefits? The reference information is incomplete, but it is likely adequate for identifying the paper through an online search.
Internationalisation of sw ed. Crisp (2017) outlines challenges to developing international sw curricula: • Differences in degrees, curriculum + learning outcomes across institutions and countries • Local accreditation issues • Differences in focus on legal aspects • Identifying mutually relevant issues between countries These are based on the author's own experience.	Good use of bullet points to succinctly summarise key points. Good use of abbreviations for commonly used words, e.g. sw for social work, ed. for education. Good use of symbol + for 'and'. Reference integrated into note, which may make it difficult to identify at a later stage. Good additional note of what this information is based on.
"While there is no doubt that international movement of students and staff has benefits for those able to travel, to be truly effective, the internationalisation agenda must also engage with students who are not able to study abroad. Incoming study abroad students may provide insights into social work practice in their own countries, but relying on them may be haphazard, particularly if they are few in number. Alternatively, internationalising the social work curriculum may rely on individual teachers drawing on their cross-national experiences (Nagy and Falk, 2000)." Crisp. The challenges in developing cross-national social work curricula.	This note is a block quote and needs to be paraphrased and shortened. The reference is incomplete and may be difficult to identify at a later stage.

Key points from this chapter

- Reading smartly can save you time: Start with the bigger picture before reading in detail
- Key information can be located in predictable places:
  - Headings
  - Abstracts/executive summaries
  - Sub-headings
  - Topic sentences
  - Introductions and conclusions
- Note-making aids recall and understanding when preparing for assignments and exams and helps you avoid plagiarism
- When making notes be succinct, use your own words, use abbreviations and symbols, and always provide the reference and page

---

Suggested solutions

ACTIVITY 2.1

Evaluating resources

Textbook

Benefits: A textbook on the topic will provide a good general overview of the issues, and may also include further readings and references.

Disadvantages: A textbook may not go into adequate detail for the purposes of this assignment (e.g. discussing differences across the UK, providing detailed information on events that impacted on this throughout recent history).

Government department report

This topic may not be addressed in governmental department reports.

Journal article

Benefits: Journal articles on this may be general but may also be very specific. They may, for example, address in detail historical events and the integration of knowledge of international social work practice and approaches, how this may have occurred across the UK, reasons for why this may or may not be the case, and how it has been received by social work educators, students, etc. This level of detail will be needed in order to write a good assignment on the topic.

Disadvantages: It can be difficult to locate articles that are specific enough for the purposes of your assignment task or that align with the issues you would like to explore further.

Social work association document

Benefits: As with a textbook, this sort of document will most likely provide a general overview of the issues and may also include further readings and references.

Disadvantages: Adequate detail of specific aspects of the issues may not be covered.

Website

Benefits: May provide both general and specific information on the topic.

Disadvantages: It is important to ensure that any websites you use to gather information on a topic are reliable, trustworthy and bias-free, as this is not always the case. See p. 38 for more on this.

For the reasons outlined above, it is a good idea to begin your research on this topic by looking at the resources in the following order:

1. Textbook
2. Social work association document
3. Journal article
4. Website

ACTIVITY 2.2

Researching the history of social work

The Wikipedia page was helpful for gaining a broad understanding of the topic, but was not helpful for understanding the topic in my local context. A journal article was helpful for understanding the local context, but was more detailed and complex. Reading the Wikipedia entry first aided my understanding.

A Google search offers journal articles, books, the National Association of Social Work's page on this topic as well as a Wikipedia page on the history of social work.

My initial choice was to use a generic search engine.

The Wikipedia entry was the number 6th option. It covers the topic generally and does not focus on specific contexts or countries.

A library search on the topic generally gave some resources that were not general.

A library search on my local context gave an excellent journal article on the topic.

The generic library search was least helpful for learning about the topic broadly. This was surprising to me.

ACTIVITY 2.3

Identifying key points

Relevant background

Increasing expectations that social work education incorporate international perspectives and prepare graduates to work in cross-national contexts is resulting in schools of social work in different countries collaborating in curriculum development. (This information is found at the beginning of an abstract.)

Research aim

This article reports on how schools of social work in different countries collaborate 'to develop elements of curriculum that could be used by all partners'.

Study methodology

There is little mention of the methodology in the abstract, though it does state that the study 'involves four Australian and four European schools of social work'.

Key findings

The collaborating schools 'struggled to develop elements of curriculum that could be used by all partners'.

The article identifies 'issues that international collaborations need to take account of in the planning and implementing of shared curriculum' but does not state what these issues are.

Further reading

Bailey, S. (2018). *Academic writing: A handbook for international students.* 5th edition. London: New York: Routledge.

Behrens, L. & Rosen, L. J. (2018). *A sequence for academic writing.* 7th edition. Harlow: Pearson Education.

Brick, J., Wilson, N., Wong, D. & Herke, M. (2019). *Academic success: A student's guide to studying at university.* London: Red Globe Press.

Godfrey, J. (2014). *Reading and making notes.* 2nd edition. London: Red Globe Press.

Greetham, B. (2018). *How to write better essays.* 4th edition. London: Red Globe Press.

Critically Evaluating Sources

In this chapter you will learn:
- What is meant by evidence-based practice in the social work context
- How to read, think and reflect critically in your academic writing
- How to bring both a sharp focus and wide lens to your critical reading, thinking and reflection
- How to evaluate the range of source materials you will need to consult when preparing different types of academic papers

What is evidence-based practice?

Evidence-based practice (EBP) means to use the current best evidence when making decisions about practice and client care. These decisions will be shaped by the underpinning values and principles of social work, namely: human rights, social justice and respect for people.

The following general definition of social work by the International Federation of Social Workers (2014) outlines why EBP matters to the profession:

> "Social work is a practice-based profession and an academic discipline that promotes social change and development, social cohesion, and the empowerment and liberation of people. Principles of social justice, human rights, collective responsibility and respect for diversities are central to social work. Underpinned by theories of social work, social sciences, humanities and indigenous knowledge, social work engages people and structures to address life challenges and enhance wellbeing. The above definition may be amplified at national and/or regional levels."

One of the key features in this definition is the use of a range of knowledge ("theories of social work, social sciences, humanities and indigenous knowledge") to engage in problem solving around human wellbeing. Social work decision-making and interventions need to be based on relevant knowledge and being able to identify relevant and good quality information plays a crucial role.

A good analogy is buying a car. Would you make your decision based on the first car you saw, or solely on the recommendation of the salesperson? What other evidence might you seek?

You might draw on your previous personal experience of owning and running a car, or some independent reviews in car magazines, which also include issues such as the cost or the environmental impact. You might consider official safety ratings or online reviews from users.

Similarly, when making decisions in social work practice, you should aim to integrate a range of knowledge or 'evidence' into your decision-making. This could include your own practical experience, observations and recommendations from more experienced staff, research on the topic, as well as considering the implications of your choice.

The following provides a helpful and holistic definition of EBP:

> "Instead of ignoring clinical expertise and client values and expectations, the EBP process requires practitioners to extend themselves beyond the realm of practice wisdom and combine these elements with the best evidence" (Rubin and Parrish 2007: 409).

In other words, when making decisions, you will need to engage with relevant sources of knowledge/evidence to inform and guide you.

There are three key steps in the decision-making process (e.g. Rubin and Parrish 2007: 407), as shown in the following visual:

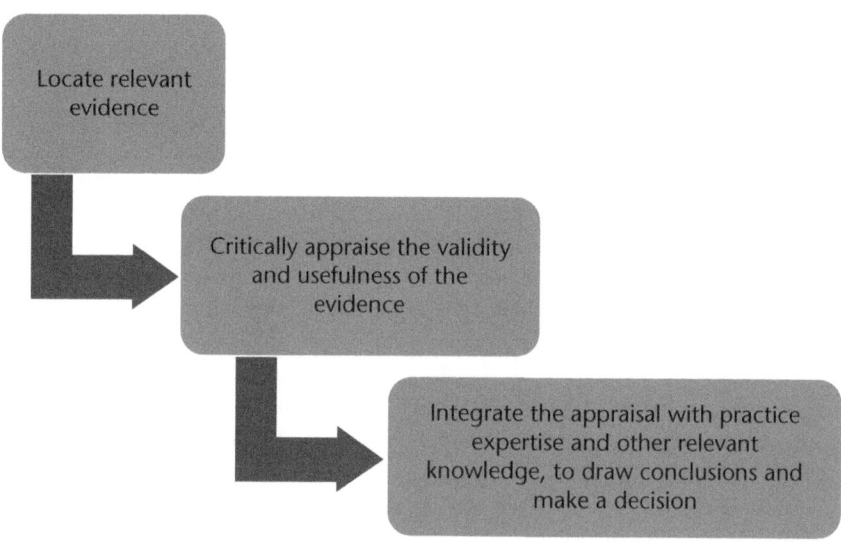

Evidence-based practice has its origins in evidence-based medicine which was defined a number of years ago as the "conscientious, explicit, and judicious use of current best evidence in making decisions about the care of individual patients" (Sackett, Rosenberg, Gray, Haynes and Richardson 1996, p. 71). In the next two decades, these ideas have been debated and developed in a range of other areas of practice. The definition has been widened to emphasise the need to critically examine research evidence, and not simply apply it – i.e. to use one's professional judgement to assess both the validity and quality of the evidence, as well as its applicability to the context. This appraisal needs to be integrated with professional expertise, alongside client values and circumstances (Rubin and Parrish 2007). There is clear recognition that what works in one setting may not be suitable in another. The idea of EBP, however, remains somewhat contentious. Some in social work prefer the term 'evidence-informed', rather than 'evidence-based', to indicate that evidence (as in research evidence) is not the only information on which we base decisions.

Evidence in social work

Social workers tend to think about evidence broadly, where it covers a range of types of knowledge. Overall, EBP requires you to be actively engaged in reading and assessing the materials you are presented with, appraising and integrating these, and not just accepting and applying. This is one aspect of what we mean when we talk about being critical.

Being well informed by evidence in our practice requires us to think about what we mean by evidence in our specific context. Social work assignments require engagement with a wide range of sources. These might include articles or book chapters reporting on research findings, assessment tools, programme/intervention tools, service user perspectives (for a discussion of other terms used, such as 'client', see pp. 188–189), and theoretical frameworks, particularly from areas such as psychology, sociology or community development.

Identifying evidence relevant to social work (Suggested solutions on p. 42)

Identify which of the sources listed below are appropriate to refer to in social work writing.

What other sources of knowledge do you think might be relevant to social work scholarship and practice? (If you are struggling to think of any others, check the reference list of a recent assignment.)

• Blog
• Cases
• Case studies

Commercial website (.com), or websites whose authorship (and therefore evidence base) is not clear, or cannot be verified

Legislation

Magazine

Newspaper reports of research

Opinion piece, for example, in a newspaper

Organisational guidelines

Podcast

Policy papers

Practice accounts of interventions

Social media

Being critical: reading, thinking and reflection

In order to develop your social work identity, it is crucial that you actively engage in thinking critically about issues of relevance to social work in their wider context (Dunk-West 2013). When lecturers ask students to be 'critical' in their writing, however (for example, writing a critical review, critical analysis, critical assessment, etc.), it often creates confusion.

Sometimes students are confused by the similarity in words: critical, criticism, critique. 'Criticism' is a widely used term that means identifying problems and faults. Critique or critical analysis, on the other hand, means to bring a more balanced assessment of strengths and limitations (Jesson, Matheson and Lacey 2011: 67).

Other times, however, students are confused about *how* to be critical. The following quote compares 'uncritical' and 'critical' thinking:

> "Uncritical thinking: automatically believing what you read or are told without pausing to ask whether it is accurate, true or reasonable ...
> Critical thinking: setting out actively to understand what is going on by using reasoning, evaluating evidence and thinking carefully about the process of thinking itself" (Chatfield 2018: 3–6).

This means that, in critical thinking, you are not setting out to find fault; rather, you are seeking to understand what is happening.

Assessing your own critical thinking skills is a good way to begin exploring the topic and help you identify your ability to think critically in your studies. The aim of the following activity is to get you thinking about critical thinking, its components, its application in your studies, and for you to come to some initial conclusions about your areas of strength as well as areas where you might need to focus your attention.

ACTIVITY 3.2

Assessing your critical thinking skills

Read the following statements and tick the box of those you feel you are able to do:

☐ Identify and locate materials relevant to my task.
☐ Question the materials that I find (asking who produced them, for whom, why, etc.).
☐ Compare and evaluate multiple sources.
☐ Weigh up arguments presented to formulate and justify my own position.
☐ Understand my own position, the evidence it is based on, as well as its limitations.

Make a note of the areas where you feel you are doing well. You might even revisit some of the assignments you have already completed, to see if you can see evidence of this in your work, or to see if this is something you have been given positive feedback on.

Also make a note of the areas where you feel you are not so confident. Is this something you have thought about before or is this new information for you?

Read the following statements and tick the box of those you feel you are able to do:

☐ Identify and locate materials relevant to my task.
☐ Question the materials that I find (asking who produced them, for whom, why, etc.).
☐ Compare and evaluate multiple sources.
☐ Weigh up arguments presented to formulate and justify my own position.
☐ Understand my own position, the evidence it is based on, as well as its limitations.

Critical thinking begins with reading. This includes paying close attention to how things are written and defined, and asking questions about the language used.

Language Focus: Reading and using terminology correctly

In the practice of social work (and when we say practice, we mean direct practice, research and policy), we are often confronted with how to understand and respond to violence enacted within relationships and families. There is a lot written about this and a considerable amount of intervention.

As you have been reading in this area, you may have noticed a range of terms being used:

• Domestic violence (DV)
• Domestic abuse (DA)
• Family violence (FV)
• Intimate partner violence (IPV)

While these terms are often used interchangeably, and all incorporate a range of behaviours – including physical, sexual, psychological abuse and, in some settings, coercive control – they have slightly different meanings.

In Australia, "…the term 'domestic violence' typically refers to violence that occurs in domestic settings between people who are, or were, in an intimate relationship, [while] the term 'family violence' also encompasses violence that occurs between other family members" (Western 2018: 84).

In England, the term 'domestic abuse' is often used. This is defined both more broadly (where perpetrators can be ex/current partners or any family member) and more narrowly (involving only those over 16 years) (Citizens Advice Bureau 2019).

In the USA, the term most commonly used is 'intimate partner violence'. The World Health Organization (2012: para. 3) (see also WHO 2017) defines intimate partner violence as "behaviour by an intimate partner or ex-partner that causes physical, sexual or psychological harm, including physical aggression, sexual coercion, psychological abuse and controlling behaviours".

The use of the term 'dating violence' (sometimes confusingly also abbreviated to DV) has also been used in more recent times. It is more typically found in US materials, although Morgan and Chadwick (2009) note the use of this term in Australia and that it brings attention to a younger cohort, not typically considered when discussing domestic or family violence.

Variation in different countries is also evident in terminology regarding violence intervention programmes. For example, in Australia, these are Men's Behaviour Change Programmes, while in the USA, you may see these referred to as Batterer or even Batter programmes. Other settings such as the UK refer to Domestic Violence Perpetrator Programmes.

When reading in any area, you will need to pay attention to what term is being used, and therefore, what the limits of this are. As can be seen from the example above, you cannot assume that all terms are interchangeable. This demonstrates how you need to bring a critical approach to all that you read.

USING TERMINOLOGY CORRECTLY

When terminology matters	How terminology matters
When you are reading 'facts and figures' on a specific issue	It is important that you are clear on the topic and population you are reading about. For example, although FV and DA capture similar experiences, IPV and DV are narrower in focus; this would be reflected in data on the extent of this problem in the community. So, you need to be very clear what definition you are using, and why. Understanding and using terminology correctly will assist you to avoid making erroneous claims. For example, in your reading for an assignment you find that 25% of women report IPV in country A, while in country B 33% of women report having experienced FV. Without being aware of the differing definitions, you may conclude, simplistically, and likely incorrectly, that IPV is a much greater problem in country B.

When terminology matters	How terminology matters
When you are reading and comparing research on a specific topic, particularly from different countries	It is important to identify who has been included as the study population and the limits of the study population. You need to be able to identify whose experiences are captured and whose are excluded. This has important implications for the conclusions that can be drawn. Here you are seeking to understand more fully what is happening, and what is being captured in what you are reading.
When you are examining and comparing legislation and/or policy	A focus on terminology will allow you to examine more clearly and closely how the issue is being framed and who and what is being targeted for attention.
When you are examining theory	Understanding the nuances of how terminology is used will also enable you to understand in more detail how the issue is being framed.

Drawing conclusions and making evidence-based decisions is the end result of a process of engaging with and understanding source materials, considering what they mean in relation to other knowledge (evaluating); then integrating these with your own knowledge and assessment of wider issues (reflection). This is summarised in the visual below:

Critical thinking processes

Critical reading	Critical thinking	Critical reflection	Evidence-based practice
Reading as enquiring – discovery "Becoming the author of one's own understanding" (Kurland, 2010) **Understanding**	Drawing on outside knowledge to evaluate the validity and value of ideas presented **Evaluating and interpreting**	Considering external sources and internal position (prior views) in your assessment Questioning how existing knowledge has been developed **Integrating**	Well informed, ethically justifiable *Conclusions *Decisions *Actions which reflect social work values **Acting**

Being a critical reader: distinguishing between fact and opinion

When you are reading for your studies, it is important from the outset to be able to distinguish whether a statement is fact or the opinion of the author. This is known as being a critical reader and is essential for your academic writing.

- A *fact* is something that can be demonstrated with evidence to be true.
- An *opinion* is a personal belief and is not founded on concrete evidence or certainty.

Sometimes an opinion is worded in a way that makes it look like a fact. You may need to look at whether the author provides a reference for their claims. Some claims are well known to be true and do not need to be referenced – e.g. the sun rises every day.

The language used can help you identify whether a statement is a fact or an opinion:

- 'This is…'
- 'It could be argued…'
- 'Many regard this as…'
- 'It should be viewed as…'
- 'This suggests that…'

Distinguishing between fact and opinion is further complicated as opinion can also be founded on credible research. The key thing to consider when reading critically is whether an opinion is based on evidence or not.

ACTIVITY 3.3

Fact or opinion? (Suggested solutions on p. 42)

- Identify whether the statements below are facts or opinions.
- How do you know they are facts or opinions?

1. Social work has always been a human-rights profession.
2. Women report being victims of domestic violence more often than men.
3. Many would agree that social workers should be vocal advocates for human rights.
4. There is a clear link between social work values and human rights.
5. More attention is needed for male victims of family violence.
6. Jane Addams was granted the 1931 Nobel Peace Prize.
7. A feminist approach is needed in services responding to family and domestic violence.
8. It has been argued that social workers pay more attention to human needs than human rights.

Being clear about facts versus opinions is an excellent starting point in your journey towards critical thinking. The next step is to think about *how* you are reading.

Reading vs. critical reading

A distinction can be made between reading and critical reading. The table below gives an overview of the differences.

A COMPARISON OF READING AND CRITICAL READING		
Guiding questions	**Reading**	**Critical reading**
What is my purpose in reading the text?	To get a basic grasp of the text	To form judgements about *how* a text works
What will I be aiming to do?	Absorbing/understanding	Analysing/interpreting/evaluating
What is my focus in my reading?	What a text *says*	What a text *does* and *means*
What questions will I be asking?	What is the text saying? What information can I get out of it?	How does the text work? How is it argued? What are the choices made, and the patterns that result? What kinds of reasoning and evidence are used? What are the underlying assumptions? What does the text mean?
What do my questions assume?	That the text is correct	That the text needs to be questioned and its meaning interpreted in context
What sort of response am I seeking to write?	Restatement, summary	Description, interpretation, evaluation
Inspired by Duncan (2019)		

The following suggested questions will guide you in considering the intentions and credibility of any text you read (i.e. reading critically):

1. What is the source? What is its reputation?
2. Does the text present a current, up-to-date, view?
3. What year was the work published? What was the social context in which it was published?
4. What is the aim of the text? What is the author's argument?
5. What 'authority' does the author have?

6. Does the author have a bias (or an agenda)? If so, is this acknowledged? What may have been missed by this author?
7. Is the argument backed up by evidence/resources? Is the argument clearly explained?
8. Do the steps of the argument follow logically?
9. Are the conclusions presented in the text replicated elsewhere? (How does it relate to any seminal works?)
10. Is there anything that you do not understand?
11. What else might you need to find out before you draw conclusions based on this text?

The following activity asks you to practise reading critically, and importantly to notice the difference between reading and critical reading.

ACTIVITY 3.4

Reading critically (Suggested solutions on p. 43)

Read the excerpt below and answer the following questions:

1. Begin by *reading*: 'What are the authors presenting?' What is the key information?
2. Engage in *critical reading* of this excerpt, drawing on the series of guiding questions posed above. (Note some will not be possible to answer without further information, such as the whole article.) Remember that the aim is to think about reading as enquiry, where you are seeking to develop your own understanding of what the material says.

Excerpt: The current accepted definition of human trafficking was developed by the UN (2000) when it adopted the ... Palermo Protocol. This protocol has shaped the legislative and policy response of Australia along with other jurisdictions, with responses focusing on prevention, protection and prosecution. Crucial concepts in the current definition are that it involves movement of people, although not necessarily across international borders, and their receipt or harbouring, with the use of deception or coercion for the purposes of exploitation (Fergus, 2005). Consent by the victim is not considered relevant, because of the duplicitous means employed.

Laczko (2005) reminds us that this definition has changed considerably since 1994 when the key features were the crossing of international borders, illegal entry into countries and money changing hands. This earlier definition is arguably now more aligned with the current understanding of people smuggling. Lusk and Lucas (2009), however, risk oversimplifying the issue by claiming the key difference is that smuggling is voluntary. Skilbrei and Tveit's (2008) research challenges this idea of the willing migrant, by highlighting similarities between those who are smuggled and those who are trafficked. Their comparison of Nigerian women trafficked or smuggled to Norway reported similar, multi-layered 'push factors': a culture of migration, combined with societal instability, leading to situations of personal desperation. These patterns are also reflected in the work of Hodge (2008), Kim et al. (2010), Roby (2005) and Rushing (2006). As well as similarities between the background circumstances of the two groups, it is also relevant to note the acknowledged increased risk of migrants (Rushing, 2006), particularly those who use smugglers, subsequently becoming victims of trafficking (Skilbrei and Tveit, 2008). (Flynn, Alston and Mason 2014: 29)

As well as being able to read, understand and evaluate the value of individual texts and studies, it is important that you also bring a wider view to this analysis, and ask questions about *how* this knowledge has been developed. This involves drawing from social work values and principles to guide your questions, for example, connecting these to issues of social justice, human rights, empowerment and representation. It is important that you can identify what patterns emerge when individual texts are considered together. You have begun to think about this in the exercise above, when questioning the author's potential bias and the reputation of the source.

Big picture skills: critical reflection

Critical reflection is where you need to think (and read) much more widely about the topic which you are investigating; this requires you to take a 'helicopter' or 'big picture' view, comparing a range of sources to see what patterns are evident, what these patterns mean, and what these patterns might suggest for knowledge in social work. The following example illustrates this skill.

Example: Critical reflection of an article

Garnham, B. & Bryant, L. (2017). Epistemological erasure: the subject of abuse in the problematization of 'elder abuse'. *Journal of Aging Studies, 41*, 52–59.

This paper focuses its critique on how the problem of elder abuse has been thought about, framed and investigated in research. The authors argue that the almost exclusive focus on measuring risk, and counting risk factors, among other things, takes the focus away from the individual and reduces them to a statistic – a 'victim' of abuse, with no voice and limited agency or power. They argue this to be a problem for both knowledge development – what we 'know' about this problem – and for how we frame our responses as social workers.

This article is an excellent example of asking wider questions, informed by social work values, to examine how the problem has been defined and examined, whose views are absent and the implications for knowledge and practice.

If you are currently working on an assignment, ask yourself the following questions:

- How are the key issues related to your topic defined, and then investigated and written about? How does this framing of the topic align with social work values and principles? For example, if you are writing a paper about risk assessment in hospital discharge, you might want to consider how different professions think about risk. Might social workers have a different focus to physiotherapists, for example? You might want to think more widely again, about how, as a society, we think about risk. Is this typically a bad thing, something to be avoided? Or something to be embraced? How do these ideas align with empowerment as a core social work principle? What are the implications of the current approach to the topic for understanding, 'measuring' and responding to risk?

- What data or information are collected in your topic area? For example, while there have been developments in research and understanding of domestic and family violence in the last decade, for a long time, there were insufficient data. Now we have large surveys seeking to map the extent of D&FV in the community, but still limited research on services – either what is used or what is effective. There is a growing body of qualitative research about women's experiences, but little which seeks the views of children affected. From a social work specific position, what would a social justice framework bring to your assessment?
- Whose views are present and/or absent in your topic area? What do you see as the limitations of the knowledge base? For example, although we have a growing knowledge base in the area of D&FV, we are typically missing the views of marginalised groups, e.g. Aboriginal women, culturally and linguistically diverse (CALD) communities and women with disabilities (Bartels 2010). As a social worker, how might you bring an understanding of human rights and social justice to your analysis of these patterns?
- What are the government or policy priorities in your topic area? Does this shape how we think about this issue, or are encouraged to think about this issue? Are there issues that you think are overlooked or ignored? (We might suggest that was the case with family violence for a very long time.)

Asking these 'bigger' questions requires you to interact with the broader knowledge base, and with a social work framework. It shows that you are seeking to understand more fully what you are reading, so as to become the author of your own understanding (in line with Kurland 2010). Bringing this wider view requires that you engage with the written works of others.

Developing and applying your own ideas by engaging with others

The table below shows some specific ways you can critically engage with the work of others (Roberts 2017). It shows the progression from simple to more complex understanding – to help you to clarify and extend your own ideas. Try to answer the questions to practice applying your learning. Note, you might need to think a bit more, read a bit more, or even just Google, to answer some of these questions.

USING CRITICAL THINKING WHEN ENGAGING WITH THE WORK OF OTHER SCHOLARS		
Characteristics of critical thinking	How others' work can help you develop your arguments	How you would see this in a specific field of practice: family violence (FV)
Being knowledgeable: Knowing the general facts	• Engaging with others' work to demonstrate knowledge	Knowing the basic landscape of FV: facts; prevalence; appropriate sources of information; relevant organisations. *Where would you locate statistical information about FV in your context?*

Characteristics of critical thinking	How others' work can help you develop your arguments	How you would see this in a specific field of practice: family violence (FV)
Being knowledgeable: Knowing the general facts	• Using others' work to support claims	Is there an official government website? Australia has the Australian Bureau of Statistics. The UK has the Office for National Statistics. New Zealand has Stats NZ. The USA has the Bureau of the Census. Are there key peak bodies? For example, Australia has Our Watch [https://www.ourwatch.org.au/] a not-for-profit that also provides relevant data.
Having understanding: Grasping the complexities (by asking critical questions)	• Evaluating others' work • Comparing and contrasting the work of others	Looking for the contentions and contradictions: Coming to grounded conclusions. *What do you see to be some of the challenges of understanding the FV field?* (Perhaps revisit some of the definitional issues we noted above.) You might, for example, think about the challenges of accurate data collection due to differing definitions; under-reporting; recognition of non-physical abuse as violence; 'measuring' violence and its consequences; as well as considering the gendered nature of FV.
Being sceptical: Questioning, both what you read and yourself	• Evaluating others' work	Asking questions about the sources you read: FV is a political area of scholarship, but sometimes author position or partiality is not obvious and needs to be examined. *How can you be sceptical and respectful in your critique?*
Seeing and noting patterns: Using reasoning and evidence	• Building on others' work • Synthesising others' work	Acknowledging key evidence and its sources. Asking questions that bring a wider focus by evaluating the available knowledge on the topic. *What do you see to be some of the big picture questions in the FV area?* *For example, are there perspectives that you think are absent?*
Being flexible: Drawing conclusions cautiously	• Using others' work to support claims • Synthesising others' work • Building on others' work	Drawing reasoned conclusions and being aware that any knowledge is simply the best available at present (Munro & Hardie 2019: 411–427). In the field of D&FV, it is helpful to recognise that that knowledge develops and changes, e.g. (1) we have more knowledge now about how the nature of male violence varies from female – it is more likely to be lethal; (2) there is a growing understanding of how longstanding responses to D&FV (liberal feminist lens) may have indirectly excluded those from minority groups, e.g. CALD or sexually or gender-diverse groups.

Locating evidence: using reliable online sources

Of the wealth of websites available, some are reliable and credible, but others are not. It is important that you can make this distinction in your academic work. When reading an online source, ask yourself the following questions:

- Check the domain (e.g. .com, .edu, .gov). Is this a government website (can be indicated by .gov)? Is it an organisation (can be indicated by .org)? Is it a commercial website (can be indicated by .com)?
- Whose interests is the information presented as? (This question is particularly relevant to a commercial website)
- What is the purpose of the website?
- Who is the intended audience? Is the content appropriately written for the audience?
- Is the language well written and professional? Do all the links work?
- Is the author of the content identified? Is the author credible, experienced, well known or qualified to write about the topic?
- Are the claims backed up by sources/references? Can these be checked independently?
- Does the online source promote a personal opinion or a biased viewpoint?
- Does the online source receive support or funding from anyone or any organisation?

It is important to bring a questioning approach to sources you locate on the internet. Locating information is easy on the internet; you really can find anything, but ease of access does not always bring the most appropriate materials. Most sources available on the web have not been subject to any review for integrity, accuracy, quality or relevance. This means that you will need to do so if you use online sources.

FIVE TIPS FOR SEARCHING FOR LITERATURE

Although a detailed account of search strategies is beyond the scope of this chapter, here are our top five tips for searching for relevant information:

1. Do not just rely on Google. As noted above, Google Scholar is a specific database that only includes scholarly material and can be a good resource. If you are a student at a university, it is best to access Google Scholar via your library; this will allow you to retrieve the fullest range of materials.
2. Search more than one database; do some research to identify those used most in social work and which are appropriate for your topic.
3. Do not search whole sentences or phrases (with connectors like 'and', 'the', 'is', etc.). Just focus on your keywords. Use 'AND' to combine these key terms (e.g. mother AND prison).
4. Think widely about your key terms and the possible terminology used in other settings. Use 'OR' in your search to capture these variations.
5. Some databases use an asterisk to allow you to search a root word and associated words, e.g. parent* will find parent, parenting, parental, etc.

It is also a good idea to seek assistance from a librarian. They can be very helpful in assisting you to develop skills in effective searching.

Evaluating an online source

Which other questions might you ask when evaluating an online source?

Applying critical reading, thinking and reflection to assignments

Studying social work requires that you write a range of assignment types. These range from reviews of existing scholarly literature, case study analyses, research papers, policy analyses and reflections on practice and decision-making. Locating source materials will vary depending on the assignment type, as these different text types all require you to engage with and draw from quite different materials.

The table below presents some general principles and ideas to help you think and engage with a range of different tasks. Always make sure, however, that you work to the specific guidelines and requirements of the assessment task you are doing. We will also address in more detail the writing of some of these types of assessment types throughout the book.

USING SOURCES FOR DIFFERENT ASSESSMENT TYPES

Assessment type	Likely source materials	Location of source materials	Questions to ask when reading *Questions relate to both 'relevance' of the material and 'quality' of the source*
Research literature review or annotated bibliography See Chapter 10	• Research articles • Government-commissioned research reports • Higher degree (e.g. PhD) theses	• Peer-reviewed journals • Government websites (local, state, federal) • Organisational websites • Library databases	How does this article specifically relate to the topic I am examining? Which specific aspects of my topic does this article address? (Think back to your key terms, concepts or variables.) What independent review has been done of this material? How do the claims relate to other, similar research? How has this study been conducted? What are the implications for the findings and conclusions presented? What else do I need to find out?

Assessment type	Likely source materials	Location of source materials	Questions to ask when reading *Questions relate to both 'relevance' of the material and 'quality' of the source*
Essay See Chapter 7	• Research articles • Books on the topic • Books and articles about particular theories • Official statistics • Reports for professionals from government, public bodies and third-sector organisations	• Peer-reviewed journals • Textbooks and monographs • Library databases • Government agencies, public bodies and third-sector organisations	Who has produced this publication and for what purpose? How recent is the publication? Might our knowledge or thinking about an issue have changed in the intervening period? Is the context for the work or ideas reported in this publication relevant for the context I am writing about (e.g. demographics of population, socio-economic context of country)? How similar or different are the issues and points being made in this publication compared with other reading I have undertaken? How compelling is the argument being made – is the argument based on strong evidence, and has the author highlighted the limitations of their evidence, or counter-arguments?
Policy analysis See Chapter 7	• Government and NGO policy documents • Critiques of policy (by advocacy groups, service providers and service users) • Media reports • Opinion pieces	• Government websites (local, state, federal) • Parliamentary speeches websites (e.g. Hansard) • Ministerial websites (for speeches and press releases) • NGO websites • Political party websites • Professional association websites (e.g. The British Association of Social Workers, The Aotearoa New Zealand Association of Social Workers, The Australian Association of Social Workers) • Newspapers (both local and national)	What is the government's stated rationale for introducing the policy? Are there hidden or unstated agendas? What philosophical or ideological ideas are reflected in the policy? (How are they conceptualising 'the problem'? What is the aim of the policy?) What are the key critiques of the policy by opposition parties or advocacy groups? (What bias/position is held by these opponents?) What contrasting ideas inform their critiques? What specific policy reforms are suggested by policy critics?

Assessment type	Likely source materials	Location of source materials	Questions to ask when reading *Questions relate to both 'relevance' of the material and 'quality' of the source*
Reflective text See Chapter 8	• Research articles • Opinion pieces • Codes of ethics and conduct documents	• Peer reviewed journals • Professional association websites (e.g. The British Association of Social Workers, The Aotearoa New Zealand Association of Social Workers, The Australian Association of Social Workers) • Media sites (both local and national)	What influences my practice? How can my beliefs and understandings be enhanced? How can my practice be developed by learning about new ideas and knowledge? What are my own opinions about these sources of information?
Case study analysis See Chapter 9	• Research articles • Books on the topic • Theoretical discussions	• Peer-reviewed journals • Textbooks • Library databases	What is this theory? Does the theory help explain the client's presenting problem (explanatory) or does it seek to provide an intervention (practice)? What is the evidence base for this theory? How has this theory been used with similar cases?

Key points from this chapter

- Critical reading, reflection and thinking skills are crucial in your studies and as a practitioner
- EBP in social work entails critically engaging with the work of other scholars, and examining the evidence presented and its applicability to the context
- A critical reader asks questions of a text as they read, to formulate their own opinion
- Critical reflection requires you to identify patterns by comparing a range of sources
- Social work students and professionals need to engage with a wide range of forms of evidence

Suggested solutions

Identifying evidence relevant to social work

Blog	Inappropriate
Cases	Appropriate
Case studies	Appropriate
Commercial website (.com), or websites whose authorship (and therefore, evidence base) is not clear, or cannot be verified	Likely inappropriate
Legislation	Appropriate
Magazine	Inappropriate
Newspaper reports of research	Generally inappropriate, but can be used as a starting point for research
Opinion piece, for example, in a newspaper	Generally inappropriate, but can be used as a starting point for outlining an argument or research
Organisational guidelines	Appropriate
Podcast	Inappropriate
Policy papers	Appropriate
Practice accounts of interventions	Appropriate
Social media	Inappropriate

Fact or opinion?

The factual statements can all be verified using published resources.

1. Social work has always been a human-rights profession. Fact
2. Women report being victims of domestic violence more often than men. Fact
3. Many would agree that social workers should be vocal advocates for human rights. Fact
4. There is a clear link between social work values and human rights. Fact
5. More attention is needed for male victims of family violence. Opinion
6. Jane Addams was granted the 1931 Nobel Peace Prize. Fact
7. A feminist approach is needed in services responding to family and domestic violence. Opinion
8. It has been argued that social workers pay more attention to human needs than human rights. Opinion

ACTIVITY 3.4

Reading critically

Reading feedback: As you are aiming to get a basic grasp of the text and understand the facts, you will be focused mostly on the information presented. As such, you may have noted the following. The authors provide a current definition of trafficking [which is...]; while they note the difference between human trafficking and people smuggling [which is ...] they highlight similarities in the people who find themselves subject to these circumstances [these are ...].

Critical reading feedback: As you are trying to form your own judgement about what the text is saying, you will be asking deeper questions. You may have considered that the article was published in a reputable peer-reviewed journal [what], reasonably recently [when], which suggests that as a source it has been subject to external and independent review, and that it presents a current view of an issue. You may have asked yourself about the aim and argument. This section sought to clarify and explain the developments over the past two decades in the definition of human trafficking, drawing on the formal United Nations definition. It also sought to problematise how some have thought about and written about this phenomenon in comparison with people smuggling. The authors draw on a range of source materials as evidence [What are these sources? Are they clearly noted, are they relevant?], to argue their conclusion that, while there are definitional differences, mostly related to border crossing, those who are trafficked or smuggled share similar push-pull factors. To be more confident about these claims, you may want to know more about the authors, but particularly about the sources they cite that are less clearly identified.

Further reading

Anastas, J. W. (2014). When is research good evidence? Issues in reading research. *Clinical Social Work Journal, 42*, 107–115. https://doi.org/10.1007/s10615-013-0452-3

Chatfield, T. (2017). *Critical thinking.* London: Sage.

Cottrell, S. (2017). *Critical thinking skills: Effective analysis, argument and reflection.* London: Red Globe Press.

Frohman, R. & Lupton, K. (2020). *Critical thinking for nursing, health and social care.* London: Red Globe Press.

Wallace, M. & Wray, A. (2016). *Critical reading and writing for postgraduates.* 3rd edition. London: Sage.

Drafting a Written Assessment

In this chapter you will learn:
- Common ways to structure a written assessment and when to use them
- The key conventions for writing an introduction, body and conclusion
- How to write a paragraph using the TEAL structure
- Why planning, drafting and revising results in a better piece of writing
- How to write clearly and cohesively using signposting and linking words

The drafting process: planning, drafting and revising

The key stages of planning (see Chapter 1), drafting and revising (see Chapter 6) are all required in order to deliver a good final product. The planning stage is a crucial first step (as discussed on pp. 9–10) for developing a well-structured and thoughtfully presented and/or argued written assessment. You should not expect to write a good text without needing to revise it (perhaps considerably), and it is very common for the first and final drafts to look very different. Initial drafts are a 'work in progress' and are typically written for the writer to clarify their thinking, organise their ideas and structure a written text. In contrast, the final draft is solely for the reader. As you start the actual writing process, remember to regularly consult your writing plan (see pp. 9–10 for details on how to develop an outline and writing plan).

It is generally a good idea to begin the drafting process with the body of the written assessment and write the introduction and conclusion sections after the body of the text is completed. This is because you might change the structure and focus of your text during the drafting process. Regardless of which order you write the sections in, always go back to check that the introduction and conclusions align with the body of the text during the revision stage (see pp. 76–78).

Structuring a written assessment

A written text can present information to the reader in a number of different ways. For example, is an argument presented according to the themes of findings, research studies, order of importance, chronology or locations? Or a combination of some of these? How is the information compared or contrasted? How are the connections and relationships of the information presented? Often the way we structure a text happens in a set way. For example, context is provided before specific examples.

Understanding the different ways to structure a text can help you to make sense of the topic you are writing about. The following table illustrates some common approaches to structuring a social work text and the types of assignments these are commonly used for. See Part 2 for guidance on structuring specific text types.

COMMON APPROACHES TO STRUCTURING A SOCIAL WORK TEXT

Structure type	This may be used to:	Type of assignment
Advantages and disadvantages	• Outline and evaluate different interventions/approaches for working with service users/communities	• Essays • Case study analyses
Cause and effect	• Show the results of certain policies, interventions, approaches, etc. • Outline an action and its effect on your thinking, beliefs, etc. in a reflective text	• Essays • Reflective texts • Placement reports
Chronological	• Describe the history of something – i.e. a field, treatment approach, policy, etc.	• Essays
Compare and contrast	• Evaluate different interventions/ approaches for working with service users/communities	• Essays • Case study analyses
Order of importance	• Indicate your evaluation of issues, or contributing factors to an issue, based on their importance • Structure information according to value – typically from most to least important	• A broad range of writing tasks
Problem and solution	• Focus on, for example, a social problem and its proposed solution(s)	• Essays • Case study analyses
Topical	• Develop a literature review where information is discussed according to topics or themes	• A broad range of writing tasks

There is no single correct way of writing a text, and the structure that you choose for your writing task needs to make sense to you and to the information that you are writing about. It is important to remember that any writing task can be approached in a range of ways.

Using headings and sub-headings to organise ideas

Using headings and sub-headings as you both read and write will help you to organise your ideas and structure your writing. Sub-headings can be removed at a later stage but are useful for guiding your writing as you complete your draft. As you read, it is a good idea to note down important and relevant information in your draft under appropriately detailed headings and sub-headings. This will give you an overview of what the key themes are in the literature and how they may best be organised. These headings and sub-headings can be modified, merged and deleted as you continue reading and reorganising your ideas to suit the writing task. If, for example, after having read a range of sources, you have a heading with only one piece of information and corresponding reference, you should consider merging the heading with another. You can then move your sections around according to how you think they are best presented.

Writing conventions differ between written assessment types

Keep in mind the key conventions used in academic writing when drafting your text. See Chapter 1 for an overview of the standard conventions for what an introduction, body and conclusion section should include.

There may be variation in the conventions and structures depending on the type of written assessment you are writing. Not all written assessment tasks will require an introduction or conclusion, for instance. Variations will be presented and discussed for a range of common social work texts in Part 2. For example, there is considerable difference between the structure of a reflective text (Chapter 8), a case study analysis (Chapter 9) and a placement report (Chapter 12). Refer to these chapters for information regarding assessment-specific writing conventions.

Structuring a paragraph

A good written text can be seen as made up of building blocks. Each paragraph is a building block that is made up of smaller blocks – namely sentences. The sentences need to be arranged in a logical way and all need to add to the main point of the paragraph. The paragraphs likewise need to be arranged in a logical way that all contribute to the purpose of the text. If you achieve this, you are on your way to developing a good solid piece of writing.

A paragraph should ideally use the TEAL (or TEEL or MEAL) structure. It should start with a strong and clear topic sentence. The topic sentence clearly outlines what the topic or main point of the paragraph is. The next component is the evidence, explanation or examples followed by the analysis. The paragraph then concludes with a link back to the main point or argument of the paper.

There are various different structures, but they all follow the same idea, which is to outline the point of the paragraph, then discuss and analyse relevant information, before linking back to the overall purpose of the written assessment.

TEAL: Topic sentence > Evidence/Explanations/Examples > Analysis > Link
MEAL: Main idea > Evidence/Explanations/Examples > Analysis > Link
TEEL: Topic sentence > Explanation > Evidence > Link

Some of these structures also include a C for comment before the L. Not all paragraphs follow one of these structures, however, and you are likely to encounter writing in your studies that does not follow these principles.

Example: A strong paragraph using the TEAL structure: community-based and individual interventions for substance use

Social work interventions can be classified as either community based or individual, both of which have different purposes, benefits and disadvantages.	Topic The topic is clearly outlined.
Community-based interventions focus on the root cause of the issue embedded in a social structure (Ife 2016). An example of a community-based intervention for substance abuse issues is access to professional treatment services or group counselling. In contrast, interventions aimed at the individual focus on the consequence the issue has on the individual (Ife 2016). An intervention targeting an individual experiencing substance abuse may, for example, make use of CBT to overcome addiction by addressing negative or destructive thoughts and feelings. To summarise, individual interventions aim to address the consequences of structural issues and support individual change and/or adaptation, while community-based interventions address the broader social and structural issues impacting on individuals.	Evidence/explanations/examples The writer outlines the main differences between the two approaches: community-based and individual interventions. A summary is also provided.
Failure to address structural issues by focusing on individual issues will inevitably mean that programmes and solutions will not fully solve the root cause of the issues (Ife 2016). At best, these approaches will prevent issues from becoming worse. Further, by addressing underlying structural issues and involving multiple stakeholders within the community network, community-based interventions can provide long-term solutions by preventing the recurrence of the issue in the future. For example, involving a local school as a part of the intervention (e.g. running cultural awareness programmes) can address the issue intergenerationally. This is a benefit that cannot be achieved through individual casework alone.	Analysis – of the evidence The analysis here examines the impacts of not focusing on the underlying issues linking these to community-based interventions. Community-based interventions are argued to have long-term benefits as they can address the underlying issues. Individual interventions are therefore less effective in the long term.

For the reasons outlined above, any approach to substance use issues needs to target not only the individual but also the wider community.	Link to the main purpose/argument of the paper The main purpose here is to outline appropriate interventions for substance use in a particular context specified.

The following activity tests your ability to identify the different components of a paragraph.

ACTIVITY 4.1

Identifying the components of a paragraph (Suggested solutions on p. 52)

• Identify the TEAL components in the following paragraphs:
• Identify whether these paragraphs belong to the introduction, body or conclusion.

Those who support the use of income management tools such as cashless debit cards (CDC) believe that substance abuse and gambling issues cause social harms, anti-social behaviours and child abuse (Forrest 2014; Price 2017). They also claim that people who commit such harms are likely to be on welfare payments and/or unemployed and may be a burden on the taxpayer. A further key argument in favour of income management concerns child safety and risk management, with proponents claiming that urgent measures need to be taken in order to protect the vulnerable (Langton 2017). For these reasons, proponents argue that it is reasonable to regulate their spending on gambling, drugs and alcohol through CDC programmes (Minderoo Foundation 2017; Price 2017). By regulating spending, therefore, these social issues will be minimised.

Opponents of the CDC argue, however, that income management does not address the reasons why people become reliant on alcohol, drugs or gambling, and income management programmes should therefore not be viewed as a solution to a social problem. Those opposed to income management programmes state that they instead violate peoples' human rights to a private life (PJCHR 2015) and impose restrictions on an individual's freedom for the purpose of behavioural change (Mendes 2015). As a result, the use of income management in the Australian context has been linked to paternalism, neoliberalism and colonialism (Bielefeld 2016) where those with authority in government interfere with subordinates under the assumption that they will be 'better off' as a result (Thomas & Buckmaster 2010). These ideas of paternalism, neoliberalism and colonialism will be discussed in detail in the following section.

TIPS: WRITING A PARAGRAPH

- Each paragraph should discuss one key point.
- The topic sentence must clearly address this key point.
- Ensure paragraphs are of roughly equal length.
- A paragraph should ideally comprise a minimum of 3–5 sentences.
- An approximate guide to words per paragraph is 100–200.
- Introduction and conclusion paragraphs are often slightly shorter than body paragraphs.
- Introduction and conclusion paragraphs should each roughly account for 10% of the overall word count. Body paragraphs should be slightly longer.
- These approximates are dependent on assignment type and the style of the writer – i.e. concise writers may require fewer words per paragraph to explore a key point than a less concise writer.

Approaches to cohesive writing, linking paragraphs and signposting

Signposting shows the links and transitions in your writing, allowing it to flow logically and help the reader navigate your assignment. It tells them what is coming up and reminds them of what has already been discussed. It also lets them know what the most important messages are from your writing. The following are some examples:

- *'A/The focus of this paper will be'*
- *'As discussed above (in specific section)'*
- *'Based on the discussion above'*
- *'In conclusion'*
- *'In this paper, I will argue that'*
- *'To summarise'*
- *'This essay will critically analyse'*
- *'This paper argues'*

Linking and signposting words and phrases

Linking words and phrases show how separate ideas relate to one another and add cohesion to a text. There are many different types of linking words as shown in the following table.

Purpose	Examples
To indicate a cause and effect relationship or show comparison and contrast	• 'An implication of this research is that…' • 'Further research is needed to explore this question…' • 'Such findings are in line with…' • 'The finding relates to…' • 'These findings raise the question of whether…' • 'This research is relevant to…' • 'This study provides support for the hypothesis that…'

Purpose	Examples
To indicate that you are talking about something additional	• 'Also' • 'In addition' • 'Further' • 'Furthermore' • 'Moreover'
To indicate that something is similar to something already mentioned	• 'Also' • 'Likewise' • 'Similarly'
To indicate that something is different from something already mentioned	• 'Alternatively' • 'An alternative is' • 'Conversely' • 'However' • 'In comparison' • 'In contrast'
To indicate that you are showing the effects of something	• 'As a consequence' • 'As a result' • 'Consequently' • 'Due to this' • 'For this reason' • 'Therefore'
To introduce examples	• 'For example' • 'For instance' • 'This can be illustrated by' • 'To illustrate this point'
To indicate a sequence, beginning or conclusion	• 'As stated earlier' • 'Finally' • 'Following this' • 'In conclusion' • 'Initially' • 'Overall' • 'This essay has demonstrated that' • 'To summarise'
To narrow the focus of your writing	• 'In particular' • 'In regard to' • 'In relation to' • 'In terms of' • 'Specifically' • 'This is particularly the case with'
To clearly indicate the transition or movement between sections or topics	• 'A further implication of this is' • 'A key factor in the discussion is' • 'Having explored … this essay will now consider' • 'The above discussion reveals that… however' • 'To further understand the issue… this section will'

ACTIVITY 4.2

Signposting and linking words (Suggested solutions on p. 52)

Compare the two paragraphs below. Which is easier to follow? Explain why.

Working with clients with addiction is a complex task. Substance abuse can result in short-term or long-term harm. Significant correlations have been found between addiction and mental illness (Kitchener, Jorm & Kelly 2013; Morgan et al. 2012; Pincock 2013). Those suffering from a mental disorder are six times more likely to have an addiction to alcohol or other drugs (Morgan et al. 2012). When treating a client suffering from addiction, it is important to assess their mental health status.	Working with clients with addiction is a complex task. One reason for this is that substance abuse can result in both short-term or long-term harm. Furthermore, significant correlations have been found between addiction and mental illness (Kitchener, Jorm & Kelly 2013; Morgan et al. 2012; Pincock 2013). For example, those suffering from a mental disorder are six times more likely to have an addiction to alcohol or other drugs (Morgan et al. 2012). When treating a client suffering from addiction, therefore, it is important to assess their mental health status.

ACTIVITY 4.3

Signposting and linking words (Suggested solutions on p. 53)

- Locate the signposts and linking words in the text below.
- Can you rewrite the short paragraph using different linking words and phrases? See the examples above.

Dual diagnosis refers to when an individual is diagnosed with mental health issues and substance use problems simultaneously (Myers, Kroes & Petrakis 2018). Commonly, however, there are various correlations and influences that can be found between substance use and mental illness. For instance, anxiety levels can increase due to caffeine intake and auditory hallucinations can be reduced by a certain amount of alcohol (Myers, Kroes & Petrakis 2018). Due to the range of variances of dual diagnosis, a tailored intervention should therefore be developed according to each individual's specific situation.

Key points from this chapter

- Producing good writing is a process that takes time: As you write a draft, refer back to your writing plan
- Use established structuring approaches to help you draft your text according to how the information should be presented most logically
- Paragraphs are an important building block in your writing. Use a TEAL, TEEL or MEAL structure to ensure you include the necessary components of a paragraph
- Using signposting and linking words will help your reader navigate your text

Suggested solutions

ACTIVITY 4.1

Identifying the components of a paragraph

These paragraphs belong to the body of the text.

T: Those who support the use of income management tools such as cashless debit cards (CDC) believe that substance abuse and gambling issues cause social harms, anti-social behaviours and child abuse (Forrest 2014; Price 2017). E: They also claim that people who commit such harms are likely to be on welfare payments and/or unemployed and may be a burden on the taxpayer. A further key argument in favour of income management concerns child safety and risk management, with proponents claiming that urgent measures need to be taken in order to protect the vulnerable (Langton 2017). A: For these reasons, proponents argue that it is reasonable to regulate their spending on gambling, drugs and alcohol through CDC programmes (Minderoo Foundation 2017; Price 2017). L: By regulating spending, therefore, these social issues will be minimised.

T: Opponents of the CDC argue, however, that income management does not address the reasons why people become reliant on alcohol, drugs or gambling, and income management programmes should therefore not be viewed as a solution to a social problem. E: Those opposed to income management programmes state that they instead violate peoples' human rights to a private life (PJCHR 2015) and impose restrictions on an individual's freedom for the purpose of behavioural change (Mendes 2015). A: As a result, the use of income management in the Australian context has been linked to paternalism, neoliberalism and colonialism (Bielefeld 2016) where those with authority in government interfere with subordinates under the assumption that they will be 'better off' as a result (Thomas & Buckmaster 2010). L: These ideas of paternalism, neoliberalism and colonialism will be discussed in detail in the following section.

ACTIVITY 4.2

Signposting and linking words

The second paragraph contains a range of signposting and linking devices (underlined) that contribute to the flow of the text and make the links between sentences easier to identify.

Working with clients with addiction is a complex task. One reason for this is that substance abuse can result in both short-term or long-term harm. Furthermore, significant correlations have been found between addiction and mental illness (Kitchener, Jorm & Kelly 2013; Morgan et al. 2012; Pincock 2013). For example, those suffering from a mental disorder are six times more likely to have an addiction to alcohol or other drugs (Morgan et al. 2012). When treating a client suffering from addiction, therefore, it is important to assess their mental health status.

ACTIVITY 4.3

Signposting and linking words

Original version

Dual diagnosis refers to when an individual is diagnosed with mental health issues and substance use problems simultaneously (Myers, Kroes & Petrakis 2018). Commonly, <u>however</u>, there are various correlations and influences that can be found between substance use and mental illness. <u>For instance</u>, anxiety levels can increase due to caffeine intake and auditory hallucinations can be reduced by a certain amount of alcohol (Myers, Kroes & Petrakis 2018). Due to the range of variances of dual diagnosis, a tailored intervention should <u>therefore</u> be developed according to each individual's specific situation.

Rewritten version

Dual diagnosis refers to when an individual is diagnosed with co-occurring mental health issues and substance use problems (Myers, Kroes & Petrakis 2018). Various correlations and influences are commonly found between substance use and mental illness, however. Anxiety levels can, <u>for example</u>, increase due to caffeine intake, and auditory hallucinations can be reduced by a certain amount of alcohol (Myers, Kroes & Petrakis 2018). Due to the range of variances of dual diagnosis, a tailored intervention should <u>then</u> be developed according to each individual's specific situation.

Further reading

Bailey, S. (2018). *Academic writing: A handbook for international students.* 5th edition. London, News York: Routledge.

Cottrell, S. (2019). *The study skills handbook.* 5th edition. London: Red Globe Press.

Gimenez, J. (2019). *Writing for nursing and midwifery students.* 3rd edition. London: Red Globe Press.

Godwin, J. (2019). *Planning your essay.* 3rd edition. London: Red Globe Press.

Referencing and Avoiding Plagiarism

In this chapter you will learn:

- Why academic integrity is important
- A definition of plagiarism and its forms
- How to paraphrase, summarise and synthesise texts
- How to correctly use in-text citations (for direct quotes and paraphrasing)
- How to write a reference list using APA and Harvard – the two most commonly used referencing styles for social work
- The benefits and disadvantages of using referencing software programs such as Endnote

What is academic integrity?

Academic integrity is the moral code of academia. It involves using, generating and communicating information in an ethical, collegial, honest and responsible manner. Acknowledging sources correctly shows your reader whose ideas you have used. If you do not acknowledge your sources, this is called plagiarism and may have significant consequences for your studies. Breaches of academic integrity can be both intentional or unintentional (i.e. accidental). Both are serious matters and should be treated in the same way.

Match the following terms to the definitions below:

ACTIVITY 5.1

Check your knowledge (Suggested solutions on p. 70)

1. Contract cheating	a. To take and use another person's ideas and/or manner of expressing them and to pass them off as one's own by failing to give appropriate acknowledgement, including the use of material from any source, staff, students or the internet, published and unpublished works.

2. Plagiarism 3. Cheating 4. Collusion	b. Unauthorised collaboration on assessed written, oral or practical work with another person or persons. c. To seek to obtain an unfair advantage in an examination or written, oral or practical work, required to be submitted or completed for assessment in a course or unit of study. This includes the resubmission of work that has already been assessed in another unit. d. When a third party assists with or wholly writes an assignment or other piece of academic work for you. A third party could be an individual (e.g. a family member, friend or private tutor) or a service (e.g. an assignment writing service, document sharing website, editing or proofreading service or tutoring company). This is known as 'contract cheating' as some form of trade is involved or 'contract' between two or more people in which there could be a form of payment. However, you could also be accused of contract cheating even if there is no exchange of money.

Why does it matter?

It is important that all degrees and qualifications are based on standards as they are essential for maintaining the academic reputation of an institution. Current and prospective students, teaching staff and the wider public need to be sure that the qualifications granted can meet the highest level of scrutiny. If those standards are lowered (because, for example, some students are found to be cheating), that qualification has no meaning and therefore no value. For this reason, it is crucial to uphold high standards of academic integrity. Academic integrity is also important to researchers and research output, which reflects on an institution.

Referencing

Referencing is an important part of scholarly practice. Referencing can take your reader on a journey of scholarly discovery and help them to learn about different researchers' perspectives. References give an insight into the type of research a student has undertaken for a piece of work. The appropriate use of references indicates the relationship between different pieces of research and the accumulation of knowledge on a topic. In addition, when done properly, using citations lends you credibility by demonstrating that you have done research and considered different ideas. Referencing also proves your understanding of a text – it shows that you have not just copied material and pretended it is your own.

Why referencing is needed

Remember that you need to distinguish between your ideas and those of others. That means it needs to be clear to the reader when they are reading the author's ideas (that is you!) and when they are reading the ideas of others (other authors/ experts). As your ideas are not clearly labelled as your own in your assignments, any idea that is not labelled by a reference is assumed to be yours. You need to show the reader which ideas are yours and which belong to someone else. This is achieved by referencing all ideas and findings which are not your own. In the text, you need to insert an indication of the source – this is called an in-text citation. An in-text citation typically includes the last names of the authors as well as the year the source was published. For example, using the APA referencing style, the in-text citation for this chapter is Davidson and Ross (2020). An in-text citation can be used within the text of a sentence (as in the last sentence) or at the end of the sentence in brackets (Davidson & Ross, 2020).

An in-text citation should be used the first time you refer to a source. If it is clear that subsequent information comes from the same source, you do not need to repeat the reference for other sentences in the paragraph, but it must be clear. Readers can then check the full reference that you include in the reference list to see what the source was. This reference in the reference list includes all information required for a reader to find that exact same text in the source.

HOW DO REFERENCES HELP US IN WRITING ASSIGNMENTS?

References:
- Give support for claims/credibility
- Provide background for your work
- Identify opposing views on a subject
- Give breadth and depth to a topic
- Highlight an expert's view

Ways to incorporate sources

There are four ways to use sources:

- Paraphrase
- Summary
- Synthesis
- Direct quotation

To use (direct) *quotes* is to use another author's words exactly as they have written them in the original text.

To *summarise* a text means to succinctly and briefly describe the general meaning of the text in fewer words than used in the original text (e.g. for a source text of 120 words, a summary should be roughly 30 words).

In contrast, *paraphrasing* a text is to restate the general meaning (or focus on one or several components) of the original text in your own words.

Synthesising texts is a more complex task as it involves combining multiple ideas from a range of sources according to findings or topics. It is a bit like weaving, where each thread represents a source. To synthesise, you will first need to be able to paraphrase and summarise.

The following table provides examples of each of these.

Example: Quoted, summarised, paraphrased and synthesised texts

The examples below are based on the articles provided in the reference list.

Quoting	McDonnell et al. (2018) argue that "it is essential for future research to examine these how [sic] children with ASD are processed by child protective services to ensure appropriate identification and supports" (p. 582).
Summarising	Duan et al. (2015) performed a cross-sectional study of 180 self-reporting parents of autistic children in China from September 2012 to September 2013. The childhood autism rating scale (CARS) was used to gauge the severity of autism in children. The aim of the study was to examine the occurrence of child physical maltreatment (CPM) in the sample of autistic children (aged 2–5) and to further explore the risk factors for severity of CPM. The results revealed that CPM is prevalent in households that have autistic children in Central China. Furthermore, a child's age and CARS score were independent risk factors of acute CPM. Therefore, the study recommends creating awareness through education specifically for families of children with high levels of autism. This is to ensure autistic children's welfare is not at risk and to assist them to reach their full developmental potential.
Paraphrasing	People from varying nations, cultural backgrounds and economic systems around the world may define CPM in unique ways (Duan et al., 2015).
Synthesising	Maclean et al. (2017) echo the findings of Duan et al. (2015) for the need to support children and their families with intellectual disabilities (ID) to ensure their safety and overall wellbeing. Similarly, McDonnell et al. (2018) and Wissink et al. (2014) assert that there is currently little research on the topic of maltreatment of children with intellectual disabilities.

When to use quotes?

Quoting is used when you reproduce something from the original text word for word. This should be used the least because you need to demonstrate your understanding and a direct quote does not always do that. Quotes (also called direct quotes) are frequently used for definitions of unfamiliar or new words and phrases. They are often taken from seminal texts or famous speeches to point out an idea or concept that is especially important to that author. Quotes are also used if the origin of a word or phrase is unique to that author.

While it is important to refer to other authors in your academic papers, quotations are not used a great deal in social work. It is often better to summarise or paraphrase, but always ensure you give the original author full credit. Use quotes when the exact words matter (as in a definition), or when the exact wording is relevant to your argument.

You may decide to use a quote in the following circumstances:

- You need to define a particular concept or treatment.
- The quotation is very well expressed.
- The quotation (or wording) is particularly significant to your argument.

The use of too many quotes, especially if they are not well chosen, will often result in lower marks. If you use a lot, the reader may think you have not understood what you have read and that is why you are quoting directly. If you use too many, it can interrupt the flow and rhythm of your writing. Copying directly from another text without acknowledging the source is a serious offence, and is equivalent to stealing. If you decide to use the exact words of someone else, there are specific rules which you must follow.

Steps to quoting

1. Carefully select an appropriate phrase/sentence to quote (e.g. powerful or unique phrasing).
2. Copy the original text, word for word.

    (a) If the quote is short (i.e. less than three lines), put double quotation marks around it and incorporate it into your own text:

    A common definition of secondary analysis is "the use of an existing data set to answer research questions" (Doolan & Froelicher, 2009, p. 204).

    (b) If the quote is longer than approximately 40 words, use a block quote. Do not use quotation marks, but indent the quote and use reduced line spacing:

    Wissink et al. (2014) concluded that:

    it appears extremely difficult in many cases to prove that it really was 'sexual abuse'. This low evidential force is associated with the lack of experts, like doctors, psychologists, psychiatrists and police officers who have been trained to use specific techniques that are needed to talk about abuse with children with (mild) ID (p. 33).

3. Insert a page number with the reference following the quote.

Modifying quotes

Quotations should be copied exactly word for word from the original source, but you can make certain changes:

- If you do not need to use all of the words in the quote, you can use ellipsis (...) to show that you have removed some words.
- If you need to change the capitalisation of a letter, enclose the letter in square brackets: [A].
- If you need to add some words to the quote without changing the meaning (for instance to clarify the meaning), enclose the additional words in square brackets [.........].
- If you believe that there is an error in the original quote (e.g. a spelling error), insert [sic] after the error (e.g. practise [sic] requirements).

When to paraphrase?

Academic writing requires a great deal of paraphrasing (or indirect quotations). Paraphrasing is when you use your own words to explain another author's ideas without changing the original meaning. The major advantage of using indirect quotations is that they show the reader that you have understood the material you have researched. This is because you need to understand something in order to paraphrase it correctly. Paraphrasing also ensures that the text flows naturally from one point to the next and allows you to write in your own voice or style. However, using indirect quotations can reduce your credibility if you incorrectly paraphrase an expert (i.e. if you have misunderstood something). Therefore, you need to make sure you keep the original meaning of the source author. For second language learners, paraphrasing can be time-consuming and requires more mastery of grammar, so extra care is needed.

Paraphrasing clarifies or explains meaning as evident in the text but without any of your own comment or opinion (i.e. without subjective interpretation). In academic writing, providing your opinion is not typically the objective of your work, or useful in responding to the assessment task at hand. Rather, the goal is to seek out and utilise the work of experts and their research to respond to the assessment task, and paraphrasing is a great way to achieve this.

In every subject area and in some styles of writing there are certain conventional or specialised phrases that you cannot paraphrase – this is called 'shared language'. Some examples of shared language you do not need to put in quotation marks include:

- Conventional designations: e.g. child maltreatment
- Preferred bias-free language: e.g. persons with disabilities
- Technical terms and phrases of a discipline or subject: e.g. sexual harassment

PARAPHRASING:

- Shows you have understood the material
- Allows you to use your own 'voice' so that the writing is not 'disjointed' or 'clumsy'
- Enables you to indicate your view of, or the focus of, the work you are paraphrasing

Steps to paraphrasing

1. Read and understand the original text.
2. Check for unfamiliar information.
3. Note the main idea/s and support sentence/s (i.e. omit non-essential words).
4. Without looking at the original text, rewrite in your own words (do not copy), explaining the author's original idea.

5. Compare your version with the original text to check that you have captured its intention and content (i.e. stay true to the original meaning).
6. Reread and edit to make it as clear and succinct as possible.
7. Insert the source reference into your writing.

TIP: WRITE FROM MEMORY

You are less likely to patchwork paraphrase or summarise if you write from memory rather than copy and paste and include a few synonyms. Writing from memory encourages you to change the sentence structure, grammar and vocabulary from the original and results in a stronger paraphrase or summary.

ACTIVITY 5.2

Referencing and paraphrasing (Suggested solutions on p. 71)

Paraphrase the following original passage from the source:

Australian Association of Social Workers (AASW). (2010). *Code of Ethics*. Retrieved from https://www.aasw.au/document/item/1201

The social work profession holds that every human being has a unique and inherent equal worth and that each person has a right to wellbeing, self-fulfillment and self-determination, consistent with the rights and culture of others and a sustainable environment.

Your paraphrase:

_____
_____
_____
_____

When to summarise?

A summary is a shortened version of a text and generally focuses on the main idea/s. In academic writing, it is an essential skill that lets you reduce complex and lengthy texts into a condensed and more readable form. For example, a summary could be a one-sentence overview of a theory. It could also be longer and more detailed, such as a summary of an entire journal article on a topic.

A SUMMARY:

- Enables you to reduce large pieces of information that you can use later
- Encourages you to identify the main ideas of a text
- Encourages you to write clearly and concisely

Steps to summarising

1. Read and understand the original text.
2. Check for unfamiliar information.
3. Identify the main argument and main points.
4. Without looking at the original text, rewrite the main ideas in your own words.
5. Compare your version with the original text to check that you have captured its intention and content (i.e. stay true to the original meaning).
6. Reread and edit your summary to make it as clear and succinct as possible.
7. Insert the source reference into your writing.

Example: Referencing and summarising a research study

The following annotations illustrate a good and a weak summary. References are provided in both APA and Harvard.

APA	McDonnell, C., Boan, A., Bradley, C., Seay, K., Charles, J., & Carpenter L. (2018). Child maltreatment in autism spectrum disorder and intellectual disability: Results from a population-based sample. *The Journal of Child Psychology and Psychiatry, 60*(5), 576–584. doi:10.1111/jcpp.12993	
Harvard	McDonnell, C, Boan, A, Bradley, C, Seay, K, Charles, J & Carpenter, L 2018, 'Child maltreatment in autism spectrum disorder and intellectual disability: results from a population-based sample', *The Journal of Child Psychology and Psychiatry*, vol. 60, no. 5, pp. 576–584, doi: 10.1111/jcpp.12993	
Strong summary	McDonnell et al. (2018) conducted a population-based sample study in the United States, aimed at linking the prevalence and features of maltreatment among children with autism spectrum disorder (ASD)-only, ASD and comorbid intellectual disability (ID), ID-only and controls. ASD is a neurodevelopmental disorder categorised by social communication difficulties, restricted and repetitive behaviours that are frequently comorbid with ID and is defined by significant impairments in intellectual and adaptive functioning. The method applied was record linkage among the Department of Social Services (DSS) and the Autism and Developmental Disabilities Monitoring (ADDM) Network. The findings showed a connection between behaviour and indicated that children with ASD + ID and ID-only were between two and three times more likely to encounter maltreatment. Overall, children with ASD and/or ID are at high risk of maltreatment. The authors conclude that empirically supported assessment and intervention methodologies for detecting traumatic stress linked with maltreatment in children with ASD require immediate attention and action.	The first sentence outlines the study, its aim and its broad methodology. The second sentence provides a necessary definition. The third sentence details the methodology used. The fourth and fifth sentences present the main findings. The final sentence describes the authors' conclusion.

APA	Posselt, M., McDonald, K., Procter, N., de Crespigny, C., & Galletly, C. (2017). Improving the provision of services to young people from refugee backgrounds with comorbid mental health and substance use problems: addressing the barriers. *BMC Public Health, 17*(280), 1–17. doi: 10.1186/s12889-017-4186-y	
Harvard	Posselt, M, McDonald, K, Procter, N, de Crespigny, C & Galletly, C 2017, 'Improving the provision of services to young people from refugee backgrounds with comorbid mental health and substance use problems: addressing the barriers', *BMC Public Health*, vol. 17, no. 280, pp. 1–17, doi: 10.1186/s12889-017-4186-y	
Weak summary	Posselt et al. (2017) conducted a research study into refugees. Refugees are defined as those seeking for clarification of visa. This study used mixed methods. The findings reflected that practitioners lack adequate training and competency in engaging with young refugees and in MH and AOD. The research confirmed the significant gaps in service provision for young refugees who are engaged with service providers because they are not effective at it.	The first sentence does not specify the study's aim or topic. The second sentence gives an inaccurate definition. It also repeats the final word from the previous sentence, which is generally avoided in good writing. The third sentence does not give enough detail about the methods used. The fourth sentence about the findings does not describe the overall results of the study. It is worded in a way that asserts this finding does not have exceptions – use of hedging language needed here (see pp. 103–104 on how to use hedging words appropriately). The concluding sentence does not explain why the service providers were not effective.

ACTIVITY 5.3

Referencing and summarising (Suggested solutions on p. 71)

Summarise in one sentence the following original passage from the source:

Maclean, M., Sims, S., Bower, C., Leonard, H., Stanley, F. & O'Donnell, M. (2017). Maltreatment risk among children with disabilities. *Pediatrics*, 139(4), doi: 10.1542/peds.2016-1817

The prevalence of disabilities in the child protection population suggests the need for awareness by agencies of the scope of issues faced by children in the system and interagency collaboration to ensure children's complex needs are met. In addition, supports are needed for families of children with disabilities not only to assist in meeting the child's health and developmental needs, but also to support parents in managing the often more complex parenting environment, including dealing with challenging behaviour.

Your summary:

_____

_____

_____

_____

When to synthesise?

A synthesis is a discussion drawing on multiple sources and may combine elements of paraphrase and summary. It is often used in literature reviews and when providing background or context for an essay. The skills involved in composing a synthesis include: understanding and summarising; critical reading of sources; establishing the relationship(s) between the sources; and selecting key ideas to help you achieve your purpose (e.g. to compare and contrast differing views on a topic).

SYNTHESISING:

- Enables you to paraphrase and summarise multiple authors' viewpoints
- Lets you draw connections between various pieces of information on a topic
- Allows you to critically assess and respond to authors' views

Steps to synthesising

1. Consider the purpose of your synthesis (i.e. making connections between similar or dissimilar ideas, critical reflection, etc.).
2. Read and understand the original text/s.
3. Underline/label key ideas and passages.
4. Formulate a thesis/argument/claim.
5. Reread sources and note points supporting your argument.
6. Develop a plan to organise the material (see p. 45 on structuring principles).
7. Write a first draft of your synthesis, including source references.
8. Revise your synthesis.

Synthesising (Suggested solutions on p. 72)

The following three original passages are on the topic of transitioning from a child/
adolescent mental health service to an adult mental health service. Reorder, paraphrase and synthesise these source sentences into one paragraph. The first sentence of the synthesis has been provided for you.

Certo, N., Mautz, D., Pumpian, I., Sax, C., Smalley, K., Wade, H. A., Noyes, D.,
Luecking, R., Wechsler, J., & Batterman, N. (2003). Review and discussion of a model
for seamless transition to adulthood. *Education and Training in Developmental
Disabilities, 38*(1), 3–17.

The Transition Service Integration Model (TSIM) takes a different approach by
emphasising the shared responsibility of services such as public schools, post-school
rehabilitation and community-based developers to collaborate, which helps avoid the
need for a navigator to bridge systems.

Nguyen, T., Embrett, M.G., Barr, N.G., Mulvale, G.M., Vania, D.K., Randall, G.E. &
DiRezze, B. (2017). Preventing youth from falling through the cracks between child/
adolescent and adult mental health services: A systematic review of models of care.
Community Mental Health Journal, 53(4), 375–382.

The Transition to Independent Process Model (TIP) model suggests the involvement
of a transition facilitator or navigator to provide one-on-one support for transitioning
youth.

Segal, L., Guy, S., & Furber, G. (2018). What is the current level of mental health service
delivery and expenditure on infants, children, adolescents, and young people in
Australia? *Australian & New Zealand Journal of Psychiatry, 52*(2), 163–172.

Community mental health occasions of service are not always delivered directly to
the young person.

Your synthesis:

The transition from Children and Adolescent Mental Health Services (CAMHS) to
Adult Mental Health Services (AMHS) is a significant challenge for children, their family
members and caregivers.

_____
_____
_____
_____
_____
_____
_____
_____
_____
_____
_____
_____
_____
_____
_____

ACTIVITY 5.5

How should you be using sources in your writing? (Suggested solutions on p. 70)

- Which way should you be using sources the most? Why?
- Which way should you be using sources the least? Why?

Order the four ways of using sources from least used to most used:

☐ Summaries   ☐ Synthesis   ☐ Direct quotation   ☐ Paraphrases

Reporting verbs

When discussing the work of others, it is important to use appropriate verbs. You may need to use reporting verbs (also called verbs of reference) when commenting on or evaluating someone's work, e.g. argue, suggest, emphasise, state, claim, report, indicate, identify and conclude. These words indicate a range of nuanced meanings. Choose your reporting words carefully, as they reflect your view of the quality or relevance of the source and whether you agree, disagree or are neutral in relation to the author's claims. Below are some commonly used reporting verbs found in the social work literature.

Language Focus: Reporting verbs

The following examples demonstrate several of the most commonly used reporting verbs in a social work context.

Appear	The published literature on CJD in which social work is even mentioned is small and a high proportion of this **appears** to mention a social worker only in passing (Manthorpe & Simcock 2018).
Argue	For substance-misuse behaviours and risk factors, this literature generally **argues** that understanding risk factors and substance-misuse behaviours is necessary for developing meaningful intervention and relapse-prevention programmes among those who are accessing treatment or for general outreach within active drug-using networks (Shier et al. 2019).
Conclude	The authors **concluded** that this was a result of the absence of familial, social and cultural connections, typically experienced within their 'collectivist' countries-of-origin (Battaglia, Flynn & Brown 2018).
Describe	Finally, a number of studies **describe** the experiences of opioid use for those that are at particularly higher risk – for both medical and non-medical purposes (Shier et al. 2019).
Find	Some scholarship has **found** links between demographic and life experience factors and opioid use (Manthorpe & Simcock 2018).
Indicate	Further information that emanates from such studies could not only **indicate** improvements to the present model, but could also act as a guide for the development of future child-care approaches (Cameron & Das 2019).

Note	The need for family support, in addition to that for the person with CJD, **is noted** across the literature (Manthorpe & Simcock 2018).
Recognise	In the United States, field education is **recognised** as the signature pedagogy of social work education (Zuchowski et al. 2019).
Report	Specifically, they **report** that the national CJD care team is able to help with the cost of counselling and psychiatric support if only private-sector counselling is available (Manthorpe & Simcock 2018).
Show	Although interaction between domestic and foreign students has **been shown** to have improved over time, due to rapid developments in globalisation, more recent findings suggest that such interactions continue to be strained (Battaglia, Flynn & Brown 2018).
Suggest	They **suggest** that this may indicate that people are unaware that such assistance is available (Manthorpe & Simcock 2018).

ACTIVITY 5.6

Identifying the meaning of reporting verbs (Suggested solutions on p. 72)

When using a reporting verb, you need to be aware of their different connotations and impact on the reader. Your choice of reporting verb can indicate your agreement or disagreement with the author or show a neutral position.

Identify where the reporting verbs (listed below) belong in the columns below. Note that some may be included in more than one column.

Agreement	Neutral	Disagreement	Highlights limitations

LIST OF REPORTING VERBS

Acknowledges	Contradicts	Explains	Proposes
Agrees	Claims	Explores	Questions
Admits	Contrasts	Finds	Reports
Alleges	Criticises	Ignores	Rejects
Affirms	Does not consider	Insists	Reveals
Analyses	Debates	Is limited to	Recognises

Asserts	Describes	Identifies	Says
Appears	Does not take into account	Justifies	Speculates
Argues	Dismisses	Maintains	States
Challenges	Discovers	Observes	Supports
Concludes	Disregards	Overlooks	Shows
Comments		Outlines	Suggests
Confirms			

ACTIVITY 5.7

In-text citations (Suggested solutions on p. 73)

Consider the following student essay extract. Where do you think the author is referring to the work of others? These are the locations where in-text references should be placed. Mark the locations using brackets (......).

According to Banks and Williams, an ethical dilemma arises when there is a difficult choice between two equally undesirable alternatives and it is unclear which choice will be the right one. Unlike an ethical problem, an ethical dilemma is not clearly prescribed by legislations, policies or practice guidelines that have to be followed. In this case, an ethical dilemma arises in regard to Fern's further care plan. Fern is under the age of 18 with limited cognitive ability and developmental delay, which means that fundamentally her parents are responsible for making decisions. As such, it is lawful for Fern's parents to bring her back home and take care of her. However, it is apparent that Fern's physical and emotional condition improved significantly in foster care; by contrast, her parents do not seem to be able to provide adequate care for her. Therefore, in regard to her safety and health, the ethical dilemma arises as to whether to respect her parents' preference and rights to take her home, or respect her well-being and her quality of life by not supporting her to return to her parents' home.

You may need to reference legislation (also referred to as Acts) or cases for some assessment tasks. The following provides examples of how to do this.

Acts and cases are cited in-text by their titles:

The Melbourne Magistrates Court is governed by the Magistrates Court Act 1989 (Vic).

In 1913 in the case of Scott v Scott, The House of Lords found that forcing Mrs Scott to be silent about her divorce proceedings violated her constitutional rights.

Compiling a reference list

The following illustrates how to reference journal articles, books, book chapters, websites and government reports using APA and Harvard referencing styles.

Example: APA and Harvard referencing

APA	Harvard
Journal article	
King, J., Edwards, N., Correa-Velez, I., Hair, S., & Fordyce, M. (2016). Disadvantage and disability: Experiences of people from refugee backgrounds with disability living in Australia. *Disability and the Global South, 3*(1), 843–864.	King, J, Edwards, N, Correa-Velez, I, Hair, S & Fordyce, M 2016, 'Disadvantage and disability: Experiences of people from refugee backgrounds with disability living in Australia', *Disability and the Global South*, vol. 3, no. 1, pp. 843–864.
Book	
Bigby, C., & Frawley, P. (2010). *Social work practice and intellectual disability.* New York, NY: Red Globe Press.	Bigby, C & Frawley, P 2010, *Social work practice and intellectual disability,* Red Globe Press, New York.
Book chapter	
Chenoweth, L. (2017). Disability. In K. Ellem, W.H. Chui & J. Wilson (Eds), *Social work and human services best practice* (pp. 66–90). Annandale, NSW: The Federation Press.	Chenoweth, L 2017, 'Disability', in K Ellem, W H Chui & J Wilson (eds), *Social work and human services best practice*, The Federation Press, Annandale, NSW, pp. 66–90.
Website	
Australian Association of Social Workers (AASW). (2016). *Scope of social work practice in disability.* Retrieved from https://www.aasw.asn.au/document/item/8865	Australian Association of Social Workers (AASW) 2016 *Scope of social work practice in disability,* viewed 10 September 2019, <https://www.aasw.asn.au/document/item/8865>
Government report	
National People with Disabilities and Carer Council. (2009). *Shut out: the experience of people with disabilities and their families in Australia,* National Disability Strategy Consultation Report. Canberra: Australian Government.	National People with Disabilities and Carer Council 2009, *Shut out: the experience of people with disabilities and their families in Australia,* National Disability Strategy Consultation Report, Australian Government, Canberra.

Referencing Acts and cases

Acts and cases get their own sections in the reference list following the references using the headings *Legislation* and *Cases*, respectively. In the following table, we provide examples of legislation and cases from Australia, New Zealand and the UK using APA and Harvard referencing. Note that, in both APA and Harvard referencing styles, all references are in italics except for the jurisdiction written in brackets.

Legislation	
Australia	*Charter of Human Rights and Responsibilities Act 2006* (Vic) *Family Law Act 1975* (Cth)
New Zealand	*The Children's Act 2014* *Child Poverty Reduction Act 2018*

UK	Children and Social Work Act 2017
	Family Law Act 1996
Cases	
Australia	Dickason v Dickason [1913] 17 CLR 50
	R v Sussex Justices: Ex parte Macarthy [1924] 1 KB 256
New Zealand	Hawking v Hawking [2014] NZFC 8194 (3 October 2014)
	Philip Dean Taueki v The Queen [2013] NZSC 146 (17 December 2013)
UK	Reilly v Sandwell Metropolitan Borough Council [2018] UKSC 16
	Re L and B (Children)[2013] UKSC 8

ACTIVITY 5.8

Referencing correctly (Suggested solutions for both Harvard and APA on pp. 73–75)

- Highlight the errors in the following written essay excerpts.
- Identify whether the referencing style is Harvard or APA.

1. As so little is known about formal peer support in a forensic setting, the current study is exploratory in nature (Alston & Bowles, 2003).
2. An exploratory approach to research is "to prepare for a more systematic research in an undeveloped field (Finestone and Kahn 1975, p. 61)".
3. In order to explore the complexity of social reality, McDermott (1966, pp. 6–7) emphasises the importance of a multi-method approach.
4. Sampling strategies are needed, as it is rarely possible to survey the entire population of interest (Alston & Bowles 2003).
5. Coleman & Unrau (2008) emphasise the importance of a systematic data analysis plan from the outset of the research project, in order to reduce the likelihood of biased results.
6. This study (Harms, Middleton, Whyte, Anderson Clarke, Sloan, Hagel and Smith 2011) focused on the perspective of the service user and did not address Indigenous family violence.
7. The narrative/storytelling approach has been used in several research studies with Indigenous people (Bennett et al 2011; Cheers et al 2006; Haldane 2009; Bennett & Zubrzycki 2003).
8. Thematic analysis as detailed by Braun and Clarke will guide the qualitative data analysis for this study, allowing for the identification analysis and reporting of themes from within the data (2006).
9. Qualitative analysis relies on interpretation of the data that has been collected, "using text and explanation to present the data" (Alston & Bowles 2003, p. 203).
10. Some have stated that "critical thinking focuses on the use of language and the practical application of rhetoric and logic" (Bowell and Kemp 2002), while others have stated that "critical thinking refers to the incorporation of critical social science into how we think about our practice" (Brechin et al. 2000).

Referencing software

When you are using a lot of references in your writing, it can be a good idea to organise your in-text citations and your reference list using a software program. The most commonly used are Endnote, RefWorks, Zotero and Mendeley. The benefits and disadvantages of using referencing software are outlined below:

Pros	Cons
• You can save time. • You can export references directly from library databases and other websites. • You can change the referencing style at the click of a mouse.	• It can take a while to learn how to use, and you may need to attend training. • The software sometimes does not work well with other applications such as Turnitin. • Unless you are accessing the software through an institution, it may cost money.

Key points from this chapter

- Academic integrity matters, so you need to ensure that you correctly attribute any idea that is not your own
- Reference lists allow your reader to easily locate the source you used. You must use a consistent referencing style such as APA or Harvard. Check with your tutor/lecturer and refer to your course handbook to see which referencing style you are expected to use
- Legislation and cases require their own separate referencing style

Suggested solutions

ACTIVITY 5.1

Check your knowledge

1 = d, 2 = a, 3 = c, 4 = b

ACTIVITY 5.2

How should you be using sources in your writing?

Paraphrases are often used the most. If you paraphrase you can show the reader that you understand and can write about the topic in your own style or 'voice'.
Paraphrases are often used in combination with summaries and/or part of a synthesis.

Direct quotations should be used the least. If too many have been used, the writer has not adequately included their own 'voice' or independent thinking on the topic.

You may also be marked down for lack of original content, poor ideas development or limited critical thinking.

Least used	Direct quotation
Most used	Paraphrases
Most used	Summaries
Frequently used	Synthesis

ACTIVITY 5.3

Referencing and paraphrasing

Sample paraphrase: According to the Australian Association of Social Workers' Code of Ethics (2010), social workers regard all people as having an intrinsic and distinctive value that encompasses rights such as individual safety and welfare, independence and self-actualisation which are in harmony with sustainability principles and others' rights and cultures.	The use of 'according to' allows the author to first identify the author of the text followed by the relevant idea. This paraphrase has kept the same meaning as the original text. This example uses synonyms and different vocabulary compared with the original (e.g. 'safety', 'welfare', 'encompasses'). This is an important feature of effective paraphrasing. Note that it is acceptable to use 'shared language' which is in common usage in social work, e.g. 'rights'. This paraphrase uses a different focus and grammar structure to the original (e.g. 'social workers' is the subject of this sentence rather than 'the social work profession' in the original. Also, the verb 'consistent' has been changed to the noun phrase 'in harmony').

ACTIVITY 5.4

Referencing and summarising

Sample summary: Maclean et al. (2017) suggest that it is necessary to appropriately support parents of children with disabilities as well as working collaboratively with other agencies to safeguard children's needs.	The use of the authors as the subject of the sentence allows the author to focus on the authors themselves as authorities on the topic. The use of the reporting verb 'suggest' shows the author's neutral attitude to the authors' claims. It is acceptable to use conventional designations in social work, e.g. children with disabilities.

ACTIVITY 5.5

Synthesising

Sample synthesis:	This synthesis has introduced the subject/theme of the paragraph to the reader with a topic sentence.
The transition from Children and Adolescent Mental Health Services (CAMHS) to Adult Mental Health Services (AMHS) is a significant challenge for children, their family members and caregivers. Nguyen et al. (2017) mention that the 'Transition to an Independent Process (TIP)' model recommends one-on-one assistance for transitional aged young people be provided from a 'navigator' or support person. Whereas, Certo et al. (2003) emphasise that multiple services in the 'Transition Service Integration Model' (TSIM) share the obligation for the youth transition process such as from school-based supports, post-school supports and long-term community supports which means a facilitator is not as necessary. However, Segal, Guy and Furber (2018) claim that youth cannot always immediately receive community-based mental health services.	The three source sentences have been paraphrased and have kept the same meaning as the original texts.
	Suitable reporting verbs have been used to state each group of authors' views on the topic.
	Appropriate signal words (e.g. 'however' and 'whereas') have been used to indicate contrasting views on the topic and the link/relationship between the authors.

ACTIVITY 5.6

Identifying the meaning of reporting verbs

Agreement	Neutral	Disagreement	Highlights limitations
Acknowledges	Agrees	Alleges	Disregards
Admits	Appears	Asserts	Does not consider
Affirms	Concludes	Challenges	Does not take into account
Analyses	Contrasts	Comments	Ignores
Argues	Describes	Contradicts	Is limited to
Confirms	Discovers	Claims	Overlooks
Explains	Explores	Criticises	
Identifies	Finds	Debates	
Insists	Maintains	Dismisses	
Maintains	Observes	Justifies	
Observes	Outlines	Questions	
Proposes	Recognises	Rejects	
Reveals	Reports	Speculates	
Shows	Says		
Suggests	States		
Supports			

In-text citations

According to Banks and Williams (2005, p. 1011), an ethical dilemma arises when there is a difficult choice between two equally undesirable alternatives and it is unclear which choice will be the right one. Unlike an ethical problem, an ethical dilemma is not clearly prescribed by legislations, policies or practice guidelines that have to be followed (Banks 2012, p. 20). In this case, an ethical dilemma arises in regard to Fern's further care plan. Fern is under the age of 18 with limited cognitive ability and developmental delay, which means that fundamentally her parents are responsible for making decisions (Family Law Act s61C 1). As such, it is lawful for Fern's parents to bring her back home and take care of her. However, it is apparent that Fern's physical and emotional condition improved significantly in foster care; by contrast, her parents do not seem to be able to provide adequate care for her. Therefore, in regard to her safety and health, the ethical dilemma arises as to whether to respect her parents' preference and rights to take her home, or respect her well-being and her quality of life by not supporting her to return to her parents' home.	When using an author's name, a reference is typically needed. Here the authors' names are in the text, so the in-text citation will just need the year and, potentially also, the page number: Banks and Williams (2005, p. 1011). The clear description of an ethical dilemma needs a reference. Both author and year are required in brackets: (Banks 2012). The citation of the Act is required here.

Referencing correctly

1. As so little is known about formal peer support in a forensic setting, the current study is exploratory in nature. (Alston & Bowles, 2003)
APA
2. An exploratory approach to research is "to prepare for a more systematic research in an undeveloped field (Finestone and Kahn 1975, p. 61)".
Harvard
3. In order to explore the complexity of social reality, McDermott (1966 pp. 6–7) emphasises the importance of a multi-method approach.
Harvard
4. Sampling strategies are needed, as it is rarely possible to survey the entire population of interest (Alston & Bowles 2003).
Harvard
5. Coleman & Unrau (2008) emphasise the importance of a systematic data analysis plan from the outset of the research project, in order to reduce the likelihood of biased results.
Harvard/APA

6. This study (Harms, Middleton, Whyte, Anderson Clarke, Sloan, Hagel <u>and</u> Smith 2011) focused on the perspective of the service user and did not address Indigenous family violence.
Harvard

7. The narrative/storytelling approach has been used in several research studies with Indigenous people (Bennett et al 2011; Cheers et al 2006; Haldane 2009 <u>&</u> Bennett & Zubrzycki 2003).
Harvard

8. Thematic analysis as detailed by Braun and Clarke will guide the qualitative data analysis for this study, allowing for the identification analysis and reporting of themes from within the data <u>(2006)</u>.
Harvard/APA

9. Qualitative analysis relies on interpretation of the data that have been collected, "using text and explanation" (Alston & Bowles 2003, <u>pp.</u> 203).
APA

10. Some have stated that <u>"</u>critical thinking focuses on the use of language and the practical application of rhetoric and logic<u>"</u> (Bowell <u>and</u> Kemp 2002), while others have stated that <u>"</u>critical thinking refers to the incorporation of critical social science into how we think about our practice<u>"</u> (Brechin et al. 2000).
APA

Harvard:	APA:
1. As so little is known about formal peer support in a forensic setting, the current study is exploratory in nature (Alston & Bowles 2003).	1. As so little is known about formal peer support in a forensic setting, the current study is exploratory in nature (Alston & Bowles, 2003).
2. An exploratory approach to research is "to prepare for a more systematic research in an undeveloped field" (Finestone & Kahn 1975, p. 61).	2. An exploratory approach to research is "to prepare for a more systematic research in an undeveloped field" (Finestone & Kahn, 1975, p. 61).
3. In order to explore the complexity of social reality, McDermott (1966, pp. 6–7) emphasises the importance of a multi-method approach.	3. In order to explore the complexity of social reality, McDermott (1966 pp. 6–7) emphasises the importance of a multi-method approach.
4. Sampling strategies are needed, as it is rarely possible to survey the entire population of interest (Alston & Bowles 2003).	4. Sampling strategies are needed, as it is rarely possible to survey the entire population of interest (Alston & Bowles, 2003).
5. Coleman and Unrau (2008) emphasise the importance of a systematic data analysis plan from the outset of the research project, in order to reduce the likelihood of biased results.	5. Coleman and Unrau (2008) emphasise the importance of a systematic data analysis plan from the outset of the research project, in order to reduce the likelihood of biased results.
6. This study (Harms, Middleton, Whyte, Anderson Clarke, Sloan, Hagel & Smith 2011) focused on the perspective of the service user and did not address Indigenous family violence.	6. This study (Harms, Middleton, Whyte, Anderson Clarke, Sloan, Hagel & Smith, 2011) focused on the perspective of the service user and did not address Indigenous family violence.

7. The narrative/storytelling approach has been used in several research studies with Indigenous people (Bennett & Zubrzycki 2003; Bennett et al. 2011; Cheers et al. 2006; Haldane 2009). 8. Thematic analysis as detailed by Braun and Clarke (2006) will guide the qualitative data analysis for this study, allowing for the identification analysis and reporting of themes from within the data. 9. Qualitative analysis relies on interpretation of the data that have been collected, "using text and explanation to present the data" (Alston & Bowles 2003, p. 203). 10. Some have stated that "critical thinking focuses on the use of language and the practical application of rhetoric and logic" (Bowell & Kemp 2002), while others have stated that "critical thinking refers to the incorporation of critical social science into how we think about our practice" (Brechin et al. 2000).	7. The narrative/storytelling approach has been used in several research studies with Indigenous people (Bennett & Zubrzycki, 2003; Bennett et al., 2011; Cheers et al., 2006; Haldane, 2009). 8. Thematic analysis as detailed by Braun and Clarke (2006) will guide the qualitative data analysis for this study, allowing for the identification analysis and reporting of themes from within the data. 9. Qualitative analysis relies on interpretation of the data that have been collected, "using text and explanation to present the data" (Alston & Bowles, 2003, p. 203). 10. Some have stated that "critical thinking focuses on the use of language and the practical application of rhetoric and logic" (Bowell & Kemp, 2002), while others have stated that "critical thinking refers to the incorporation of critical social science into how we think about our practice" (Brechin et al., 2000).

Further reading

Bailey, S. (2018). *Academic writing: A handbook for international students*. 5th edition. London: Routledge.

Behrens, L. & Rosen, L. J. (2018). *A sequence for academic writing*. 7th edition. Harlow: Pearson Education.

Brick, J., Herke, M. & Wong, D. (2020). *Academic culture: A student's guide to studying at university*. 4th edition. London: Red Globe Press.

Creme, P. & Lea, M. (2008). *Writing at university: A guide for students*. 3rd edition. Maidenhead: Open University Press.

Hamp-Lyons, L. & Heasley, B. (2006). *Study writing*. Cambridge: Cambridge University Press.

Swales, J. & Feak, C. (2012). *Academic writing for graduate students: Essential skills and tasks*. 3rd edition. Ann Arbor: Michigan University Press.

Williams, K. & Davis, M. (2017). *Referencing and understanding plagiarism*. 2nd edition. London: Red Globe Press.

Editing and Proofreading

In this chapter you will learn:

- The distinction between editing and proofreading
- How these processes improve the quality of your writing
- Practical approaches to editing and proofreading
- How to maintain a consistent voice throughout a text
- How to correctly use abbreviations, acronyms and capital letters

Why is editing and proofreading important?

Editing and proofreading enhances a piece of written work. This is the stage where the writer steps back and looks critically at what they have produced. Chapter 1 showed you how to start planning a text. This chapter will now show you how to finish off the task in a way that will give you the best possible end result. Careful editing and proofreading will improve the quality of your assignment, so make sure you give this final stage the time and attention it deserves. You'll be surprised how obvious it is to a marker when it has been skipped.

Revision can be a lengthy process and can be done multiple times – each resulting in very different versions of the original draft. Often, the more revisions a written assessment receives, the better the end product. It is a very good idea to allow some time between finishing a draft and starting the revision process. Time away from a piece of work allows you to gain some distance from the writing and see it with a new perspective. Factor this time into your writing process, and aim to have a complete draft several days prior to the assignment deadline to give you enough time to edit and proofread your work before submitting it.

A commonly used strategy for both editing and proofreading is to print out the draft and make notes or corrections on the hardcopy. For some, it may be easier to identify errors or organisational issues on a printed draft, as some find it is easier to follow a text when looking at a paper copy rather than reading on screen (Ross et al. 2017). See also pp. 109–110 for tips on essay revision.

What is editing?

Editing involves looking at the structure of a text and how information is presented (see p. 45 for more on structuring a social work text), whether the voice or style is consistent and appropriate for the task and the audience, whether the argument or focus of the text is clearly conveyed to the reader and whether all the components of the text add to its overall purpose. Editing may require rewriting sections of the text.

In summary, the key functions of editing include:

- Structure
- Voice
- Style
- Argument/focus
- Relevance

A key aspect to editing is to ensure that all of the text is relevant to the task or argument and that unnecessary details, facts or examples are not included. While these may be interesting, you should only include material that is relevant for your purposes. Each paragraph should contain one main point relevant to the task or argument. One way of checking this is to add a short note of no more than 3–4 words next to each paragraph stating what its main point is. You can then check how each paragraph fits within the overall text.

Within each paragraph, ensure that each sentence plays a key role (see pp. 46–47 on paragraph structures such as TEAL). Ensure that you can identify the topic sentence, the evidence, explanations, elaboration and the links. If some sentences do not fit, consider whether they are adding to the paragraph in a meaningful way. If not, delete them.

For more editing and proofreading tips, see also pp. 109–110.

CHECKLIST: EDITING A TEXT

Check that you have addressed all of the items listed below as you edit a text.
- Does the draft align with the task description?
- Does the draft fulfil the marking rubric criteria?
- Is the argument clear and well reasoned using appropriate evidence (see Chapter 3 on critically evaluating evidence)?

- Is the information logically organised?
- Is the draft clearly structured?
- Does the introduction paragraph clearly outline the argument or purpose of the task and the structure of the text?
- Are all the paragraphs relevant to the argument or purpose of the task?
- Are signposting and linking words used appropriately? (See Chapter 4)
- Is there any repetition?
- Do the introduction and conclusion paragraphs align?
- Do the paragraphs follow coherently from one another?
- Does the conclusion paragraph summarise the key points only and not add anything new?
- Is the language and expression consistent and appropriate throughout the text?

Example: Comparing a draft and edited essay excerpt

The following excerpt is taken from an essay draft about aged care. This essay discusses the considerations and care approaches needed for an increasingly ageing population.

The edited version shows the improvements made to the original.

Original version	
The community is the primary base of care for older people. Recent reforms in aged care have emphasised consumer-directed care (CDC) to give choice and control to the service user and enhance their independence, wellbeing and reablement (Braddy & Erhardt-Rumpe 2018). CDC is well implemented when it ensures a good relationship with the older person and their quality of care through care coordination, communication and continuity of care (Prgomet et al. 2017).	The topic sentence could be either the first or the second sentence. As a result, the paragraph does not have a clear argument and is difficult to follow.
	Further evidence and examples are needed to back up the claim in the third sentence.
	A link is lacking at the end of this paragraph to the main argument. Without it, the paragraph ends abruptly and is incomplete.
As modern Western family structures change, a whole-community approach will be needed (Hughes & Heycox 2010). Health services should identify carers and the level of their involvement as well as build supportive social networks (Hughes & Heycox 2010). Eventually, the whole-community approach should aim to address negative stereotypes towards ageing so that older people can better participate in society. Health services can engage in inter-sectorial work with non-government organisations such as Men's Sheds and Lively, which aim to enhance social connectedness and intergenerational communication.	In the second paragraph, the first sentence is the topic sentence, though it is incomplete with some further detail required.
	Good explanation and use of evidence and examples to support the writer's point.
	A concluding link is needed at the end of this paragraph.
	Signposting and linking words are needed to ensure the flow and linking of the sentences in this paragraph.
	The voice and style are consistent and appropriate throughout the two paragraphs.

Edited version

Consumer-directed care (CDC) has been found to enhance health care for older people. This is recognised in recent reforms in aged care which highlight how CDC gives choice and control to the service user and enhances their independence, wellbeing and reablement (Braddy & Erhardt-Rumpe 2018). CDC is well-implemented when it ensures a good relationship with the older person and their quality of care through care coordination, communication and continuity of care (Prgomet et al. 2017). This requires that hospital social workers have a strong partnership with the older cohort to not only support their care choices to sustain their independence and autonomy, but also deal with any challenges to implementing CDC. These challenges may relate to patient and family involvement in decision-making, quality assurance (Ray et al. 2015), cost-effectiveness of services and the needs of a larger population (Berkman et al. 2006). Hospital social workers need to balance these competing demands while counselling service users and monitoring their CDC.

As modern Western family structures change, a whole-community approach will be needed to cater for the needs of older people (Hughes & Heycox 2010). This means that health services should identify carers and the level of their involvement as well as build supportive social networks (Hughes & Heycox 2010). Eventually, the whole-community approach should aim to address negative stereotypes towards ageing so that older people can better participate in society. For example, health services can engage in inter-sectorial work with non-government organisations such as Men's Sheds and Lively, which aim to enhance social connectedness and intergenerational communication. The efforts described above may assist in adapting to the needs of aged care as caring roles and social structures in society change.

The sentence: 'The community is the primary base of care for older people.' has been omitted as it did not relate to the focus of the paragraph.

The first sentence functions as a clear and direct topic sentence.

The first and second sentences are linked together with the words 'This is recognised…'.

The evidence provides a balanced view of the benefits of CDC to service users and the challenges of implementing CDC for hospital social workers.

A concluding sentence at the end of the paragraph summarises the key issues outlined in the paragraph.

In the second paragraph, the first sentence is the topic sentence.

Good use of 'This means' to link between sentences.

Good explanation and use of evidence and examples to support the writer's point.

Good use of 'For example' as a signpost.

A concluding sentence at the end of this paragraph summarises the implications of the information discussed in the paragraph.

Signposting and linking words are used appropriately throughout.

The voice and style are consistent and appropriate throughout the two paragraphs.

What is proofreading?

The focus of proofreading is to look for surface errors such as spelling, punctuation and grammatical errors, formatting issues, sentence structure and word choice issues, referencing errors, as well as inconsistencies with headings and subtitles. Proofreading does not require rewriting of the text.

One way to approach the task is to look for 1–3 different items at a time (e.g. abbreviations, capital letter usage and punctuation). Once you have ticked a category off your to-do list of editing, you can move on to the next items. This may take a little longer, but it often makes the proofreading task a little less daunting and more straightforward.

Another proofreading strategy is to read the text aloud while taking note of any errors. Alternatively, use a ruler on a paper draft to slowly and methodically read over a single line at a time. You may find it easier to proofread a draft written with double-spaced lines. It is worth testing out these options to find the one(s) that work best for you and produce the best work. When you are revising a document on your computer, try and remove anything that might distract you from the task at hand, such as open web pages or applications. You can also use the 'focus' function in Microsoft Word, which creates a view of your document that removes visual distractions from your screen.

Assign your proofreading to a time of day when you are most alert and when there are fewest distractions. Work in short bursts, and take breaks when you are tired or lose concentration.

CHECKLIST: PROOFREADING A TEXT

Check that you have addressed all of the items listed below as you proofread a text.

- Grammar
- Spelling errors
- Spelling conventions (e.g. are you using British, Australian, NZ or US spelling consistently?)
- Punctuation
- Use of capital letters
- Abbreviations and acronyms (e.g. are they spelled out the first time?)
- Sentence structure
- Word choice (e.g. is this consistent, respectful and in line with social work values?)
- Formatting (e.g. have you followed the task instructions?)
- Headings and subtitles (e.g. are these used logically and consistently?)
- In-text citations and references (e.g. is the correct style used? Are all in-text citations included in the reference list and vice versa? See Chapter 5)

Language Focus: Using acronyms and abbreviations

- Spell out abbreviations when they first appear followed by the abbreviation in brackets directly after. Then use the abbreviation consistently throughout the text.
- Do not use an abbreviation if the word is used fewer than 3–4 times in the text.
- Avoid using too many abbreviations in a text as it can be confusing to the reader.
- Avoid using abbreviations in a title. An exception is words that are commonly known through their abbreviation rather than the full words (e.g. HIV, AM/PM or NATO).
- When using the indefinite article (a/an) before an abbreviation, choose the form that matches how the abbreviation is pronounced (e.g. a UK citizen, an MRI).

Language Focus: Using capital letters

Overusing capital letters can be jarring to read as it feels like you are SHOUTING at the reader. For this reason, keep their use to a minimum.

You should usually capitalise the first word only in a sentence, bullet point, heading or sub-heading. For example:

- Theories and approaches in mental health
  o Biopsychosocial model
  o Strengths-based approach

You should generally use capital letters for proper nouns (e.g. names of people, organisations, countries, job titles) and principal words only (i.e. not 'a', 'an', 'the', 'of', 'and', etc.). For example:

- John Smith
- Minister of Social Services
- The Department of Home Affairs
- The United Kingdom

Do not use capital letters for professions or fields of practice, such as social worker, child protection worker, social work and child protection (note that job titles are capitalised).

Be wary of capitalisation conventions in different countries. For example, in the United States, it is usual practice to put punctuation marks between the U and S when abbreviating (e.g. U.S.). However, in Australia, New Zealand and the United Kingdom it is acceptable not to do so (e.g. NZ, UK).

Using correct terminology

It is important that you use the correct terminology and that you use language that is in line with social work values and is respectful. This means that language should not be discriminating, judgemental or biased. For instance, rather than refer to social work practice with 'an old client' or 'an aged client', instead use the term social work practice with an 'older person' (See boxed text below). Throughout this book, we include examples of such language in a range of different fields of social work practice (see for example pp. 29–30, pp. 110–111, p. 122, p. 165, pp. 188–189).

Language Focus: Describing the ages of service users

There is some variation around the definitions of certain terms, particularly in different countries and over time. The following outlines the most commonly used general terms for different age groups:

- Infant: a child under 1 (WHO)
- Child: generally someone aged under 18 or 19 and under (WHO). This varies according to whether the definition is for legal, social or biological purposes.
  - In some cases, someone under 16 or 21 (US)
- Adolescent: someone between 10 and 19 (WHO)
- Young person: someone between 10 and 24 (WHO)
- Minor: someone under 18 (Australia, England, Wales); or under 16 (Scotland)
- Adult: older than 19 (WHO); aged 18 and above (Australia, UK); aged 20 and above (NZ)
- Middle-aged person: someone between 45 and 65
- Older people: aged 65 and above (worldwide)

Other terms used for older people include *senior citizen* (UK and US), *seniors* (US), *older person* (with sub-categories *young old, middle old, very old*), *old-age pensioner (OAP)* (UK) or *pensioner* (note that these last two include information on retirement status).

Do not refer to older people as 'the aged' or 'old people', as these are considered impolite.

In your writing, define the terms you use to avoid any confusion.

ACTIVITY 6.1

Editing practice (Suggested solutions on p. 86)

Read the essay excerpt below and identify how you might edit it. Remember that there are many ways to organise, structure and write a text.

Social work practice which focuses on social justice, human rights and advocacy will be even more important with an increasingly ageing population. As people age, their health status and the capacity to make choices decreases (Ife 2012). This means that it will be crucial to support the ageing population's increasing vulnerabilities and respect their self-determination. This can be achieved with the professional care, advocacy and coordination skills of hospital social workers.

In the near future, an increased number of older people are anticipated to remain in, or return to, the workforce to supplement their often diminished retirement income (Silverstone 2005). As a result, the prevalence of age discrimination in the workforce can become a barrier to improving their productivity (O'Loughlin & Kendig 2017). Financial pressures resulting from chronic diseases and limited informal support can increase the risk of elder abuse (Berkman et al. 2006). These societal changes may increase the risks of older people being mistreated, which is why the advocacy role of hospital social workers will become increasingly crucial.

Finally, I would argue that care coordination skills will be extremely important for hospital social workers. A growing number of older people having chronic illnesses meaning that they may use multiple health services at the same time (Berkman et al. 2006). The Australian Association of Social Workers [AASW] (2015b) states that best practice for working with these patients is through coordinated care between multidisciplinary teams. Building on social work skills and knowledge, hospital social workers are well-positioned to ensure the quality and continuum of care with coordination skills among different stakeholders.

Hospital social work and the field of social work are not well prepared for an ageing society. The literature shows the overall paucity of research in gerontological social work and a general lack of educational opportunities for social work students in this field (Richards et al. 2014). Through collaboration with academics and policymakers, hospital social workers need to engage in more research output and educate young practitioners to be competent to work in this field.

Maintaining a consistent writing style

Maintain a consistent writing style and voice throughout your text. For example, if you use the first person in your writing (e.g. 'I will argue that…') (which is generally acceptable – though some academics still argue that it should be avoided. If in doubt, check with the person marking your paper if they have a preference), make sure that it is used consistently throughout and does not make its first appearance on the second to last page or only once on the first page as this is jarring to the reader.

Balance the use of active and passive sentences according to your writing needs and avoid predominantly using just the one type. The passive voice is often used to avoid making mention of the subject performing the action, and this is done for a range of reasons, for example, the subject may not be important for the purpose of the text, or the subject may be unknown. An example of a passive sentence is: "The service user was provided with a personalised plan" or "The surveys were developed based on previous literature". Try not to overuse passive structures, especially if it means creating very long sentences.

Choice of vocabulary plays a role in maintaining the same level of formality throughout a text. Formal language avoids colloquial words, avoids abbreviations and uses precise terminology, while informal vocabulary is more relaxed, and the kind of personal language you might use in a casual conversation. Use academic language and ensure it is appropriate, specific and formal. For example, use 'in addition to' rather than 'besides', 'receive' rather than 'get', 'conduct' rather than 'do' and 'furthermore' rather than 'also'.

ACTIVITY 6.2

Using appropriate vocabulary (Suggested solutions on p. 87)

Identify the words or phrases below that may be inappropriate for academic writing. Explain why.

- On the one hand... On the other hand
- In relation to
- Look at
- Health outcomes
- Without a doubt
- Beliefs
- Think
- A lot, a lot (of)
- Make sure
- Sort of/kind of

- Bad
- Do research
- Mention
- Perspectives
- See
- Justify
- Thing
- Pay attention to
- So
- Lady/guy

Using too many direct quotes may affect the writing style and voice of your text. Direct quotes will use another author's voice and style which includes sentence structure and vocabulary. Using too many quotes or 'other voices' can therefore create a disjointed text.

It is important to use the correct tense in academic writing as different tenses serve different purposes. Advice is offered for using the correct tense for different text types. The following table outlines how tense is generally used in social work writing.

Language Focus: Using the appropriate tense

The present tense is often used to generally describe an ongoing situation, studies and research.	The older person **lives** alone but requires ongoing support from a carer. Overall, the research **indicates** that while migrants from NESB struggle to find equivalent employment, those from the Middle East have specific difficulties. (Rynderman & Flynn 2014, p. 270) In later work, comparing employment outcomes for migrant professionals in Canada and Australia, a similar pattern **is evident**. (Hawthorne, 2006). (Rynderman & Flynn 2014, p. 270) One of the most stressful times for international students **is** during placement (Taylor, Craft, Murray, & Rowley, 2000), and the challenges they **face** can negatively affect their engagement with their studies. (Goldingay, 2012). (Ross, Ta & Grieve 2019)
The past tense is used to describe past events and research methodology.	The older person **fell** and **injured** themself while in the shower and is no longer able to live alone due to risk of further injury. I **wrote** some detailed reflections **yesterday** about my first home visit to an older person who was recently discharged from hospital. This research **was conducted** in late 2016 using a cross-sectional design employing an online survey. (Ross, Ta & Grieve 2019)
The past tense may also be used to describe past studies and research.	Braman and Wood (2003) in particular, **focused on** the need to help children increase their social connections and decrease their isolation. (McCrickard & Flynn 2015, p. 41)
The present perfect indicates that a situation or piece of research started or occurred in the past but is still relevant or continuing.	The older person **has refused** to accept home support services. The case notes say that the social worker **has referred** the service user to the financial counsellor. More recently, social workers **have highlighted** the need to collaborate with others in the transformation of current economic, social and political arrangements (Peeters, 2012), while Jones (2013) **has suggested** that one of the pressing tasks for social work educators is to give ecological considerations a central place in transforming the social work curriculum. (McKinnon & Bat 2013, p. 154) Data **have revealed** that the participants emanated from socially and financially well-established backgrounds, but that 'push' factors in their country of origin were important in their decision to migrate to Australia. (Rynderman & Flynn 2014, p. 281)

Proofreading practice (Suggested solutions on p. 89)

Proofread the reflective writing excerpt below and highlight any errors you can find.

An ethical dilemma I observed through direct client work while on placement involved a residential aged care client who was a victim of elder abuse from her daughter and subsequently owed the Health Services Nursing Home a huge amount of money. I met with the client and also attended a meeting with the finance department regarding the clients' situation.

There is a clear conflict between my social work practice and values advocating for and supporting social justice for this client and the organisation wanting to recover this money from this client and not taking into account the stress and emotional impact that this would cause the client. Through reflection, and discussion with my supervisor, I was able to verbalize a clear understanding of the ethical dilemma I face when supporting a client while maintaining loyalty to organizational policy.

Key points from this chapter

- Revision is crucial and needs to be factored into the writing process
- Editing looks at the larger components of a text
- Proofreading looks at the smaller details
- Find a strategy for revision that works for you

Suggested solutions

Editing practice

| Social work practice which focuses on social justice, human rights and advocacy will be even more important with an increasingly ageing population. As people age, their health status and the capacity to make choices decreases (Ife 2012). This means that it will be crucial to support the ageing population's increasing vulnerabilities and respect their self-determination. This can be achieved with the professional care, advocacy and coordination skills of hospital social workers. | This paragraph outlines the issues faced by older people generally. A topic sentence is lacking. Avoid starting two consecutive sentences with the same word – in this case 'This'. The final sentence in this paragraph links to the important role of hospital social workers which lists three main roles. |

In the near future, an increased number of older people are anticipated to remain in, or return to, the workforce to supplement their often diminished retirement income (Silverstone 2005). As a result, the prevalence of age discrimination in the workforce can become a barrier to improving their productivity (O'Loughlin & Kendig 2017). Financial pressures resulting from chronic diseases and limited informal support can increase the risk of elder abuse (Berkman et al. 2006). These societal changes may increase the risks of older people being mistreated, which is why the advocacy role of hospital social workers will become increasingly crucial.	The second paragraph elaborates on the issues faced by an ageing population.
	Again, the final sentence links to how hospital social workers can assist – in this case, through advocacy.
Finally, I would argue that care coordination skills will be extremely important for hospital social workers. A growing number of older people having chronic illnesses meaning that they may use multiple health services at the same time (Berkman et al. 2006). The Australian Association of Social Workers [AASW] (2015b) states that best practice for working with these patients is through coordinated care between multidisciplinary teams. Building on social work skills and knowledge, hospital social workers are well-positioned to ensure the quality and continuum of care with coordination skills among different stakeholders.	In paragraph two, the topic sentence comes at the end – it should be clearly stated first and then elaborated on.
	A signposting word such as 'Further' could be used before 'Financial pressures'.
	In the third paragraph, there is a change in voice, with the use of the first person 'I'. This is somewhat jarring as it has not been used in the previous two paragraphs.
	The abbreviation AASW should be surrounded by parentheses (round brackets).
Hospital social work and the field of social work are not well-prepared for an ageing society. The literature shows the overall paucity of research in gerontological social work and a general lack of educational opportunities for social work students in this field (Richards et al. 2014). Through collaboration with academics and policymakers, hospital social workers need to engage in more research output and educate young practitioners to be competent to work in this field.	The final paragraph reads as a conclusion to this section and links the discussion above with the overall argument of the essay.
	A reference is needed for the claim made in the first sentence.
	'Hospital social workers' is spelled out rather than abbreviated to 'hospital social work'.

ACTIVITY 6.2

Using appropriate vocabulary

Words and phrases inappropriate for academic writing are underlined with explanations provided.

On the one hand... On the other hand	This is too informal for academic writing. Instead use phrases such as 'One argument in favour of this is...' and 'Arguments against this include...'. See Chapter 5 on signposting for other alternatives.	Bad	An unhelpful and vague word to describe something negative. Instead use a word that accurately captures what aspect is negative – e.g. 'poor (performing)', 'not useful', 'negative outcomes', 'inefficient', 'limited'.

In relation to		Do research	Informal phrasing. Appropriate academic language is 'conduct research'.
Look at	Informal phrase. Generally, phrasal verbs are more informal than their single verb counterpart. Here, alternatives are 'explore', 'discuss', 'evaluate'. See Chapter 1 on question verbs for other alternatives and Chapter 10 on verbs to describe other people's research.	Mention	Inaccurate when used to describe an author's statement. To mention something is to state something briefly, possibly without prior planning or deliberation. See Chapter 1 on question verbs for other alternatives and Chapter 10 on verbs to describe other people's research.
Health outcomes		Perspectives	
Without a doubt	An informal and inappropriate phrase to indicate certainty. Certainty should be hedged using appropriate academic language. See Chapter 7 on hedging language.	See	Informal. Instead use 'observe'.
Beliefs		Justify	
Think	Informal and vague. Use an alternative such as 'states', 'claims', 'it is my belief', 'I will argue'.	Thing	Vague, informal and inaccurate. Use a precise term or an alternative such as 'aspect', 'component'.
A lot, a lot (of)	Informal and vague. Use a more precise term such as 'a majority', 'half', 'over half', 'many', 'in most cases'.	Pay attention to	
Make sure	Informal. Instead use 'ensure'.	So	Informal. Instead use an alternative such as 'For this reason' or 'as a result'. See Chapter 5 on signposting for other alternatives.
Sort of/kind of	Informal and vague. Use a precise term or an alternative phrase such as 'in some ways...', 'This is similar to... in that...'.	Lady/guy	Inappropriate and informal. Instead use man/woman or male/female.

ACTIVITY 6.3

Proofreading practice

Errors are underlined and explained in the right-hand column.

An ethical dilemma I observed through direct client work while on placement involved a residential aged care client who was a victim of elder abuse from her daughter and subsequently owed the <u>H</u>ealth <u>S</u>ervices <u>N</u>ursing <u>H</u>ome a <u>huge</u> amount of money. I met with the client and also attended a meeting with the finance department regarding the clients<u>'</u> situation.	The first sentence is too long and could be divided into two sentences.
	Incorrect form of the indefinite article 'a' used.
	Incorrect usage of capital letters on 'Health Services Nursing Home'
	Possessive marker missing 'client's'.
	Vocab: the use of 'huge' is inappropriate and informal. Use an alternative such as 'considerable' or 'large'.
There is a clear conflict between my social work practice and values advocating <u>for</u> and supporting social justice for this client and the organisation wanting to recover this money from this client and not taking into account the stress and emotional impact that this would cause the client. Through reflection<u>,</u> and discussion with my supervisor, I was able to verbali<u>z</u>e a clear understanding of the ethical dilemma I face when supporting a client while maintaining loyalty to organi<u>z</u>ational policy.	This sentence is too long and, as a result, unclear; It needs to be divided into two or three sentences and reworded slightly for clarity.
	Comma error.
	The use of 'z' in words such as 'verbalise' and 'organisational' follows US spelling conventions.

Further reading

Boyle, J. & Ramsay, S. (2017). *Writing for science students.* London: Red Globe Press.

Brick, J., Herke, M. & Wong, D. (2020). *Academic culture: A student's guide to studying at university.* 4th edition. London: Red Globe Press.

Greetham, B. (2018). *How to write better essays.* 4th edition. London: Red Globe Press.

Smith, D. & Sutton, H. (1994). *Powerful proofreading skills tips, techniques and tactics.* Menlo Park: Crisp Publications.

PART

II

Key Types of Assessment

Writing an Essay

In this chapter you will learn:

- How to answer an essay question
- How to develop an argument
- How to structure and shape an essay
- What to include in the following sections:
  - The introduction
  - The body
  - The conclusion
- Rules about argumentation, counter-argumentation and expression

What is an essay?

An essay provides an answer to a question or puts forth an argument. The goal in writing an essay is to show that you can think critically and draw upon the ideas of others to build a coherent narrative and case. This means going beyond demonstrating your understanding and recall, to also include an analysis and synthesis of ideas from different sources, then critically evaluating them. This includes identifying what different authors agree upon, on what issues they differ and in what ways, and who makes the most persuasive argument and why.

A key to a successful essay is to make your point clear from the beginning and use the rest of the essay to elaborate. Once the reader gets to the end, the conclusions should be obvious to them. However, that does not mean your argument should be simplistic. It ought to be a nuanced argument that considers the detailed nature of the topic, exploring some of its challenging, controversial or murkier aspects. A good essay is never one-sided. It considers different perspectives, opposing arguments, alternative theories and contradicting evidence. By the end, you will put forward your own evaluation of the situation or issue under consideration. Convince your reader by demonstrating that you have fully and carefully considered the case and come to the most sensible conclusions based on a thorough interrogation of the matter.

Answering the essay question

The first rule of writing essays is: *answer the question* (as discussed on p. 3). Sometimes the 'question' is written as a statement, such as: 'Discuss the challenges of social work with unaccompanied asylum-seeking children.' Whatever its form, your assessors have set you this exercise in this way and part of the assessment process is checking whether you can meet the requirements of a given task. The most beautifully written and insightful piece of work is likely to get a low grade if it is off track. To avoid this, carefully read the question, break it down into its component parts, base your answer around it and, when you revise your essay, check whether every section is contributing towards its answer. You need to ruthlessly cut out those portions that have strayed from the path, no matter how good they may be (as discussed on p. 77). These portions can be kept in a separate document for later in case they are relevant to a future task. If you are unsure how to answer the question, ask a member of the teaching staff for clarity.

When deciding how to answer the essay question, look at the learning outcomes and assessment criteria for the essay. This will provide an indication of what you are being assessed on and what you need to demonstrate in your essay (see p. 3 on understanding the task and pp. 7–8 on marking rubrics).

Three essay types

There are several different types of essay questions. Three of the most common types are:

- A question with an answer
- Compare and contrast
- Describe/analyse/critically discuss

The following outlines some tips for answering these three essay question types.

A question with an answer

Essay questions phrased as questions help you to be clear about whether your essay is on track. Your answer should remain in the terms of the original question and answer it comprehensively. An example is as follows:

> **Essay question example: A question with an answer**
>
> What legal frameworks inform the response to victims of human trafficking in the United Kingdom?

In this case, the essay should describe the legal frameworks in the United Kingdom, so it might help to structure the essay around the different pieces and types of legislation. Here, the essay might have a section on migration law, criminal law and law specifically on the treatment of victims of human trafficking or modern slavery. It should also explain how these pieces of legislation shape the treatment of victims of human trafficking, such as the nature and length of support. To gain critical depth, the essay could discuss some of the tensions or contradictions between the legal frameworks (e.g. where victims of human trafficking may be treated as both victims and criminals). It may also make sense to argue that an understanding of the legislation and response needs to take account of the wider social and political context; this seems appropriate, and may enhance the quality of your essay, so long as you clearly explain how this is relevant. In the end, the key test is whether you have fully answered the question in an informed manner.

Compare and contrast

A 'compare and contrast' essay question invites you to describe and discuss both similarities (compare) and differences (contrast). While there is likely to be a near-infinite number of points of similarity and difference, your task is to identify those that you deem as most important to your topic. The following is an example of a compare and contrast essay task:

Essay question example: Compare and contrast

Compare and contrast the policy positions in England and Scotland in relation to the integration of asylum seekers.

For this example, the essay could start by defining the issues that are similar across the two national contexts, such as the Geneva Convention Relating to the Status of Refugees 1951 and Protocol 1967, and UK-wide policy and legislation that relate to asylum and migration (e.g. Immigration and Asylum Act 1999). The essay could then move into explaining how responsibility for certain aspects of policy that relate to the integration of asylum seekers in Scotland differs from England, such as around education, health and housing. The essay could describe similarities and differences in the politics and specific policies between the two countries (Ndofor-Tah et al. 2019; Scottish Government 2018), perhaps picking up on other relevant issues such as demographics and public attitudes towards migrants. Overall, the essay should give the reader an understanding of the key similarities and differences, ideally with an informed explanation for, and discussion of, this situation.

Describe, analyse and critically discuss

Essay questions that ask you to describe, analyse or critically discuss an issue can be treated as asking you to define, describe, analyse and critically reflect on the topic. For more on this, refer to Chapter 1 on understanding what question words mean.

Essay question example: Describe, analyse and critically discuss

Critically discuss the role of social workers in assessing the age of unaccompanied asylum-seeking children.

In this case, the essay could start by defining 'unaccompanied asylum-seeking children' and 'age assessment'. It could then describe what social workers do in this process. Following this description, the essay should explore key issues that are worthy of interrogation. For instance, it could explain the importance of age assessment (e.g. how an individual's rights and treatment depend on whether they are judged to be a 'child' or 'adult'), describe ways of assessing age and their relative strengths and limitations and discuss the tensions that social workers may experience in undertaking these assessments. To be 'analytic' or 'critical', the essay could consider different perspectives, ethical frameworks, research evidence or theories in relation to these issues. After considering these different perspectives and weighing the evidence, the essay should draw some overall conclusions in relation to the topic.

Structuring the essay

An essay can be thought of as a well-planned journey that gets you from your origin to your destination, making all the necessary stops along the way. When deciding what is relevant and what is not, keep in mind that your essay should demonstrate your knowledge and understanding of a topic and/or make an argument. This means that before you start typing you need to have a plan (see pp. 9–11 on developing an outline and writing plan). Clarify the focus and scope of your topic, and where you wish to take the reader. Think about each section and paragraph as a stop along the way. Is each stop necessary to get to the destination? That is, does your reader need to understand this issue in order to appreciate your argument?

Thinking about your essay this way will help you decide what information is needed and what is extraneous. What details of a research study does your reader need to know in order to judge the value of its evidence? What aspects of the sample, research methods and context are relevant to your argument? This does not mean 'cherry picking' evidence to support your argument, i.e. for support rather than illumination. Instead, carefully consider the evidence and structure your own argument around it. See p. 45 for more details on how to structure a writing task.

As a general guide, aim to use approximately 10% of your word count for both the introduction and the conclusion, leaving the remaining 80% for the main body of your work.

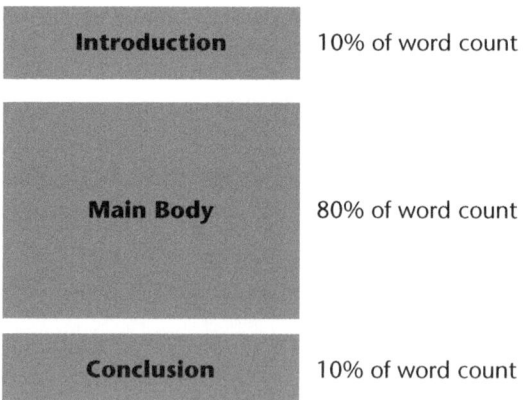

Introduction	10% of word count
Main Body	80% of word count
Conclusion	10% of word count

An overly long introduction runs the risk of repetition in the main body of the essay, whereas too short an introduction may mean that the reader is grasping to understand the focus of your work. Similarly, a good conclusion can leave a very good impression of your work. In our experience, conclusions are often an after-thought with some students. They are either a summary of what has already been said, rather than a take-home message, or they are very brief, indicating that students have either run out of words or energy, and usually both.

A typical essay contains many different types of information, which are often placed in their own sections or parts such as introducing the argument, analysing data, raising alternative or counter-arguments, and concluding. Introductions and conclusions have fixed places, but other parts do not, and this may depend on whether you have been provided with a structure to follow, or been given the freedom to lay out the evidence and your arguments in a way which makes sense to you.

Sometimes students like a structure provided for them for the security of not leaving something out. As a marker though, it is great to read essays which address the question set in different ways based on the argument and evidence being presented by the student. Try not to be overwhelmed if you have not been given a structure for your essay – see it as an opportunity to be creative. For organising principles, see p. 45, and for organising a literature review specifically, see pp. 170–171.

Take the example of a counter-argument; this may appear within a paragraph, as a free-standing section, as part of the beginning of a section, or before the ending of the main body of your work. Alternatively, background material (such as historical context, statistical overview of an issue, a summary of relevant theory or criticism, or the definition of a key term) often appears at the beginning of the essay, between the introduction and the first analytical section, but might also appear near the beginning of the specific section to which it is relevant. It can be useful to think of the needs of your reader – what questions might they have about the topic or issue, and how can you provide illumination for them?

Using the hourglass

The hourglass is a standard shape for an essay. An hourglass is wide at the top, narrow in the middle, and widens again at the bottom. Similarly, an essay can start with a general issue or broad context, narrow down towards a more specific topic, and in the middle carefully consider very particular and refined points, before broadening out at the end to reflect on the wider relevant implications and applications of the issue.

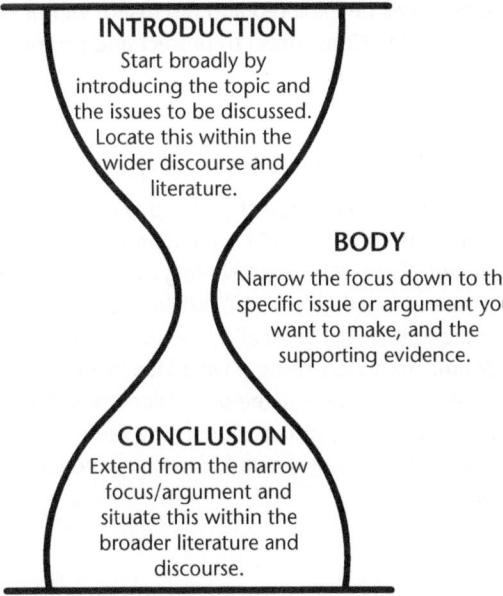

INTRODUCTION
Start broadly by introducing the topic and the issues to be discussed. Locate this within the wider discourse and literature.

BODY
Narrow the focus down to the specific issue or argument you want to make, and the supporting evidence.

CONCLUSION
Extend from the narrow focus/argument and situate this within the broader literature and discourse.

The introduction

Some say that, when writing an essay, you should 'Say what you're going to say, say it, then say what you said'. This is boring and a waste of words. Introductions matter, but they should do more than simply state what the essay is about. Poor introductions either paraphrase the essay question or state what the essay is about in a very general and abstract way. A good introduction will state the focus, scope and central thesis of the essay, and will make the reader want to read on.

Titles

If you have the scope to give your work a title, see this as an opportunity to be creative and descriptive, rather than choosing a generic title such as 'Refugees'. Use the title to grab your reader's attention, give them some clarity about your topic, highlight your argument or put a question in their mind. Consider the title of this article by Lynn and Lea (2003): '"A Phantom Menace and the New Apartheid": The Social Construction of Asylum-Seekers in the United Kingdom'. This title is memorable, evocative, yet clarifies the focus of the article. A title "offers a powerful first impression" (Sword 2011: 63), and first impressions matter, so try to do this in a way that fits your essay, whether this is with humour, stating a controversial position or posing a puzzle.

Focus

The introduction will state what the essay is going to discuss in specific rather than general terms. For instance, if the essay topic is 'Describe how the European Convention of Human Rights has shaped a particular area of social work practice', rather than state 'This essay will describe how the European Convention of Human Rights has shaped a particular area of social work practice', it might state, for instance, 'This essay will examine how the European Convention of Human Rights has shaped the social work response to an often powerless and marginalised group – asylum seekers in the United Kingdom. In doing so the usefulness of the Convention and some of its limitations will be explored and discussed, with a view to considering how social workers can use the Convention to protect and promote the rights of service users such as asylum seekers.'

Example: An introduction from a student essay

One of the most pressing contemporary challenges is the vast number of forcibly displaced people across the world. In 2017, the number of forcibly displaced people globally reached 70.8 million, representing the highest number of displaced people ever recorded (UNHCR 2018). Whilst most displaced people are hosted in developing countries (UNHCR 2018), many European countries, such as the United Kingdom, are experiencing an increase in asylum applications as well (Refugee Council 2018). Asylum is the protection offered to a person fleeing persecution in their home country (Sturge 2019). The term 'asylum seeker' refers to a person who has applied for asylum and is awaiting a decision to receive refugee status (Sturge 2019).

Scope

The introduction should provide a sense of what is within or beyond the scope of the essay. This can be as simple as stating the main aspects and issues that will be covered. Again, this should not be done in general terms (e.g. 'I will discuss policy and legislation, theory and research, and implications for practice'), but rather in more specific terms (e.g. 'I will analyse how the European Convention of Human Rights has influenced the development of asylum policy and law in the UK, discuss key legislation of relevance to social workers, review research on social work with asylum seekers in the UK, and draw out the implications of the Convention for social work policy and practice.'). It should also be clear what your essay will not do – telling the reader this at the beginning has the benefit of helping them to set their expectations about your work, while also helping to keep you on track.

Thesis

In many types of essays, you will need to put forward a thesis. A thesis is a statement or theory that is put forward as a premise to be maintained or proved. State this in your introduction. If you do not know what your point is, you need to keep reading and thinking until you do. Your essay ought to have something to say that's worth hearing. Try formulating it into a sentence that begins with something like: 'In this essay I will demonstrate/show/argue/illustrate...'. If all you are going to do is 'describe' or 'discuss', then you probably haven't figured out what your point is yet. However, do not get carried away and set out to 'prove' something for the sake of being original.

A strong thesis may argue for or against something in a committed way: 'I will demonstrate that ethical social work practice is impossible within the current migration system'. A nuanced thesis is no weaker, it just presents the argument as having multiple facets: 'I will show that social work with asylum seekers provides an ethical and valuable service to people fleeing war and persecution who are able to reach a safe country, but global social work across borders, as well as international interventions to address political instabilities and economic inequalities, is necessary to meet the needs of and to protect internally displaced people and refugees who are seeking safety.' As a rule of thumb, a good, common place for your thesis statement is at the end of your introduction, acting as a launch pad for the main body of your work.

Engagement

Make your essay interesting. Tell your reader from the start why this topic is important, or demonstrate it by using a 'hook' that will grab your reader's attention from the start. Is there a prominent incident that directly relates to your topic? Perhaps there is a recent film or TV show that dramatises issues closely related to your essay? Consider using a quote from a politician, someone famous, or perhaps from a service user or someone with relevant personal experience. You may even have some personal or professional experience that you are willing to (briefly) mention to begin the essay. Yes, we know your marker *must* read your essay, but make them feel as if they *want* to.

Example: An interesting start

The following are examples of interesting introductions outlining the context of the topic.

History in the service of politics: Constructing narratives of history during the European refugee "crisis"

Politicians around the world often refer to "our proud history of supporting refugees" (Taylor 2017). However, there is no inherent reason why politicians must refer to history in deciding the response to refugees, and the historical record regarding responses to refugees is not straightforwardly positive. So how is history drawn upon in political debates regarding refugees? This article addresses this question through analysing politicians' references to history in such debates. The aim is to contribute to political, psychological, and historical work by developing a framework for examining the discursive functions of history, reformulating the distinction between "psychological" and "rhetorical" functions of historical analogies, and reflecting on the implications of hegemonic historical narratives for refugee history and policymaking. (Kirkwood 2018, p. 297)

Recent years have seen a considerable increase in the number of refugees resettled in Australia. These refugees tend to have multiple and complex physical and psychological health issues (Department of Health and Human Services Victoria 2016). In regard to mental health issues, refugees tend to have post-trauma stress disorder, depression, and anxiety. In relation to physical health, commonly seen issues include sexual health, infectious diseases and immunisation issues. Some social issues are also potential risk factors, including housing, employment and poverty (Mehrotra 2015). However, despite their poor health, this vulnerable group also reports more barriers accessing the health care system than their Australian equivalents.

Revisiting the introduction

Once you have completed your first draft of your essay, it is worth going back to your introduction and considering whether it needs to be rewritten. This is because, as you have written your essay, testing your thinking against the evidence, perhaps changing direction or modifying the idea you started with, you want to ensure that your introduction reflects what you did rather than what you said you would do. Clear, focused beginnings rarely present themselves ready-made; they must be written and rewritten, with a clarity that engages readers and establishes your authority on the topic. See also pp. 76–79 on editing your work.

The essay body

A first draft of your essay is unlikely to be the final draft. An important aspect of writing an essay is to provide a structure that allows your reader to be led through the individual issues in a logical way which tells a bigger story. Therefore, the way you present your arguments and evidence should help the reader to grasp both the big ideas and the nuances of the topic.

One way of helping you to help the reader is to make an essay map at the beginning to guide your writing. This requires you to anticipate what your reader wants and needs to know, and where your reader will expect background information, an explanation and exploration of issues, and the evidence to support the many important points you are seeking to make. Essay maps are not concerned with paragraphs so much as with sections of an essay. They anticipate the major argumentative moves you expect your essay to make.

Essay map

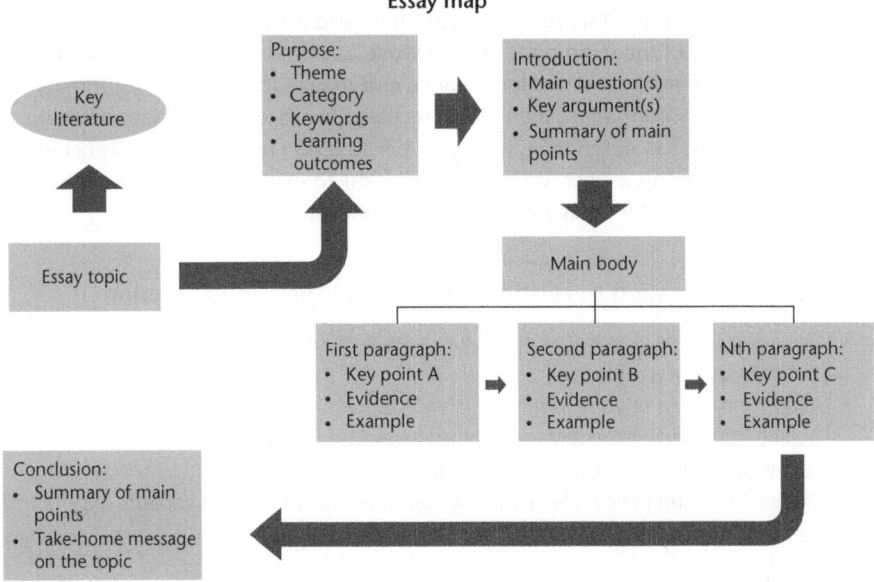

Key literature

Purpose:
• Theme
• Category
• Keywords
• Learning outcomes

Introduction:
• Main question(s)
• Key argument(s)
• Summary of main points

Essay topic

Main body

First paragraph:
• Key point A
• Evidence
• Example

Second paragraph:
• Key point B
• Evidence
• Example

Nth paragraph:
• Key point C
• Evidence
• Example

Conclusion:
• Summary of main points
• Take-home message on the topic

TIPS: MAPPING AN ESSAY

State your over-arching argument or thesis in a sentence or two, then write another sentence saying why it is important to make this claim. In other words, try to capture what a reader might learn by exploring the claim or argument with you. You are trying to anticipate the take-home message for your reader in having engaged with your work.

Then write another signposting sentence: "To be convinced by my argument, the first thing a reader needs to know is . . ." Then say why that is the first thing a reader needs to know and name one or two items of evidence you think will make the case. This will start you off on identifying the golden thread of your argument that needs to run through your essay from the introduction to the conclusion.

Begin each of the following sentences using signposting language such as: "The next thing my reader needs to know is . . ." Once again, say why, and name some evidence. Continue until you have mapped out your essay.

Providing context

The first part of an essay should provide the context. This is likely to be the most descriptive aspect of your essay as you seek to set out the nature of the issue being considered, define some key terms and essentially provide the foundation for exploring the evidence base informing how we understand an issue and the debates and discourses around the topic in subsequent sections.

In weaker essays, students spend too much time setting the scene of 'what', which is likely to be largely descriptive, and not enough time on the following sections which are more discursive. As such, think about this section as being no more than a third of the main body of your work. If it does take up more than this, the essay will be perceived as lacking balance and may read as merely a summary or description of key information. If you have received feedback on previous written work that says it is too descriptive, it may be because you have spent too much of the word count on this aspect. While it is important to explain the context, this merely sets the scene for what will come in the following sections.

Types of information to consider including in the context section

- Define key terms (e.g. define an asylum seeker and clarify how this differs from the definition of a refugee).
- Include statistics relating to the prevalence and incidence of the issue (e.g. outline how many individuals seek asylum each year in your country, number of asylum seekers in total in your country).
- Outline laws and policy relevant to the topic and indicate which aspects are relevant to social work practice.

Presenting issues and arguments

You will need to identify the key issues and arguments to present to the reader. This will require that you have read sufficiently to understand the issues and arguments relevant to your essay. Try to avoid starting to write and read as you go along – this is likely to be reflected in your work whereby ideas and the work of different authors will be presented discretely, rather than in an integrated and cohesive fashion. This is sometimes referred to as a 'walk-through essay', as the student follows the structure of their sources rather than establishing their own. Refer to p. 45 for more on organising principles, and pp. 170–171 for organising and structuring a literature review.

TIPS: READING AND LEARNING FROM THE SOURCES

For every source you read, write two paragraphs for each in a new document. The first paragraph should be what you think the key messages are from the article, report or book. The second paragraph should be about some data (statistics or quotes) which you think support the key messages in the first paragraph. Remember to put the reference details at the top of the page to help you when you have to write your reference list. See also Chapter 2 on note-making.

> Once you have done this for all the key literature you have found and read, write one page identifying:
> - The points that all or the majority of authors agree on
> - The points they disagree about (if at all)
> - Any unique points made by an author (you might have several unique points)

Authors might agree on the core issues, but might differ in terms of how they understand the issue, and the arguments they present around this. Try to undertake most of your reading before you start to write – and to capture the key points of each journal article, research report, policy document and book for each source, rather than trying to copy out large chunks of information (see p. 18–20 on note-making). It can be a challenge to present the issues and arguments in a clear, logical and coherent fashion. Consider the story you are seeking to tell on your topic and present the issues and the evidence to support your story. This evidence might be the citations of the authors whose work you have read, but is also likely to include some statistics, findings and quotes – though be careful not to rely too heavily on quotations. Refer to Chapter 5 for more on quoting, summarising and paraphrasing.

Qualifying statements: hedging and boosting language

The language that you use to make an argument shows the strength of the evidence and how confident you are in your claims. This is done by using either hedging or boosting language. In academic social work writing, it is much more common to use hedging language rather than boosting language.

Using cautious language to hedge your claims

When you are discussing evidence to support your claims, it is important to be cautious with your statements. By quantifying the strength of your claims, you show your reader that your claims may have exceptions and are not always the rule. This is also called cautious or tentative language.

There is a range of approaches to this, including:

- Adjectives (e.g. certain, likely, limited, little, possible, probable, strong, uncertain, unlikely, weak)
- Adverbs (e.g. apparently, clearly, for the most part, generally, largely, likely, mainly, maybe, often, perhaps, possibly, presumably, sometimes, typically, usually)
- Clause constructions (e.g. It could be suggested…, It could be the case that…, It is important to…, It may be…)
- Modal verbs (e.g. could, may, might, will, would). See p. 151–152 for more on modal verbs
- Nouns (e.g. assumption, a/the majority, a/the minority, likelihood, possibility, tendency)
- Quantifiers (e.g. all, any, every, few, many, most, several, some)
- Verbs (e.g. appear, assume, estimate, indicate, reveal, seem, suggest, tend). See p. 65–67 and p. 171–173 for more on reporting verbs

The following are examples of hedging language typically found in social work writing:

- Social workers <u>could</u> consider whether using a family member as an interpreter is likely to be more or less helpful for a service user, than using a professional interpreting service.
- <u>Generally</u>, within immigration services, age assessment is seen as an inexact process for accurately gauging the age of a child.
- Research <u>indicates</u> that many refugees are keen to return to their country of domicile when safe to do so.

Using boosting language to assert your claims

Boosting language is the opposite of hedging language and shows your reader that you are extremely confident in your claims. You should use boosting language in your writing sparingly and with caution. Boosting is generally indicated in the following ways:

- Adverbs (e.g. always, clearly, conclusively, definitely, evidently, obviously, undoubtedly/without doubt/there is no doubt)
- Clause constructions (e.g. It is clear that..., Research shows that..., Studies confirm that...)
- Verbs (e.g. know, prove, shows)

The following examples of boosting language may be found in social work writing:

- <u>Clearly</u>, leaving one's own home and country is never a decision taken lightly, especially when the move is out of necessity rather than free choice.
- There is a <u>definite</u> link between children's experiences of forced migration due to civil conflict and later expressions of poor mental health.
- Decades of research <u>confirm</u> that forced migration is much more likely in periods of civil unrest, war, famine and natural disasters, and that international agencies and governments need to respond quickly in the aftermath of such events to reduce the movement of significant numbers of people.

ACTIVITY 7.1

Identifying hedging and boosting language (Suggested solutions on p. 112)

Read the examples below and identify the hedging and boosting language used to quantify the statements.

1. There is strong evidence to suggest that child refugees are at risk of experiencing harm while in transit.
2. The findings indicate that age verification is imprecise.
3. Government policy undoubtedly poses a high barrier that asylum seekers must reach in order to confirm their status as refugees.
4. Many countries express a receptiveness to help refugees even though their immigration policies indicate otherwise.
5. It is clear that the majority of refugees are living in low and middle income countries, rather than high income states.
6. Child refugees often undertake the role of carer and protector for younger refugees, whether related or not.

ACTIVITY 7.2

Using hedging language to qualify statements (Suggested solutions on p. 112)

Qualify the statements below by using hedging language.

1. Refugees are suspicious of dealing with government officials for a variety of reasons.
2. Unaccompanied asylum-seeking children should be placed with a relative at the earliest opportunity.
3. Providing micro-loans to women in refugee camps to start their own business is a way of reducing gender-based violence and abuse for many women.

Using counter-arguments to strengthen your discussion

When you write an academic essay, you are making an argument: You propose a thesis and offer some reasoning, supported by evidence that suggests why the thesis is true or relevant. However, there will also be alternative points of view or arguments which could be made, and it is important that you engage with these – both to show that you are able to present a broad view on a topic, but also to then disassemble the counter-argument, which in turns makes your own argument stronger.

Using counter-arguments presents you as the kind of person who weighs alternatives before arguing for one, who confronts difficulties instead of sweeping them under the carpet, and who is more interested in discovering the truth than winning a point. This is a very helpful skill to develop for professional practice, whereby, for example, in court, you might be presented with alternative hypotheses or outcomes to the one being proposed by you and your agency. You will need to engage with dismantling the logic of these counter-arguments in ways which allow a judge to see you as thoughtful and reasonable in your approach to issues, and to have confidence that you can be trusted to make well-reasoned and informed recommendations and decisions.

The following example is a paraphrased extract from a research article (Kirkwood 2018: 310), demonstrating how arguments and counter-arguments can be interwoven to advance the depth and subtlety of your writing. The article provides an analysis of politicians' references to history when discussing the response to refugees. This paragraph follows from the main points that politicians draw on historical narratives about the nation to strengthen their arguments.

As is shown in this article, politicians talked about history in ways that portrayed the United Kingdom as a nation that stands up for people who face persecution, making a strong argument that the UK should provide support to Syrian refugees.

Argument

However, despite this consensus across political parties on the historical narrative about the UK's support for refugees, **Counter-argument** and therefore the need to support Syrian refugees in the present day, this made little obvious difference to the UK Government's policy in relation to Syrian refugees. That is, they retained the position of accepting up to 20,000 Syrian refugees living in refugee camps over a five-year period and would not accept those who had already travelled to the European Union. This shows that while historical narratives can be powerful for legitimising broad political responses, they do not necessarily determine the specifics of policy.

One exception is that Lord Alfred Dubs, who was himself brought to the UK via Kindertransport as a child fleeing persecution in Nazi Germany, was able to bring forward an amendment to the **Counter-argument** Immigration Act 2016, which permitted unaccompanied refugee children to come to the UK from European countries. This shows that individuals may draw on their own personal identities, which can be linked to **Refined thesis** wider historical narratives, in order to draw support for specific policy actions.

The first sentence starts the main argument. The next three sentences provide a counterpoint to the overall argument of the piece. An exception to the argument is then provided, illustrating the complexity of the topic. However, it ends with an evaluation of the overall situation, which adds a layer of subtlety to the argument. This brings seemingly contradictory evidence to the topic, and integrates it into the discussion so that the reader can gain a more nuanced understanding of the subject. Such an approach in your essays can demonstrate that you have sought out potentially contradicting evidence, explored alternative perspectives, and tested your main theses, which can help you draw conclusions that have more explanatory value and give the sense that your argument is relatively robust.

Using counter-arguments in essays

It can be helpful to consider that a counter-argument in an essay has two stages:

1. You *turn against* your argument to challenge it
2. You then *turn back* to re-affirm it

Begin by imagining a sceptical reader, or cite an actual source, who might resist your argument by pointing out:

- A problem with your argument, e.g. that a different conclusion could be drawn from the same facts, a key assumption is unwarranted or perfunctory, a key term is used unfairly, or certain evidence is ignored or played down
- One or more disadvantages or practical drawbacks to what you propose
- An alternative explanation or proposal that makes more sense

You introduce this turn against your argument with a phrase such as "One might object here that…" or "It might seem that…" or "It is true that…" or with an anticipated challenging question: "But how…?" or "But why…?" or "But is this not just…?"

or "But if this is so, what about...?". You can then state the case against your own argument as briefly, but as clearly and forcefully as you can, using available evidence to back up your argument where possible.

The next step is to return to your own argument, which must involve a careful engagement with the issues, rather than a cautious or flippant dismissal of the counter-argument. In reasoning about the proposed counter-argument, you may:

- Acknowledge its relevance or plausibility but suggest why on balance it is relatively less important or less likely than what you propose, and therefore does not overturn your argument.
- Concede its relevance and acknowledge that it complicates your idea accordingly – restate your thesis in a more exact, qualified or nuanced way that takes account of the objection, or start a new section in which you consider your topic in light of it. This will work if the counter-argument concerns only an aspect of your argument; if it undermines your whole case, you will need a new thesis.
- Refute it, showing why it is mistaken – an apparent but not real problem.

Signpost clearly to the reader what you are doing by using sentences such as the following: "The next thing my reader needs to know is . . .". Once again, say why, and name some evidence. Continue until you have mapped out your essay.

Not every objection is worth entertaining, of course, and you should not include one just to include one. However, in good essays, some imagining of the viewpoints of others, or of resistance to one's own ideas, often occurs. The key is to engage in debate and discussion without losing sight of your own thesis. This is why a first draft of an essay is unlikely to be the final draft, as you go back over your work and sharpen the focus, argument and counter-argument. For more on this see Chapter 6 on revising your work.

While a counter-argument can appear anywhere in the essay, it most commonly appears:

- Within the introduction – before you propose your thesis – where the existence of a different view is the rationale for your essay, and the reason it needs writing
- As a section or paragraph just after your introduction, in which you lay out some common arguments or beliefs before turning away to present your own thesis
- As a quick move within a paragraph, where you imagine a counter-argument not to your main idea but to the sub-idea that the paragraph is arguing or is about to argue
- As a section or paragraph just before the conclusion of your essay, in which you imagine what someone might say in contrast to your own point of view

Typically, presenting a counter-argument within your essay will strengthen your work, but be careful about how you do this and to what extent. Using an occasional counter-argument will sharpen and energise your essay, but using too many will have the reverse effect by obscuring your main idea or suggesting that you are ambivalent or unsure about your own standpoint.

TIPS: REFERRING TO OTHER PEOPLE'S WORK: TO QUOTE OR NOT TO QUOTE

Quotations can fulfil a number of useful, and sometimes useless, functions in an essay, as discussed on p. 57–58. Firstly, they can show that you have read some-thing, which is reassuring for the reader but does not necessarily demonstrate your understanding.

More importantly though, a reference can be used to either support a point you have made, or to illustrate an issue for the reader. When using a quotation to support a point you are making, it is important that you make the point rather than adding the quote and hope that the reader somehow discerns the very important point you are seeking to make. If using a quote to illustrate an issue, this might include the words of a participant in a research study that demonstrates a complex issue or brings the issue to life.

A good reason to use a quote is that you wish to comment on the specific way the issue was described, such as discussing technical definitions, criticising descriptions or analysing rhetoric.

The temptation is to always think another writer has said something so much better than you could ever, and therefore to use quotations like sprinkles on a cake – liberally and without much thought. Our advice is to be judicious and to be very sparing about using quotes.

Try and paraphrase what the author is saying in your own words instead of a quote, and use only a small number that add something to your work through either supporting a central argument you are making, or illustrating a key aspect of the topic. One function of an essay is to demonstrate your understanding of the topic; it is difficult for a marker to assess your understanding if too much of the writing is in other people's words.

Finally, avoid quoting or referencing what an academic staff member said when they presented a class on this issue. Instead, look for the primary material they based their teaching material on. This might be their own published work, which is fine.

The conclusion

The conclusion is your final opportunity to impress a reader and to leave them feeling better informed and persuaded by your argument. Too often we see essays with either a very short conclusion or none at all. This is a strong sign that the student has run out of energy and/or words.

While it can be helpful to remind readers of the main thrust of your argument, a stronger conclusion can do more than merely pull together the key threads of your work. While you should avoid introducing new arguments into your conclusion, it can provide an opportunity to reflect upon the implications of the argument, analysis or discussion you have provided in the main body of your work. A conclusion can outline what your argument implies, involves or suggests. For example:

> "This essay has discussed factors influencing global migration, arguing that both pull and push factors are occurring in tandem. As such, it is

imperative that policy makers engage with the varied reasons for migration, and the often contradictory rhetoric issued by politicians, who want
to attract migrants to bolster the economy, but purely on their own
terms, while limiting opportunities for other types of migrants."

Think carefully about your final sentence, as it is the last thing the reader will see,
and it can have a lasting impression. Use it to provide a 'take-home message' – the
key argument you want your reader to take from your work. This should represent
the golden thread of the thesis you have presented throughout your essay – and it is
important that this links with the introduction. This is why you might need to go
back and edit your introduction to reflect the way your essay and thesis have
developed as you have written your work.

Revising the first draft

Your first draft of an essay is likely to be good, but not as good as it could be. As
such, it is worth planning to have sufficient time to complete a first draft: leave it for
a good 24–48 hours, and then return to it to do some further work before submission. It is likely that with fresh eyes you will identify presentational issues (e.g.
mis-spelling of words, missed references, poor sentence construction), while also
seeing afresh whether your structure, argument and counter-argument hold
together. Refer to Chapter 6 for more tips on revising a written text.

It is also important to consider the feedback you have received on previous
essays – have you seen regular comments about the lack of referencing or inaccurate
referencing? Have you been advised to consider sentence construction or the use of
colloquialisms? Your work will improve if you engage with the feedback you have
received from previous work and seek to incorporate this advice into future work.

TIPS: EDITING AND PROOFREADING YOUR OWN WORK

- Ask someone to read your essay and give you feedback – and be open to
  receiving this advice and using it.
- Construct a backward outline of your essay. Identify the main idea(s) in each
  paragraph. Rank their importance in advancing your thesis. Consider connections
  between and among ideas.
- Rethink your thesis. Based on what you did in the previous step, restructure your
  argument: reorder your points, remove sections or arguments which are irrelevant
  or redundant, add additional points of clarity or complexity, and the implications
  of such.
- At this point return to your introduction and conclusion to ensure that they start
  and bring together the golden thread of your thesis.
- Read your assignment aloud – your ear can sometimes pick up what the eye
  cannot see in terms of the flow of language.

- Make sure all of your words are doing important work in making your argument – and use fewer, rather than more words to make your point. Avoid using two sentences to say what you can say in one, and do not use ten words where five will do.
- Try and mix up your use of words – even small, apparently innocuous words like 'says' are worth your attention. Instead of 'says', use a word such as 'argues', 'acknowledges', 'believes', 'claims', 'contends', 'reveals', 'states' or 'suggests'. Words like these not only make your sentences more interesting and lively but also provide useful information: if you tell your readers that someone 'acknowledges' something, that deepens their understanding of how or why they said that thing; 'said' merely reports.
- Go through your references to ensure that they are accurate, are all included in your reference section, and are presented in the style and to the standard of your course.
- For more editing advice, see Chapter 6 OR pp. 76–85.

Language Focus: Asylum seekers, refugees and migrants

There may be confusion around the definitions of these terms, yet it is very important to use them correctly. In relation to asylum seekers, refugees and migrants, it can be difficult to establish the correct use of terms, partly because different actors will use them in different ways, partly because the topic can be politically charged and the use of different terms has political connotations and partly because it is not always obvious which particular term should be applied to an individual or group. The following attempts to clarify what each of these terms refers to:

> 'Asylum seeker' refers to "someone whose request for sanctuary has yet to be processed" (UNHCR 2020a).

> 'Refugees' refers to "people who have fled war, violence, conflict or persecution and have crossed an international border to find safety in another country" (UNHCR 2020b) or those "unable or unwilling to return to their country of origin owing to a well-founded fear of being persecuted for reasons of race, religion, nationality, membership of a particular social group, or political opinion" (Geneva Convention Relating to the Status of Refugees 1951 and Protocol 1967).

Generally, 'refugees' have been recognised as refugees under the 1951 Geneva Convention, while 'asylum seekers' are in the process of seeking recognition of refugee status but are yet to be assessed. Sometimes the term 'refugee' is applied to people who have fled persecution but have not been formally recognised as having refugee status, either because such formal processes are inaccessible to them or as a more political move to recognise their circumstances despite the lack of formal recognition.

'Migrant' is often used to refer to someone who moves to a new country by choice, often for work, education or family reasons. They can choose to return to their country of origin should they wish to. It is sometimes also used as an umbrella term to include anyone who has moved between countries, in which case it would include asylum seekers and refugees.

General writing advice

Writing is a skill, and like any other skill, it requires practice, patience and a little trial and error. Throughout your academic studies, you will receive feedback along with a mark for your work. The mark is important, but the feedback is more important. What are you doing well, as you should keep doing it? What do you need to do differently, and are you clear about what this might look like? If you do not understand your feedback, seek advice from the person who marked your work, from your personal tutor or from the learning support staff in your institution. We often think our feedback is clear, but students sometimes have a different view, and your feedback about our feedback is also helpful to us in making sure our feedback is constructive, precise and focused on *how* you can improve, not just *what* needs to improve.

Be patient with yourself, and be a risk taker; try out some of the suggestions provided in this chapter. It might not work the first time, but keep at it. As a skill, your ability to write will improve over time, and we have seen many students whose work has improved over the course of their studies as they get feedback and use that feedback to develop their ability to craft an argument and to present it. Learning to write clearly and persuasively is a skill that will help as you move into professional practice, so see your essay as an important aspect of your professional development, rather than just an academic exercise that must be endured.

Key points from this chapter

- Different essay question types have different requirements and will need to be organised and structured in different ways. Three common essay question types are:
  - A question with an answer
  - Compare and contrast
  - Describe, analyse and critically discuss
- Use an essay map to help organise your thoughts, clarify your argument and structure the essay
- An essay should be shaped like an hourglass:
  - Wide at the top = general context
  - Narrow in the middle = specific topic
  - Wide at the bottom = reflect wider implications
- Your essay should build an argument, but it will be strengthened by engaging with alternative points of view or arguments – i.e. using counter-arguments

- Writing a good essay takes time: You will need to plan, write, rewrite and revise your essay
- Writing is a skill, and will improve with time if you can act on the feedback you receive about your work

Suggested solutions

ACTIVITY 7.1

Identifying hedging and boosting language

1. There is strong evidence to <u>suggest</u> that child refugees are at risk of experiencing harm while in transit.	Hedging language
2. The findings <u>indicate</u> that age verification is imprecise.	Hedging language
3. Government policy <u>undoubtedly</u> poses a high barrier that asylum seekers must reach in order to confirm their status as refugees.	Boosting language
4. <u>Many</u> countries express a receptiveness to help refugees even though their immigration policies indicate otherwise.	Hedging language
5. <u>It is clear</u> that the majority of refugees are living in low and middle income countries, rather than high income states.	Boosting language
6. Child refugees <u>often</u> undertake the role of carer and protector for younger refugees, whether related or not.	Hedging language

ACTIVITY 7.2

Using hedging language to qualify statements

Statements	Possible solution
1. Refugees are suspicious of dealing with government officials for a variety of reasons.	<u>Some</u> refugees are suspicious of dealing with government officials for a variety of reasons. *(Quantifier)*
2. Unaccompanied asylum-seeking children should be placed with a relative at the earliest opportunity.	<u>Consideration should be given as to whether</u> unaccompanied asylum-seeking children should be placed with a relative at the earliest opportunity. *(Clause construction)*
3. Providing micro-loans to women in refugee camps to start their own business is a way of reducing gender-based violence and abuse for many women.	Providing micro-loans to women in refugee camps to start their own business is a <u>possible</u> way of reducing gender-based violence and abuse for many women. *(Adjective)*

Further reading

Bailey, S. (2018). *Academic writing: A handbook for international students*. 5th edition. London: Routledge.

Behrens, L. & Rosen, L. J. (2018). *A sequence for academic writing*. 7th edition. Harlow: Pearson Education.

Bottomley, J., Pryjmachuk, S. & Cartney, P. (2018). *Academic writing and referencing for your social work degree*. St Albans: Critical Publishing.

Cottrell, S. (2017). *Critical thinking skills: Effective analysis, argument and reflection*. 3rd edition. London: Red Globe Press.

Greetham, B. (2018). *How to write better essays*. 4th edition. London: Red Globe Press.

8

Writing a Reflective Assignment

In this chapter you will learn:

- What critical reflection is
- The purpose of reflective writing and its importance in social work practice
- About different types of reflective texts used in social work contexts
- How to structure and write reflective texts
- How to link reflection with theory and the literature
- The language, grammar and style associated with reflective texts

---

What is critical reflection?

Critical reflection can be understood as a process for considering ideas, knowledge, assumptions and beliefs in order to improve our personal selves and our professional practice. It is an active, thoughtful process where we scrutinise what we think or believe. The learning that comes from critical reflection can provide us with new ways of working, new knowledge or confirm what we may already think or know. The critical reflective process can make us more aware of the relevant issues in a specific situation, and this may lead us to question socially, culturally and politically constructed knowledge and values.

An essential component of critical reflection is to examine our own subjectivity (D'Cruz and Jones 2004). Our subjectivity is affected by experiences, social positioning, biases, gender, cultural backgrounds, abilities, values and beliefs. Critical reflection, therefore, involves examining our (perhaps) deeply held, hidden or taken-for-granted beliefs and assumptions.

Critical reflection requires that we take a step back from a situation, view it from a distance or another perspective and ask thoughtful questions. Although critical reflection can sometimes be an uncomfortable process, it can also be a transformative process, as we come to understand our views within different contexts (Askeland and Fook 2009). Critical reflection is therefore an essential task of a social work student or social worker.

As a social work student, critical reflection can play a significant role in how you use your experiences as learning opportunities. Critical reflection requires that you evaluate an experience, belief or the information presented to you. It requires you to consider why and how you think the way you do and what has informed your decision to think or act in particular ways. It also requires you to consider how you might practise differently in the future given your new learning.

What is involved in critical reflection?

Critical reflection may be an individual exercise or part of dialogue with another person such as a supervisor, or in a group, for instance in peer supervision. Having critical conversations with colleagues can also be considered a critical reflection process. A potential challenge when reflecting with others can be a power dynamic, for example, between a student and their supervisor. We may feel less comfortable exploring our assumptions and beliefs in a relationship that is unequal, or when the supervisor is also an assessor or line manager. Similarly, organisations can alternatively either encourage or discourage critical reflection of the approaches, policies, legislation and practice being employed.

A culture of power over staff or students can inhibit both engagement in critical reflection and the implementation of improvements in current practice or systems. In these environments it is important to seek out alternative means for critically reflecting with others, for example, external supervision or peer supervision with people outside of the organisation.

WHEN ENGAGED IN CRITICAL REFLECTION, YOU SHOULD:

- Consider how your own lived experience affects your understanding of other people's life experiences
- Identify the possible biases introduced by your own lived experience, values and worldview
- Consider how your own values and worldview connect (or not) with the relevant professional code of ethics and conduct
- Decide on new ways of thinking and being for future situations

Reflection provides us with an opportunity to link different theories and ideas with our practice. You can do this by carefully considering what theories or social work approaches might have informed your decision-making in a particular situation. Sometimes this is not so obvious to us, especially when we first start out as a social work student or newly qualified social worker. Taking time to explore what you thought and how you reacted or acted in a range of situations will help you better understand your practice and enable you to consider how your practice could be improved.

Reflection can also assist us in developing a personal philosophy of practice or integrated practice framework (O'Donoghue, Nash and Munford 2005). This framework includes your values, beliefs, preferences around theories and models and the skills you utilise in your social work practice. Sometimes we are very aware of these aspects of ourselves and our professional practice, although often some components are almost sub conscious and can be difficult to articulate. Our practice framework is not static and will evolve over time as we develop as practitioners. It may also change depending on our life experiences and the fields of practice we work in.

Reflecting on values

Thinking about how your own values impact your practice is especially important. Your values reflect what is important to you and motivate you in your work and daily life. These are different for all of us. It may be useful to spend some time noting down what you consider to be your core values and think of situations in which you have seen these values influence your actions or decisions. Can you think of a situation where your values were different or opposed to someone else's? Did you hold firm to your values or consider a compromise? Did this value conflict create tension with someone else? If you are unsure of your core values, there are simple tests online that can guide you.

In practice, our values guide our thinking, preferences for certain theories and models, and often our views of others and their actions. We need to be careful to respect the values of others, even when we may disagree with them. When we are on placement or working, our values may be inconsistent with the values held by the organisation or the management. Sometimes our values can also be different from those of the service users or others we are working alongside.

ACTIVITY 8.1

Practising reflection

Thinking about your own values and preferred theories, models and skills, reflect on the following questions:

- What has informed my preferences?
- Have I chosen the theories and models intentionally or just because these are ones I think I should be using?
- Am I aware of my values and how they influence what I say and do?

Self-awareness, especially about our values, is critical to social workers because what we say and do directly impacts those who we work alongside. Critically reflecting on our integrated practice framework before, during and after we are working with others enables us to become more insightful, deliberate and effective practitioners.

DIFFERENT TERMINOLOGY ABOUT REFLECTION

There is a range of different terms about reflection in social work. These are sometimes used interchangeably or inconsistently applied (Askeland & Fook 2009; Fook 2007). The following definitions are frequently used in social work studies and practice:

Reflection or reflectivity: Broadly, the process of learning from experience; examining the underlying foundations of one's thinking; ability to consider how beliefs or actions may influence a situation (Askeland & Fook 2009; Fook 2007).

Reflexivity: Closely linked with reflectivity, this is an ability to locate yourself in a certain situation and appreciate how your own self can influence practice or research; may include questioning how knowledge has been constructed (D'Cruz et al. 2007).

Critical reflection: Either examination on a deep or hidden level or reflection connected to critical social theory and consideration of influence of social structures (Askeland & Fook 2009; Fook 2007).

Reflective practice: Practice that is improved upon through an individual's awareness of their hidden assumptions and how this links with relevant professional theories of practice (Schön 1991).

The process of reflection

Reflection is a process that can occur in a range of ways. We might reflect during a situation as well as after it has occurred. We can think of this as reflection-in-action and reflection-on-action (Schön 1991). If we are reflecting during a situation, we may be considering how a person is responding to what we have said, ours and their body language, or other factors that are affecting the situation, e.g. the physical space we are in or whether there are other people around. Through our reflection-in-action we may change our practice approach, for example, how we are responding to a person, the way we are phrasing our sentences or the words we are using.

The reflection-on-action process may occur immediately after an event or some time later. Often, we use supervision as a safe place to reflect more deeply and thoughtfully as our supervisor can guide us through a reflection process and ask us more probing questions than we might ask of ourselves.

There are several models that can guide us through a reflective process, including Kolb's experiential learning theory (1984), the What? So what? Now what? model of reflection (Rolfe et al. 2001) and Gibbs' reflective model (1988). The model we choose to assist us with the reflective process is generally a matter of personal preference. Each model offers similar stages of reflection.

Briefly, Kolb's widely used cyclical model of reflection (1984) has four steps:

1. Have an experience
2. Review the experience
3. Develop conclusions from the experience
4. Plan next steps and test new ideas

Rolfe and colleagues' model of reflection (2001), which we will consider in more detail below, is also relatively simple. It comprises the following questions:

- What? – What was the experience?
- So what? – What lessons did you learn, or conclusions did you reach from the experience?
- Now what? – How are you going to change your behaviour or the way you relate to people given your learning from this experience?

Gibbs' model (1988) is frequently used in social work contexts and provides a straightforward set of six cyclical steps to work through:

1. Description – What happened?
2. Feelings – What were you thinking and feeling?
3. Evaluation – What was good and bad about the experience?
4. Analysis – What sense can you make of the situation?
5. Conclusion – What else could you have done?
6. Action plan – If it arose again, what would you do?

As you work your way through any reflective process, you will need to ask yourself a range of questions and revisit your experience, values and beliefs a number of times. As mentioned earlier, doing this in supervision can be very useful.

The following is an example of a student's reflection on their placement experience based on the six steps of Gibbs' reflective model.

Example: A reflection using Gibbs' reflective model

Description: My placement is in an agency that works alongside Indigenous peoples, with a focus on supporting them to find employment. I am now at week 6. Over the past 2 weeks I have co-worked with my field educator with a 25-year-old woman who I'll call TK. TK has not had any form of employment for 10 years, since she left high school. She is not keen to be in paid work but has been told by the government welfare agency that she has to actively look for work or else her welfare payments will be stopped. She does not have any children, she lives by herself and she describes her usual day as being fun, hanging out with mates and gaming. She seems very happy with this lifestyle and is angry that she has been told to find work. TK said this was how her parents and grandparents had lived so why couldn't she?	Brief description but with some details to identify some of the relevant facts of the situation. Note the use of less formal language: 'She is not keen to be...'.
Feelings: I realised after meeting TK a couple of times that I did not have much empathy for her or her situation. I actually thought she was lazy and self-entitled and should have to get some work and not just take the government's money! I also found myself getting annoyed with her because about three times in a row she did not show up for our meetings and did not call to say she would not be coming. This meant we wasted time waiting for her. I highly value honesty, integrity and punctuality, and TK did not seem to exhibit any of these.	Key feelings identified and explanation as to where these feelings might originate. Initial exploration of own values in relation to the client's. Note the use of less formal language: 'and not just take the government's money!'.

Evaluation: I found working with TK quite frustrating. I talked about it a lot in supervision and unpacked some of my feelings and assumptions. I know that I value hard work, self-motivation and punctuality; all things TK did not seem to value herself. I also think that people should all contribute usefully to our society so we can make it a positive functioning place. TK did not seem to value that either. I realised that I did not understand the upbringing that TK had had or what this would have been like for her and how this might have influenced her own worldview about life, work and the government. I have learned about social inequities for Indigenous populations, but I had not really thought how it could impact on employment as we mostly hear about health, education and incarceration statistics. Overall, I found the situation quite negative, both in terms of my own reactions to TK and also because TK did not seem to want to compromise at all around finding some work.	Further exploration of assumptions and values. Acknowledgement of difference. Indication of the negativity in this situation and what this was concerned with.
Analysis: I think I could link back my feelings to neoliberal theories and the idea that people should work hard and support themselves with minimal government intervention. I also wonder how Indigenous models like Te Whare Tapa Wha could help me to better understand and work with TK. I'm still thinking about that. Critical theory can also help me consider the impact of structures in society on individuals and how power and privilege can affect individuals. I have struggled a bit with the idea of self-determination from our codes of ethics and how this works in a situation like TK's. Do we just say to her she can do what she likes even though the consequences may not be good for her?	Connections made with relevant theories and models so the situation could be examined more closely. Recognition of the complexity of this situation. Note the use of less formal language: 'I have struggled a bit...'.
Conclusion: I have not quite reached a conclusion yet with this situation with TK because we are still working with her. I think though, that I need to work harder at recognising my values and biases and try and put these aside and be more non-judgemental so that I can build a better relationship with TK. I do not think she trusts me yet.	Thoughts about different approaches or what needs to be different.
Action plan: As my next step, I think I need to spend more time getting to know TK, who and what is important to her, what she enjoys doing (apart from hanging with mates) and what she sees her strengths as. That way, maybe she'll be able to identify something that might motivate her to learn something new or get into a workplace she might enjoy. I think this is important with whoever I work with next – try and put my judgements to one side and get to know who they are first. I need to remember my way of thinking or doing is not the only or best way.	Consideration of what approach could be taken next and recognition of the role of self in practice.

Applying Gibbs' reflective model

Choose a recent situation to reflect on. It could be something that occurred with a friend or family member, in class or on placement.

Using Gibbs' reflective model, note your thoughts under each stage of the model ending with an action plan of what you might do differently should a similar situation arise in the future.

Reflective writing

Writing reflectively is an essential skill for social work students to develop. Writing down our reflections can help us better understand ourselves and our practice. It enables us to closely examine what occurred in a situation, our response to it, what may have informed our response and what the implications of our response might be. Thinking about what we might do differently in a similar situation is often the final part of our reflection. We can think about this approach simply as the What? So what? Now what? model of reflection (Rolfe et al. 2001).

There are many different types of reflective text in social work. This is because personal reflection and awareness of one's beliefs, biases and culture and how that may influence interactions with service users and colleagues is a crucial component of being a good social worker. The different types of reflective texts you may encounter throughout your studies include:

- Reflective journal entries
- Reflective eportfolios or portfolios
- Reflective essays

As a student, you may also be required to reflect on:

- Assessment feedback
- Case studies
- Placement experiences
- Individual or group work experiences
- Articles or book chapters

What does reflective writing look like?

Reflective writing is generally:

- Personal
- Inclusive of feelings and beliefs
- A way to explore a situation or experience in depth
- An opportunity to gain a better understanding about yourself
- Structured and may include secondary source material, e.g. academic references

Sometimes, students can find writing reflectively challenging, as you write in a different style from formal academic writing. For example, when you are doing reflective writing you can use 'I' and share your ideas and opinions. This is illustrated in the two annotated examples of reflective texts below: (1) a reflective essay and (2) a reflection on a placement experience.

Writing a reflective essay

When you are writing a reflective essay, consider using a structure that includes a description, analysis and implications. This approach also aligns with Rolfe's reflective model. The description may include your feelings and perceptions of the issue or situation you are reflecting on (the What?). The analysis (the So What?) is your reflection on what resulted from the situation or issue, lessons learned or conclusions made. The final stage is implications (the Now what?), where you consider how what you have learned may affect your actions or practice in the future. In a reflective essay, you would be expected to follow usual essay conventions, for example, essay structure and appropriate inclusion of relevant literature and referencing.

Example: An excerpt from a reflective essay

I recently attended a workshop on the topic of long-term unemployment of Indigenous populations. This workshop provided me with insight about how to consider the specific issues relevant to Indigenous peoples related to long-term unemployment.	Clear introduction outlining the topic of the essay.
Before the workshop, my assumption was that laziness can be a part of the reason for their current situation. Objectively speaking, as a person who had been raised in an upper middle class, non-Indigenous family, and with considerable work experience and education, I was not able to empathise with this client group. This assumption of laziness relates to a social value where I come from: there is a saying, 'no work, no food', which sees diligence or hard work as a virtue.	The student outlines her previous beliefs relevant to the topic and explicitly links them to her socio-cultural upbringing and social values.
However, there were two comments in particular in the video we were shown in the workshop that helped me to compare two different views on the topic and reassess my own perspective. One man said 'If you were born in [town] and got out of it, you did very well', and another man advised those who are long-term unemployed to 'Keep on going, and be positive'. The first speaker stated that the long-term unemployment of Indigenous populations is a consequence of perplexing social-economic and political factors, which often marginalises this group from society. On the other hand, the second speaker was implying that individual effort could reverse the situation.	The student describes the change in their thinking about this topic and explains what caused it. Two differing perspectives on the issue are briefly presented.
I am now aware that questioning my previous assumptions and trying to see the issues from a broader systemic perspective, including increasing my cultural understanding, will help me to identify any biases or judgements I may hold.	Links are made to future practice and personal philosophy of practice.

Central to a social worker's professional practice is the need to make ethical decisions based on core social work values including respect for diversity (ANZASW, 2019). Continual critical reflection on personal values, prejudices and assumptions is crucial if non-judgemental and non-discriminatory decisions are to be made in social work practice (AASW 2010b). Therefore, I will address each case from a social worker's perspective, in order to uncover any unconscious assumptions I hold.	The student addresses social work practice values and links relevant literature to this topic and to their own future professional practice.

Language Focus: Writing about Indigenous populations and considering cultural diversity

Social workers work alongside a diversity of people. It is important that we use language in our reflective writing that is culturally appropriate. We need to be careful not to stereotype or either intentionally or unintentionally colonise or be racist. In some countries, for example, the UK, it is important to be aware of how we label and discuss situations involving migrants and refugees (see Chapter 7), Black and other ethnic minority communities. In other countries, such as Australia and Aotearoa New Zealand, it is important to be mindful of the language associated with Indigenous populations as illustrated in the examples below.

The Australian context

Indigenous refers to Aboriginal and Torres Strait Islander people of Australia
Aboriginal refers to the Indigenous peoples of Australia excluding Torres Strait Islander people
Torres Strait Islander refers to the Indigenous peoples of the Torres Strait Islands
Elder refers to a community leader in Indigenous cultures
Country (with a capital) refers to the ancestral lands of Indigenous Australians
Language (with a capital) refers to the ancestral languages of Indigenous Australians
Always capitalise the words *Indigenous*, *Aboriginal* and *Torres Strait Islanders*.
Use the terms *Indigenous*, *Aboriginal* and *Torres Strait Islander* as adjectives.

The Aotearoa New Zealand context

Tangata Whenua refers to the Indigenous Māori population – literally the 'people of the land' in Aotearoa New Zealand.
Māori are the Indigenous peoples of Aotearoa New Zealand.
Country (with or without a capital) is not usually used when referring to Aotearoa New Zealand.
Language (with or without a capital) is not usually used when referring to the languages of Māori (te reo Māori).
Macrons should be used appropriately when using te reo Māori (Māori language).

Reflecting on a placement experience

Many students will be required to reflect on aspects of their placement experiences. This may include journaling or using tools such as an eportfolio. It is important to give your reflective writing a structure, and in order to do this, selecting one of the reflective models above is helpful.

Be honest and transparent in your reflection but only share what you are comfortable with your lecturer reading if it is for an assessment. Provide enough detail for the reader to understand your context, what occurred, your response to it, your feelings and beliefs, what informed your decision-making and what your further development might need to be.

Where possible, make links with relevant social work literature or research to strengthen your evaluation and analysis of the situation as well as your decisions for your next learning steps. For example, if you are reflecting on an interaction you had with a family, you could consider how ecological systems theory can help you understand the dynamics of the situation. If you reflected on this theory while you were with the family, consider how it guided your conversation or decision-making.

Remember that reflections not only deal with difficult or challenging situations. We can also learn from reflecting on something that went well or was positive.

Example: A reflection from a placement experience (using the What? So what? Now what? reflective approach)

One of the main reasons that I wanted to complete a placement with this agency was so I could become more confident and comfortable within a Te Ao Māori [within a Māori world] setting. Before beginning placement, I was extremely shy about saying a karakia [set form of words, e.g. prayer or incantation] to open and close sessions, bless food, open and close meetings etc. But due to attending karakia in the morning with the rest of my team and also deciding to open and close my supervision sessions with a karakia I have really grown in confidence. I can now say the karakia I have learned without needing to read them. Waiata [song or chant] was also something I was nervous about, yet I love singing, and at my agency they sing every day. This can occur any time during the day, mostly in the mornings and lunchtimes. I now know at least three waiata off by heart, which I am really proud about.	Clear explanation about the topic of the reflection. Awareness of the student's feelings and the connection with their learning goals. The student outlines what has been learned.
From the beginning of placement, I was uncomfortable being in a Māori space, which is a bit bizarre considering that I am Tangata Whenua [Māori], as well as another ethnicity. I noticed my uncomfortableness (and so did my supervisor) because sometimes instead of joining in with karakia and waiata in the mornings I stayed at my desk and said I had university work to complete. About week 3 of my placement, my supervisor asked me about this and I had to really reflect on what was bothering me.	Links with feelings and awareness of their own self in the situation. The student highlights a consequence of their choices.

We talked in supervision about my upbringing and that I have not really had as much exposure to things Māori and I am much more comfortable with my other ethnicity. We talked about Ko Wai Au? [Who am I?] The idea of cultural identity, situating yourself, understanding who you are and where you belong (Paniora 2008). I think for me I'm still figuring that out, although this placement was important in terms of immersing myself within this realm of Māori tikanga [customary system] and being brave to this experience. This is important not just for me personally but also because, as it says in the ANZASW Code of Ethics (2019), social workers "acknowledge the importance of whakapapa [genealogy]", not just for our clients but also I think we need to understand this for ourselves as well.	The student analyses the situation and links to relevant literature/research. Provides justification of why the learning is important. Note the less formal language used, such as 'a bit bizarre' and 'I think for me, I'm still figuring that out'.
Learning about my whakapapa [genealogy] is an ongoing process, but I have some family members who I want to keep learning from about this. Although I now feel confident saying an opening and closing karakia, I want to extend my learning in this area by learning other karakia, especially ones for different purposes, for example, blessing the kai [food].	The student focuses on their future learning areas.
Over my 12-week placement, I became more open to pushing myself out of my comfort zone, and learning karakia and waiata were examples of this. I also grew in confidence about being on the marae [area in front of the meeting house, but more generally referring to the tikanga associated with being near and in the meeting house], and what this involved for me as being part of the tangata whenua of the agency and also a male.	The student recognises their personal and professional development.
There were a few activities that I was anxious about trying during my placement, and I hope to build the courage in the future to do these (Mau Rakau [use of Māori weaponry], Kapa Haka [Māori cultural performing group]). I will need to be active in finding other safe spaces where I can learn and grow in these areas and continue to challenge myself to get involved.	Openness about future learning and awareness of what is required to support this learning.

Reflecting on a case study

Students may be asked to complete reflections on case studies. As with other reflective tasks, using a reflective model will provide a structure for the reflection process. Firstly, consider what information you have been given and what this tells you about the situation. Then reflect on what information is missing or needed to make fuller judgements or decisions. It is important to identify all the people who are involved in the case study and what their roles and relationships are. Consider the values, beliefs and assumptions that people in the scenario may have. Examining what theories, models or knowledge have been noted or could have been utilised in the case study will add depth to your reflection. As you will see in the example below, full sentences may not be required in this type of reflection.

ACTIVITY 8.3

Critical reflection of a case study (Suggested solutions on p. 128)

When we need to reflect on a case study, the What? So what? Now what? model can be helpful.

Read the case study below and write down your thoughts (i.e. reflection). Put yourself in the role of the student:

- What? (description of events or what you are reading)
- So what? (unpacking the event or what you are reading)
- Now what? (what have you learned)

Case study

Sam, a young Pākehā [of white European descent] social work student on placement in a generic child and family social service, was assigned Aroha, a Māori woman about their own age who had recently returned from overseas with her two children. Aroha had previously been drug dependent for 3 years. She had never sustained full- or part-time employment for more than 3 months since she had left high school. She and her children were living in poor circumstances with little money or household items. They received welfare assistance from the government. They all had health problems. Aroha self-referred to the agency as she had previously been a client there before she went overseas. Aroha wants to find appropriate employment to support her and her children.

At the end of their first meeting together, Sam suggested that she contact the woman's whānau [extended kin] in another part of the country but Aroha adamantly refused this. She said she had not had contact for more than 5 years and that when she had previously asked them for help with her drug use they had refused to assist. Sam asked her field educator, Michelle, who was also Pākehā, for support with this idea. Michelle did not feel she could support Sam's idea because she believed Aroha had the right to determine her own course of action. Sam decided later that day to make a 'discreet' phone call to a whānau member, who according to the previous case files had once had a strong relationship with Aroha. The phone call was not positive with the whānau member refusing to have anything to do with Aroha and strongly telling Sam to mind his/her own business. Sam now has to explain the phone call to Aroha and Michelle.

Consider the following questions to get you started:

- What are the key points/events in this case study?
- How might ethnicity or culture shape some of the beliefs or assumptions in this event?
- What was your initial response to what Sam decided to do?
- What other options do you think Sam had in this situation? What might the pros/cons of these be?
- What theories, models, code of ethics or conduct could inform Sam's decision-making?
- If this was you as the student, what might you have done differently?

Because reflection requires that you uncover, examine and evaluate your sometimes hidden or unconsciously held thinking, behaviours and beliefs, it can be an unsettling or personally confronting practice. It is not unusual that questioning your thinking can cause you to feel vulnerable (Béres & Fook 2020). It is OK for us to feel a bit uncomfortable when reflecting as this enables growth, both personally and professionally. Keep this in mind as you go through the process of reflecting.

The language and style of reflective writing

When you are engaged in reflective writing, it is important that your style is clear, succinct and reasonably formal. Remember it is still academic writing.

It is appropriate to use first-person pronouns, e.g. 'I experienced...', 'In my view', 'This affected me strongly'.

It is common to alternate between present and past tense in reflective writing:

- Use the past tense to describe actions that took place in the past and that are complete
- Use the present tense to describe current or continuing thoughts or feelings
- Use the present tense to discuss how your experiences or thoughts link to the research

Use language that clearly indicates the order of experiences, e.g. 'Last week, I encountered...', 'Following this experience...', 'The next day...', 'Prior to this...', 'After some time...'.

Do not use the verb 'feel' to hide your opinion or judgement, e.g. 'I felt the service user was not making an effort'. Instead, acknowledge that you are expressing your opinion or making a judgement and reflect on that, e.g. 'As the service user only gave yes or no responses it seemed to me they were making minimal effort to engage with me'.

DECONSTRUCTING AND RECONSTRUCTING THE LANGUAGE WE USE

"Questioning why we use certain words, terminology, or phrases, and exposing the biases inherent in these, is called 'deconstruction', and it is by deconstructing the language we use, and the stories or narratives which we tell about these experiences, that we can begin to understand more about our own experiences and how we might want to 'reconstruct' them in order to make our desired changes or improvements". (Béres & Fook 2020, 12)

Understanding the central role and power of language is important in both social work education and practice. Reflecting should be a transformative and empowering process for service users, social workers and colleagues. This is why the process of reflecting should be about analysis of actions and how this can lead to positive changes in future practice. For example, keeping your use of language 'strength-based', through articulating the resilience, assets and skills of service users over any deficits or dysfunction, is one way to maintain empowering language in your reflections.

ACTIVITY 8.4

Using appropriate language (Suggested solutions on p. 129)

Identify which of the sentences below are appropriate or inappropriate. Explain why.

1. Having seen the client's apartment, I feel that he is not interested in keeping it clean and tidy.
2. Should a similar situation arise in the future, I would consult with my supervisor before calling a client I had not met before.
3. The author was upset when the client became agitated and started yelling at the author.
4. Reading the assigned article made a significant impact on me and has strongly influenced my thinking about Indigenous issues.
5. The service user felt agitated when the nurse outlined his options.
6. All Indigenous people get addicted to alcohol and drugs easily.
7. I sat alongside the client at the appointment and encouraged them to speak about their situation as the Code of Ethics suggests to enable self-determination.
8. I felt uncomfortable speaking out at the staff meeting but knew I needed to so that the client's perspective could be heard by the multidisciplinary team.

Key points from this chapter

- Reflection requires that you examine your beliefs, values and biases
- Reflecting is a learning opportunity that links your experiences or practice with theory
- Reflection is a process that may occur immediately or some time after an event and requires honesty
- There are several models for reflective writing suitable for social work writing, such as:
  - Gibbs' reflective model (1988)
  - The What? So what? Now what? model of reflection (Rolfe et al. 2001)
  - Kolb's experiential learning theory (1984)
- Different forms of reflective texts may have different styles or structures, though all reflective writing should follow academic writing guidelines

Suggested solutions

ACTIVITY 8.3

Critical reflection of a case study

What? (Description) • The client, Aroha, self-referred to the agency as she wants to find employment. • Sam, a social work student, has been asked to work with Aroha. • Sam wanted to connect Aroha with her whanau, but Aroha disagreed, as did her field educator. • Sam contacted a whanau member anyway, but the phone call was not positive. • Sam now has to talk to Aroha and her field educator about this phone call.	Key people and events are noted.
So what? (Analysis, Conclusions) • Aroha has previously been drug dependent. She has three children and minimal history of employment. • Aroha self-referred, which suggests she was happy with her previous engagement with the agency. We do not know what this engagement was for. • We do not know why Aroha has decided to seek support for employment at this point in time. • Aroha does not appear to have strong connections with whanau. • We do not know about other support systems she may have either in the city or elsewhere. • We do not know Aroha's short- and long-term aspirations. • Aroha is Māori, but we do not know how connected she is with her culture. • Sam seemed to make assumptions that Aroha should be connected with her whanau. • Sam appeared to make their decision to phone the family member based on assumptions rather than listening to the client or supporting their self-determination. • Sam did not seem to have all the information about Aroha's ecosystem. • It is not clear why Sam chose to ignore both Aroha and Michelle's directives. Does this suggest that Sam is not open to listening to other people's points of view?	The identified risk and protective features are outlined, and important missing information is highlighted. This raises questions that could be considered as the case study is developed or in the final 'now what' section. Matters relating to Sam's abilities, knowledge or attributes are suggested.
Now what? (Implications, Next steps) • Sam would have been wise to gather more information about Aroha's support and cultural systems. • The agency might have had an assessment tool to help Sam gather information, or the ecological systems approach could have been of value. • Sam should have considered the relevant codes of ethics and conduct, especially relating to self-determination and understanding diversity. • If I were the student, I would have gathered more information from Aroha, built a trusting relationship with her over a longer period of time and questioned Michelle in supervision about her reasons for not supporting a phone call.	Ideas about what Sam could have done differently or in addition to their actions are suggested. A final comment is made about what the reader would have done as initial steps if they were in Sam's position.

ACTIVITY 8.4

Using appropriate language

1. Inappropriate. This statement is judgemental and uses the verb 'feel' as a way of hiding this.
2. Appropriate. The writer outlines a future plan based on past experience.
3. Somewhat inappropriate. It is acceptable to use the first person in reflective writing. Using 'I' instead would be clearer.
4. Appropriate. Good reflection on the change brought about by reading an article. Appropriate descriptive terms 'significant' and 'strongly' used.
5. Inappropriate. The writer cannot know how the service user felt but is making an assumption. Instead the writer should use the word 'seemed'.
6. Inappropriate. The writer is stereotyping and making assumptions.
7. Appropriate. Description of what they did and research/knowledge that supported their action.
8. Appropriate. Acknowledged feelings and justified reason for their action.

Further reading

Béres, L. & Fook, J. (eds.) (2020). *Learning critical reflection: Experiences of the transformative learning process*. London: Routledge.

Fook, J. & Gardner, F. (2007). *Practising critical reflection: A resource handbook*. London: McGraw-Hill Education.

Gardner, F. (2014). *Being critically reflective*. London: Red Globe Press.

Harms, L. (2015). *Working with people: Communication skills for reflective practice*. 2nd edition. Ebook. Oxford University Press.

Pockett, R., Napier, L. & Giles, R. (2011). Critical reflection for practice. *Skills for Human Service Practice: Working with Individuals, Groups and Communities*, 9–19.

Tanguay, E., Hanratty, P. & Martin, B. (2020). *Reflective writing for nursing, health and social work*. London: Red Globe Press.

Writing a Case Study Analysis

> **In this chapter you will learn:**
> - What a case study analysis looks like
> - The process of writing a case study analysis
> - How to analyse a case study
> - How to link a case study to theory
> - How to develop an intervention plan with clients

What is a case study analysis?

In social work education, the aim of a case study analysis is to test your ability to carefully and objectively analyse given information about a situation and apply a range of theories to it. This will allow you to explore how relevant the theoretical concepts are to the case and encourage you to think about the situation from a practice perspective as well as more broadly. A case study should outline a scenario or situation that presents typical and complex issues faced by a client (service user). You will need to consider the case in light of social work practice, values and ethics, and develop potential interventions. Focusing on one case in detail can clarify the links between social work theory and practice.

The key components of a case study analysis are shown in the following figure. Note that these components are arranged to indicate that they are equal in importance.

The key components of a case study analysis

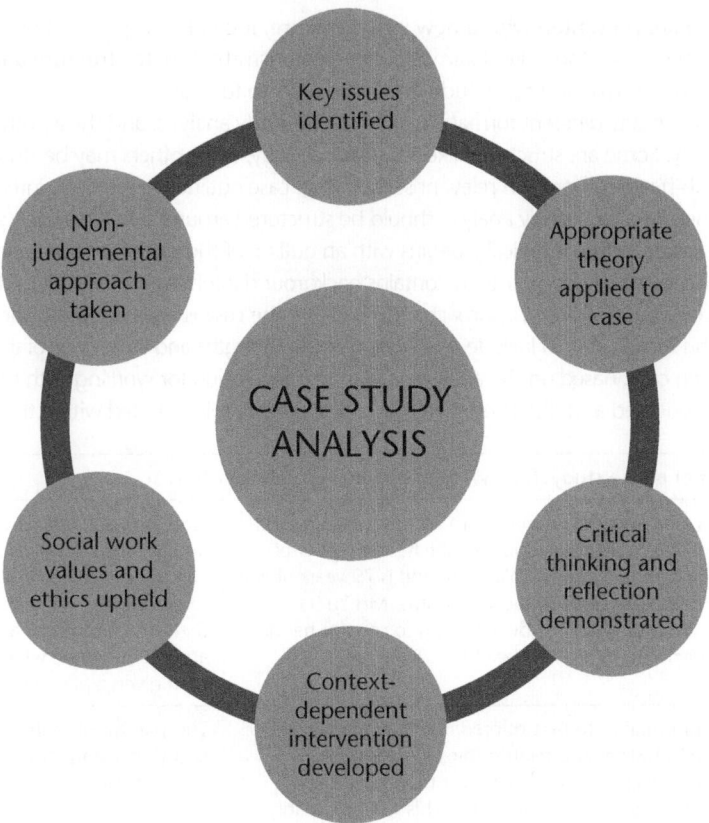

A sophisticated level of analysis demonstrates the following:

An understanding of:	The ability to:
• The case and its context • The social work setting and its focus • A range of theories • Case-related knowledge and social work ethics and values	• Select and apply appropriate theories to the case and context • Develop an intervention that is sensitive to the client's context • Make a clear and well-argued case for your choices • Use appropriate language • Use relevant and recent literature including evidence-based research

This chapter will show you how to achieve this level of analysis, with examples and exercises at each step to illustrate how to integrate all of these components into your analysis. The skills and knowledge covered in this chapter will be crucial for when you start practising as a social worker.

What does a case study analysis look like?

When you are presented with a new written genre, it can be helpful to see examples of what those texts look like. Examples can demonstrate how to structure a text, what sort of information to include and even how to format it.

There are many different formats used for a case study analysis, and the length can vary considerably. Some are structured like a traditional essay, while others may be structured around sub-headings for each relevant section (e.g. case outline, assessment, intervention, etc.). Generally, a case study analysis should be structured around what has been specified in the task description. It typically begins with an outline of the case, the issues and the theory or approach chosen. It then contains background information relevant to the case and the relevant theory and approach. This is where the case is analysed using the chosen theory. This section should include a discussion of the strengths and limitations of that theory to the given case. Based on the analysis, a plan or intervention for working with the client should be outlined and discussed. Often, a critical reflection is included within the text.

Analysis of a case study: family/social history and relationships	
Mrs Yu is a 74-year-old woman from an Asian background with English as a second language. She has a number of significant health issues. Mrs Yu's husband is 79 years of age and is her primary carer. In recent months, Mrs Yu has become increasingly dependent on him to care for her due to her deteriorating physical health.	Note how the first paragraph outlines the facts of the case. Following the description of the relevant facts, the writer has then structured their analysis around four areas which are each given a paragraph.
Further information to be explored in relation to Mrs Yu's family/social history and relationships includes the presence of children, relatives and/or friends, and if any what their levels of involvement are. This will help clarify if there are any informal supports and emotional supports available for the patient. This is particularly important given the care burden that is currently being placed on Mr Yu.	This paragraph outlines the client's existing family and social relationships.
A further consideration that should be taken into account is the role of Mrs Yu's first language. Interpreters or translators may be required by health providers and service staff to communicate with her. In the Australian context, Mrs Yu has a right to such services (Australian Commission on Safety and Quality in Health Care 2019).	The client's language background and needs are described.
Mrs Yu's cultural orientation and information such as migration history are also important to know, as cultural factors influence the care process and patient perceptions of illness (Berkman et al. 2003; McInnis-Dittrich 2014).	Relevant cultural and migration information is included.
In order to develop an appropriate intervention plan for Mr and Mrs Yu, it is important to discuss with them their wishes (e.g. do they wish to remain living in their home?). The next step is to identify the informal and formal supports they have access to (including family and social relationships) and any barriers they may have (e.g. linguistic, cultural, physical needs). Based on this information, the social worker can identify appropriate services available (e.g. local government services such as meals-on-wheels or daycare assistance) that may decrease the care burden of Mr Yu and assist the couple to remain in their home.	The final paragraph discusses the development of an intervention plan to suit the client's identified needs.

Now that you have an understanding of what a case study analysis looks like and should include, the following sections will take you through each of the steps involved in developing a case study analysis. The nine steps involved in writing a case study analysis are illustrated in the following figure. It is important to go back and forth between these steps as needed.

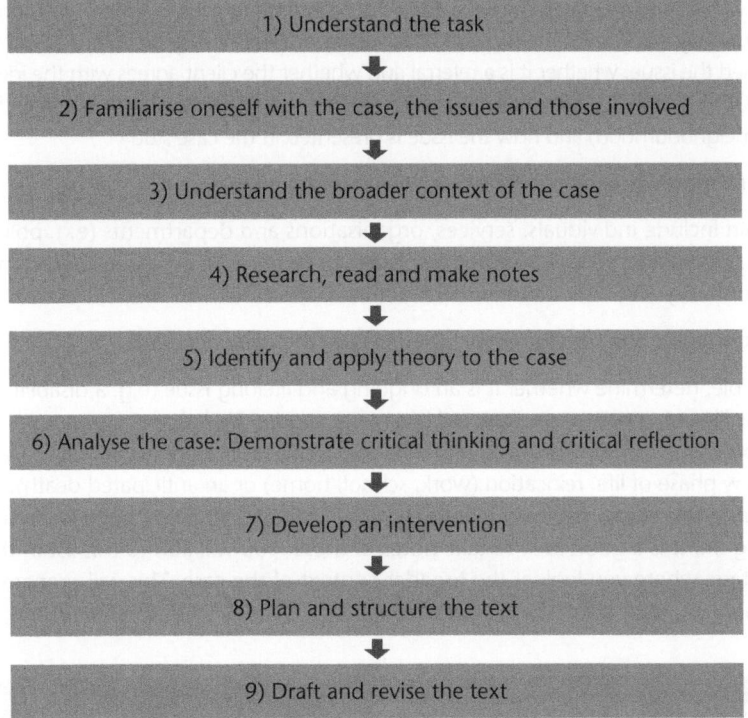

The nine steps of writing a case study analysis

1. Understanding the task

The first step is to read the case study and task instructions carefully. Identify any terms you are unfamiliar with. Do you have enough understanding of the context of the case to write about it? If not, write down the topics you will need to research. Are the task requirements clear? Have you been provided with a task rubric? See Chapter 1 for further details on this step.

2. Familiarising yourself with the case, the issues and those involved

After you have read and understood what is required for the task, the next step is to understand the case itself. This involves:

- Familiarising yourself with the case study and the case setting

First you will need to identify the client/family and the setting (e.g. hospital, prison, sexual assault centre or child protection). Then you will want to identify the role and responsibility of the social worker (this is an important consideration in your case analysis as it can make some issues more salient than others) and the role of others involved in the case (e.g. intake officer, discharge planner or a case worker assessing a client for eligibility). These can add another dimension to the case study analysis.

- Identifying the presenting issue(s)

The next factor to identify is the issue and who is presenting with it. If there are more than one, you may want to list the issues in order of importance. It may be helpful to know who identified the issue, whether it is a referral and whether the client agrees with the identified issue. Other factors to consider include who else is involved in the issue (e.g. other children in the neighbourhood) and how the issue is presented in the case study.

- Identifying who else is indirectly involved in the case

This can include individuals, services, organisations and departments (e.g. police, courts, workplace, school, neighbours, carers or family). This may be related to the chosen theory and direct and indirect factors in the case.

- Determining the timeframe for when events/the issue occurred

If possible, determine whether it is an ongoing and lifelong issue (e.g. a disability or chronic illness), a new or unexpected issue (e.g. sudden illness), a re-occurrence of an issue previously presumed solved (e.g. financial debt) or a future event (e.g. a transition to a new phase of life, relocation (work, school, home) or an anticipated death).

During this stage, you may identify topics or theories that you need to do further reading on. It is a good idea to take notes of these. You will add to this list in the next stage where you look at the broader context of the case. This will prepare you for when you start researching your topic.

CHECKLIST: ASSESSING YOUR UNDERSTANDING OF THE CASE

1. Who is the client/family?
2. What is the agency setting?
3. What are the key issues of the case?
4. Can you distinguish between the presenting issue, recent events, any underlying issue and the symptoms of the issue for the client?
5. What are the client's needs, feelings, beliefs and thoughts about their situation?

ACTIVITY 9.1

Identifying the key issues of a case (Suggested solutions on p. 153)

Read the case study about Antonia and Stavros and identify 3–4 of the main issues to explore in a literature search. State these as questions.

For example: What are the confidentiality issues when working with a child? Does a social worker need to inform the parent who contacted you of all their conversations and the issues discussed?

CASE STUDY: ANTONIA AND STAVROS

You are a social worker employed at a local clinic where your role is to attend to child and youth welfare issues. You receive a phone call from the very distressed mother (Antonia, 42 years) who is concerned about her youngest son (Stavros, 12 years). Antonia tells you that her son spends too much time on his computer and becomes aggressive whenever he is called away for meals or to complete chores. He has stopped attending family outings altogether. The family is Australian/Greek and values regular contact with grandparents and extended family. Antonia overheard her son tell his older sister (Chloe, 16 years) that he has 400 friends on Facebook. His grades at school have dropped since his father decided to buy him a laptop computer to help with his school work.

Antonia is also concerned that Stavros has stopped playing with his friends after school. She has noticed a change in his sleeping patterns and has had to ask him several times very late at night to turn off his computer to go to sleep. In the past year, Stavros' father (Mikkos, 48 years) moved out of the family home after several years of suffering from mild depression. Mikkos recently moved in with a woman he has been seeing (Breeanna, 38 years), after several months of living with his parents.

Antonia is finding it difficult to exert authority with Stavros, who is increasingly ignoring her. Stavros spends most of his time in his bedroom and on the computer and does not appear to be doing any school work or socialising with his friends. He often complains of being tired and feeling unwell and has recently missed school because of nausea and dizziness. Antonia would like you to meet with her son to re-engage him with his social life and his school work.

Antonia sounded very agitated when she was outlining Stavros' change in behaviour, but also seemed unable or unwilling to take action to regulate his time on the computer.

You recall that you have had some conversations with Chloe, his sister, after she had a panic attack a few weeks after her father Mikkos moved out of the family home. The panic attack occurred after she ran up the stairs to return to her class after one hot lunch break.

You vaguely remember that there were some issues with bullying in Stavros' year level earlier in the year and wonder if he was in some way impacted by that situation.

3. Understanding the broader context of the case

Case studies generally introduce a client, the social work practice setting and the client's specific issues. The issues are typically described within their historical, social and political context. When analysing a case study, therefore, you will need to identify the following contextual factors:

- The social work setting in which the client is being seen by the social worker
- The historical, political, social and other relevant background considerations present in the case

A good case study analysis will take into account the context of the challenging issues and potential changes possible in the situation. It will also demonstrate an understanding of the relevant issues (e.g. family violence, substance abuse, homelessness or poverty), as well as the potentially complex interrelationships within a particular setting (e.g. the individuals involved, agency rules and types of relationships present in the case).

CHECKLIST: KNOWLEDGE REQUIRED TO ANALYSE THE ISSUE

1. What do you know about the relevant issues of the case?
2. What are the contextual factors contributing to the client's difficulties?
3. What topics/issues raised in the case do you need to do more background reading on?
4. What is the interrelationship between the intra-personal, interpersonal relationships, social, economic and cultural contexts?
5. How self-aware is the client about their difficulties? (e.g. they may be overusing substances but not aware of this)

For your analysis, it is helpful to identify which levels the various elements of the case belong to as outlined in the table below. Note that these levels are drawn from critical ecological system theory and represent a key difference in approaching a case from a contextual social work perspective. Some models include the exo (structural) level as outlined in Chapter 11 (p. 191).

Levels of analysis: micro, meso, macro and chrono

1. **The micro level**
   The micro level looks at the individual and their friends and family.
2. **The meso level**
   The meso level looks at the broader level of the client's neighbourhood, school and community.
3. **The macro level**
   The macro level looks at the social and political factors that may affect a client. The societal component includes cultural, ethnic, political, economic, religious, racial and gendered relations. The political component involves understanding the legislation, policy and/or programmatic aspects related to the case.
4. **The chrono level**
   The chrono level looks at events in time. It takes into account the impact of new technologies such as social media, the internet and also previous events that impact people now, such as wars, forced migration and episodes such as famines or epidemics.

ACTIVITY 9.2

Identifying the level of engagement (Suggested solutions on p. 153)

Read the case study about Antonia and Stavros above and identify 1–2 issues at each level of engagement.

Micro: _____

Meso: _____

Macro: _____

Chrono: _____

You will need to continually check that you have all the knowledge needed to explore the relevant issues. For example, if the case is of an ageing person with special support needs, what do you know about this topic? You will need to have knowledge of:

- Best current practice in working with a client in the given setting
- Challenges in working with a client in the given setting
- The way knowledge in the field of practice can be applied to the case study
- The theories that are most often applied in the given setting
- The theoretical principles that might best explain various aspects of the case
- New developments in thinking or research about issues in the case (e.g. the influence of childhood trauma on drug use or crime)
- Any gaps in the research on this topic

If you are unfamiliar with a topic, you will need to take notes and do some research and reading. This is the next step.

4. Researching, reading and making notes

You will most likely need to do some background research, reading and note-making (see Chapters 2 and 3) before you begin your analysis of the case and proceed to the next steps. This is where you will need to check your knowledge of what is known about the relevant issues of the case (e.g. drug addiction, family violence, sexual assault, internet addiction and how it impacts on people). Things to look for when reading on a topic include identifying practice wisdom and advice on how to take into account the factors that relate to the issue (e.g. in relation to family violence).

Your reading will inform your choice of theory, your analysis and intervention. Reading about a topic or theory will influence your thinking about a case and your analysis, which may in turn spark your interest in reading further about a related area. For this reason, reading and analysis often occur at the same time, with one step informing the other in a circular way. Make sure you keep good notes when reading. For more detail on these steps, refer to Chapters 2 and 3.

You will be expected to use a range of resources to assist with your analysis of a case. Typically, this will involve sources such as agency policies, processes and procedures, and research studies relevant to the issues raised in the case.

5. Identifying and applying theory to the case

Once you have read the case study, identified the key points to focus on and developed a solid understanding of the context of the case, you will need to start thinking about which social work theories or approaches are most suitable to apply to the case. The purpose of a theory is to help explain something. Familiarity with a range of social work theories at the direct or indirect practice level is needed. Given that social work is a contextual and value-driven profession, some theories are ubiquitous and necessary, such as critical ecological systems theory (Coady and Lehmann 2016). Your unit or social work subject will generally indicate what the level of focus is and whether it is predominantly micro, meso or macro or whether the chrono level also plays a part – though each case links to all of these levels and theories should identify their interactions.

Depending on whether the core issues of a case study belong to the micro, meso or macro levels, a range of different social work theories can apply.

ACTIVITY 9.3

Identifying relevant theories (Suggested solutions on pp. 153–154)

Fill in the blanks in the table below to check your knowledge of various theories commonly used in social work practice. You may add theories that are not listed that you have come across in your studies.

Theory	Description	Levels of engagement
Critical ecological systems theory	A holistic, person-in-environment approach	Micro, meso, macro, chrono multi-level: Focus is on the interaction between systems.
Attachment theory	Early caregiving relationships help children meet their emotional needs for comfort, security and protection. This early bonding assists individuals with personal development throughout life.	Micro: Focus is on the relationship between the caregiver(s) and child.
Client-centred theory		Micro: Focus is on the interpersonal relationship between the client and social worker.
Narrative therapies	A collaborative, non-pathologising and non-blaming approach to enable clients to separate themselves from their problem.	

Theory	Description	Levels of engagement
Cognitive behavioural therapy		
Solution-focused therapy		Micro: Focus is on the client achieving their goals and solutions.

Your selection of a theory should be based on whether the theory is relevant, whether it helps you to understand and explain the case and whether it provides advice on how to approach the case. Once you have identified the theory, you need to justify your choice of theory and relate the theory to the case. You need to explicitly indicate how it can assist with developing a hypothesis about the interrelationship between issues that you have identified in the case (e.g. does the chosen theory explain what is known to reinforce addictive behaviour?). A good analysis will identify any gaps or limitations of the theory and suggest alternative theories or approaches to complement the analysis. You will also need to outline the implications for the client as proposed by the theory.

Example: Applying social work theory and developing an approach to a case study: Maya's family

This critical reflection presents an interpretation of the case of Maya, a Syrian refugee girl, and her family, by adopting the lifespan, life course, and multi-dimensional approach.	This brief introduction outlines the theories applied to the case.
Maya may be facing several underlying issues and challenges. Based on a lifespan approach, middle childhood is a crucial stage for emotional and social development (Harms, 2010). For this reason, further examination of Maya's linkage with others' needs may be required. On the surface she seems to get along with others, but may also have a fear of opening up to them. In relation to her relationship with her mother, Maya appears to be eager to receive validation from her, whilst also showing concern about her mother's physical condition and her reluctance to disclose her sexual assault.	The choice of the lifespan approach is justified, critically evaluated and linked explicitly to details from the case study.
Cognitive development regards middle childhood as 'the concrete operational period', where children learn to be less egocentric and acquire an understanding of the 'self' through interaction with others (Ginsburg & Opper 1979, p. 129). Applying this perspective may be meaningful to understand age-related differences in Maya's thinking and emotions, however, this case cannot be analysed using the lifespan approach alone.	The justification of applying this perspective is provided (understanding age-related differences) and its usefulness explained in relation to Maya's case. A limitation of the lifespan approach is introduced.

Although it outlines the typical milestones (Zastrow & Kirst-Ashman, 2010), 'normative' experiences and behaviour, the lifespan approach cannot fully explain culturally and socially related aspects of each individual (Harms, 2010). For this reason, it is helpful to integrate a life course approach to interpret Maya's specific case: what do her dark drawings indicate? How are the adversities she is experiencing influencing her? How does she see her new life in Australia?	The limitation of the lifespan approach is explained in detail and directly linked to Maya's case (does not adequately account for culturally and socially related aspects). An additional approach to further investigate Maya's case is introduced.
A goal in working with Maya should be to develop a relationship with her and support her to develop her relationship with her mother. Further goals are to assist her to develop her strengths and build social networks.	The goal of the intervention is clearly outlined.
In terms of proceeding with the case, a social worker could use narrative therapy (Geldard & Geldard, 2012) to explore together with Maya her experiences and how they have shaped the way she views the world, herself and her future, and how she relates to others. Using this approach in counselling may help Maya to realise that she is not the problem, but rather 'the problem is the problem' (Geldard & Geldard, 2012, p. 128). Narrative approaches have been documented to be helpful when working with children (White & Morgan, 2004).	An approach to working with the client is outlined, and the choice is justified by linking to relevant references.

Checklist: Assessing your application of theory to the case

1. What are one or two theories that help you to understand and explain the case?
2. How do the theories enable you to understand the client in their context?
3. Do these theories help you to develop a hypothesis about the interrelationship between the various factors of the case? Explain.
4. Are there any gaps or limitations of these theories to the case? What are they?
5. How do the chosen theories complement each other in your analysis?

6. Analysing the case: demonstrating critical thinking and critical reflection

Once you have the required knowledge, you can begin your analysis. It is important to demonstrate critical thinking throughout your case study analysis. This can be achieved in a range of ways:

- Justifying your choice of theory/approach to apply to the case
- Critically evaluating the usefulness of these in relation to the case
- Acknowledging gaps or limitations of the chosen theory/approach

What does this look like? As discussed in Part 1, there is a difference between criticising and critical thinking and analysis. Refer to Chapter 3 for further details regarding how to critically analyse an issue.

Thinking critically is often initially associated with finding fault with something or someone; however, in the academic context, critical means making judgements and evaluations. Indeed, in social work, the trick to analysing a case study is to recognise the common and frequent judgements made of people due to their status, behaviour or difficulties. Unpacking these assumptions is the next step. This requires being clear about what is a fact, and what is an assumption, an opinion or a value judgement – particularly if that judgement is not tempered with compassion and knowledge about structural causes of, for example, poverty or suicidal ideation. Identifying valid information to use in the context of the case study is important in making an informed analysis.

Criticism in social work is often associated with blaming clients for their situation without taking into account more broadly the factors that contribute to a client's difficulties. As such, criticism is not considered appropriate in a case study analysis, as a social worker should not criticise a client or blame them for their situation. For example, you might feel that a parent is not doing a good job parenting their young children because the house is much messier than you are used to in your own living arrangements. The state of the house might be an indicator of some disorganisation in the occupants' life, or it might be an indicator of stressful events and is not a major risk factor in the situation. Critical analysis takes into account the circumstances of the client at a certain point in time while noting what might be worthy of further investigation at the time or at a later stage.

Rather than basing your thinking about a case solely on your own assumptions, you should identify these to ensure they do not unduly influence how you approach a case. In writing a case study analysis, your thinking about these issues is indicated through your use of your language. You will need to describe circumstances and behaviours and arrive at a tentative conclusion, while still being aware that these factors will need further investigating. In a sense you are highlighting how you are evaluating the circumstances and situation for possible meanings and exploring these further.

Critical analysis is not about restating the content of the case study. A description of the case without any consideration of your engagement with it, by analysing or applying theory to the case, is simply not doing anything worthwhile with the information provided. A critical analysis should include identification of your own assumptions about the situation, and objective analysis based on available informa-tion. You will need to make connections or links between various events in the case study without claiming a causative relationship between these events. An analysis should acknowledge possible links and indicate how these might be explored further. This can be done by highlighting how the analysis of information has promoted you to think more critically or deeply about the case.

Example: Critical thinking, criticism and summary

Critical thinking	Criticism	Summary
Stavros' behaviour and physical symptoms have many hallmarks of an adolescent who is becoming too involved in using social media. From a human development perspective, he is seeking peer support and having 400 friends on Facebook is one tangible way he can show his achievements in this regard.	Stavros is rude and inconsiderate of his mother.	Stavros and his mother do not get along.
Antonia is new to parenting on her own, and this presents a major change for her. Previously, disciplining was possibly supported in some way by Mikkos (Stavros' father).	Stavros' mother is not good at parenting because Stavros does not listen to her.	Stavros' mother is not good at getting Stavros to do the things he should be doing, such as going to bed on time, visiting family and attending school.

When analysing a given case, it is important to consider how your own life experiences and values may impact on your interpretation of the case. It is a good idea to reflect on any possible biases you may have that result from your own lived experience and values. Indeed, case study analyses often ask you to explicitly provide a critical reflection of your analysis. A valuable skill in professional practice is the ability to discuss these aspects and how they interrelate with a social work understanding and interpretation of a case. Your arrival at a curious and empathic response to a case depends on this ability. Case study analysis is therefore a task used to assist future social workers to develop empathy, compassion, critical thinking and self-reflection skills in social work practice settings. For more on critical reflection, refer to Chapter 8.

Identifying judgement, bias or personal opinion

A case study analysis should be based on facts and EBP rather than personal opinions or biases resulting from your own lived experience and values. You will need to ask yourself whether your interpretation of a case may be affected by your personal opinions (which may be influenced by your upbringing, religious, cultural and political beliefs, etc.). This requires self-awareness, self-reflection and honesty and can be a difficult task – even for social workers who have worked in the field for many years. Some biases are not conscious and require uncovering. This may require the assistance of others, such as supervisors or tutors, to highlight the influence of unquestioned beliefs, and judgements on our relationship to ourselves and others. It is an important skill and one that will require attention continually throughout your education and your professional life. This is particularly relevant to adhering to the values of the social work profession.

The following activity demonstrates how bias and judgement can be reflected in writing.

ACTIVITY 9.4

Identifying bias and judgement in writing (Suggested solutions on p. 154)

Read the following statements and decide whether they are objective or whether they reflect the author's judgement or bias.

1. The client seems unwilling to take responsibility for their care.
2. The health support staff has raised concerns with the client's family several times about the client's lack of adherence to their care plan.
3. The client's living conditions suggest limited interest in maintaining a clean and tidy apartment.
4. The client has no interest in maintaining her rental property.
5. The client reports being too tired to do housework. She prioritises activities other than housework in order to keep attending her workplace regularly.
6. The client seems uninterested in taking care of her apartment.
7. The client seems overwhelmed by the prospect of cleaning up her dishes.
8. The client appears to struggle with the simplest tasks.

7. Developing an intervention

Based on all of the work you have done so far, you then need to plan how to proceed working with your client. It is important that you directly base this intervention on your understanding and analysis of the case. The intervention you use needs to be context dependent: one size does not fit all in social work.

In planning the intervention, you will need to identify the goals with your client and work with your client towards these goals. In an analysis, you consider how to achieve these goals through collaboration with the client. You will need to think about what the goals are of working with the client, both short term and long term. You may also need to contemplate what priorities the client might have that are different from, for example, the imperatives of the agency or social norms.

There are several options for working with Stavros and Antonia, both separately and together, as outlined in the table below. These options are presented in their logical sequence and are linked to relevant social work theories.

Interventions: Working with Stavros and Antonia

Stavros	Antonia	Stavros and Antonia
Meet with Stavros to establish a trusting relationship in order to discuss what is happening to him at school and at home. Theories: Attachment and critical ecological systems theory.	Meet with Antonia (if she agrees) in order to explore with her how the separation is impacting her life. Theories: Attachment and critical ecological systems theory.	If possible (and both agree), bring Stavros and Antonia together to discuss their situation. This will require careful negotiation. Theory: Narrative therapy.
Explore Stavros' feelings about his father leaving the family home. Explore any goals he might have about his relationship with his father and his mother (as well as Chloe and the wider family). Use an eco-map to highlight sources of support. Theories: Attachment and critical ecological systems theory, task-centred and solution-focused theory.	Explore Antonia's feelings about what is happening with her and her children. Theories: Attachment and critical ecological systems theory, task-centred and solution-focused theory.	Explore what Stavros and Antonia find supportive in their relationship and what they would like to change. Theories: Attachment and critical ecological systems theory, task-centred and solution-focused theory.
Explore any issues around Stavros' friends and any possible bullying behaviour at school or on social media. Discuss the time he spends on Facebook and encourage him to assess the impact on his life. Theories: Attachment and critical ecological systems theory, task-centred and solution-focused theory.	Explore any issues where Antonia feels she wants to make changes – especially in relation to parenting Stavros. Theories: Attachment and critical ecological systems theory, task-centred and solution-focused theory.	Identify any goals or changes Stavros and Antonia wish to work toward. Theories: Attachment and critical ecological systems theory, task-centred and solution-focused theory.
Explore how Stavros would like to proceed. Identify some goals Stavros has for himself personally, and for his interactions with others.	Explore Antonia's support system and identify her goals. Use an eco-map to explore her networks and supports.	Consider including Chloe once the counselling work with Stavros and Antonia is working. If considered appropriate by everyone involved, perhaps include Mikkos (if he agrees) to work through identified family issues at a later stage.

Stavros	Antonia	Stavros and Antonia
Refer Stavros to any services if required. Promote clubs that he may be interested in joining in order to encourage him to build relationships and supports for himself. Theories: Critical ecological systems theory, task-centred theory and strength-based theory.	Refer Antonia to counselling services, financial services or any other relevant services as required. If on-going parenting with Mikkos is an issue, consider promoting couple counselling. Theories: Critical ecological systems theory, task-centred theory and strength-based theory.	Refer Stavros and Antonia to family therapy if required. If desired by them, assist with planning ways to be together as a family that is not pressured or difficult – e.g. a regular outing or birthday dinners. Theories: Attachment and critical ecological systems theory, task-centred and solution-focused theory.

8. Planning and structuring your text

The planning stage of any writing task is crucial (see Chapter 1): It makes the drafting process easier and the end result much better quality. Unfortunately, many students skip this step as they are eager to get started and add to the required word count for the task. Creating the plan and structure helps you get a clear overview of what you are doing and whether you have included everything that is needed for the task.

In order to plan your text, you need an idea of how to structure a case study analysis and the components that need to be included. As the format of a case study analysis can vary considerably, it is important that you follow the task requirements you have been given very carefully. Your case study analysis should generally include the following components:

1. Introduction: outline of the case
2. Background information
3. Chosen theory: overview
4. Application of theory to case, demonstrating critical thinking, including strengths and limitations
5. Intervention: discuss plan, goals, include potential issues, challenges
6. Conclusion

These can be structured in a range of ways: for example, the key points can be analysed in order of importance, or they can be analysed according to the levels of engagement (e.g. micro, meso, macro and chrono).

One possible structure for a case study analysis is as follows:

Structure of a case study

Introduction	Outline the case Identify the key issues State the main theory to be used Outline the proposed intervention
Body	Describe the case in more detail Provide relevant background information Analyse key issues using the chosen theory, demonstrating critical thinking Discuss limitations of the theory in understanding or analysing the case Identify alternative theories to bridge these gaps Discuss your proposed intervention for working with the client Justify the intervention demonstrating critical thinking Critically reflect on the case and its analysis
Conclusion	Summarise the key points of your analysis Make recommendations

9. Drafting and revising your text

Now that you have understood the task, researched the topic, analysed the case and planned and structured the text, you need to begin writing. A simple approach is to use the structure from your plan. In a blank Word document, create a heading for each of the sections outlined in your essay plan, and for each section write what you think is relevant according to your plan.

When re-stating or describing the case study, make sure to paraphrase it in your own words. Presenting it as stated in the assignment task reduces your opportunity to demonstrate your interpretation of the case and often leads to repetition of content. It also does not indicate what meaning or sense you have made of the case in relation to your views, social work ethics, social work theory and practice settings. See Chapter 5 for more guidance on summarising and paraphrasing a text.

Implying a relationship vs. implying causation

When writing up a case study analysis, you want to avoid overstating the cause and effect relationships identified in the case. It is important that you indicate possible relationships between various elements of a case study, but without indicating that 'this necessarily causes that'. The way you discuss and analyse cause and effect relationships is very important in social work and cannot be too deterministic for a range of reasons.

For instance, if you state that Stavros, in the above example, has withdrawn from both his extended family and his school friends because his father left the family home, you are claiming a direct cause and effect relationship between these events. In reality, this may be inaccurate, and the causation might be far less direct. This assumption may also neglect other potential causes (such as possible bullying at school). If you state that Stavros' withdrawal from family and school friends coincides with the changes in his family home, you are drawing a link between these events but not claiming a causative relationship.

You could say that, because Stavros is now the oldest male in the household, he is ignoring his mother in order to assert his role as the dominant male in the household. This again suggests a strongly causative relationship between his gender and his behaviour towards his mother. It is important to check your assumptions when you state that one event likely caused another event. It is best to be cautious and tentative with such claims (see also Chapter 7 on using cautious language and hedging claims). It is possible to hold these ideas as possibilities to be further explored with the client and their family or other professionals involved in the case.

ACTIVITY 9.5

Describing a relationship vs. causation (Suggested solutions on p. 155)

The table below outlines some statements about Stavros' case study. Identify whether these indicate a possible connection or a causative connection between events.

It is rare that a social worker would make a causative connection between events without further investigating the situation. Mostly, social workers are tentative about these relationships and pose them more as a possibility than a causation.

Stavros withdraws from his extended family and school friends...	... coincided with his father leaving the family home.
	... because his father left the family home.
Stavros increasingly ignores his mother...	... because he is now the oldest male in the household.
	... while also increasing his use of his computer and social media.
Stavros' sleeping patterns are changing...	... because he is now a teenager and all teenagers change their sleeping patterns.
	... perhaps influenced by his increasing computer use at night before bedtime.
The panic attack that Chloe, Stavros' sister, had...	... similar physiological effects to her running up the stairs on a hot day.
	... was caused by her father leaving the family home a few weeks earlier.

Refer to the chapters in Part 1 on drafting (Chapter 4) and revising a text (Chapter 6). By this stage in the writing process, you should have a range of resources to acknowledge and reference (Chapter 5). During the revision stage, remember to go back to the task requirements and rubric and check that your work fulfils the expectations outlined.

Examples of a case study analysis

Below is a case study followed by two analyses of the case. The first provides an example of a solid case analysis and highlights the components that make it strong. The second analysis is weaker and highlights the areas that could be improved. These examples will help you to identify the components that can strengthen your analysis as well as illustrating which things to avoid.

CASE STUDY: BEN'S FAMILY

You are one of the social workers at a local service. Ben's (7 years.) mother, Judy (35 years.) recently came to see you to tell you about Ben's medical condition. After a few months, Judy took Ben to the doctor as he was suffering from dizziness, headaches, clumsiness and blurred vision; he was eventually diagnosed with a brain tumour.

Judy was distraught and blamed herself for not seeking medical advice sooner. She felt she should have known something was wrong sooner, because Ben's behaviour had changed in recent times. He was not as happy or physically active as he had usually been.

Judy is worried about Ben's younger sister, Louella (6 years.), who attends the same primary school as Ben. She is concerned that Louella is becoming more introverted at school and not spending as much time with her friends as she used to. Judy worries that Louella is not coping with Ben's illness.

Judy's husband, Michael (40 years.), has previous negative experiences of hospitals due to prolonged childhood hospitalisation and multiple operations following a serious car accident. He is not coping with the many hospital visits required for Ben's treatment and has asked Judy to take over that aspect of Ben's care.

Judy and Michael's parents live several hours' drive away and are in poor health. Judy has a small group of close friends, but she does not want to burden them with her problems. She seems tired and stressed.

You meet with Louella and discover that she is lively and funny. When playing a game, she tells several stories about sadness and loss. Louella also tells you about her brother and how he is no longer like he used to be: he can no longer run, climb or play. She tells you that her parents are very busy now and that she has to be good or else her brother might not get better.

Example: A strong case study analysis

There are several key issues in this case: Louella is experiencing a degree of stress as a result of her home life. She has noticed that her parents are stressed and busy. She has modified her behaviour believing that it may influence her brother's recovery. Judy is experiencing stress due to the extra workload of caring for her sick son and taking him to doctors' appointments. She does not have adequate family support and is reluctant to ask her friends for assistance. Her husband is not taking on his share of the hospital appointments due to his past negative experiences in a hospital.	A descriptive and non-judgemental overview of the key issues in the case.
An approach that would be applicable to this case is critical ecological systems theory (Coady & Lehmann, 2016). This theory looks at how an individual interacts with other groups in their system.	An appropriately chosen and justified social work theory. The theory is introduced and explained briefly.
In this case, Louella's experiences are the result of the interaction between herself and the situation outlined in the case (her environment).	Adequate application of the theory to the case, though, could be elaborated on further. For example: "Critical ecological systems theory focuses on the interaction between the individual and their environment. In this case, the effect of Louella's brother's illness is that some of her social and emotional needs may not be met due to stress on the family as a whole."
Judy's response to her son's illness and the guilt that she feels can be explained using critical ecological systems theory. This theory describes issues and their causes as reciprocal, as all people, situations and environments are interrelated and "...everything in a system is constantly influencing everything else" (Rothery, 2016).	Good application of the theory to the case. A page number is missing for the quote.
In Judy's case in particular, we should concentrate more on the person part of the system rather than the external environment as we would with Louella. Critical ecological systems theory sees a person as a subsystem of needs, biology, capacity, beliefs, strengths and responses interlinked with the resources and demands they have access to. For example, Judy's response can be seen as a result of her needs and beliefs as a mother in relation to her children's safety (that she is responsible for Ben and should have noticed his illness), her capacity and choice to use the resources available to her (when to seek medical assistance) and her guilt-based response to the situation. We must also take into account Judy's husband's dislike of hospitals, which may change her beliefs and responses to compensate.	Demonstrates critical thinking and good application of the theory to the case. The writer is showing that they understand that different aspects of the theory are more applicable to different parts of the case. The writer's reasoning is clearly demonstrated.

A limitation of using critical ecological systems theory alone is that it does not provide the social worker with specific interventions for a particular case, nor does it give detailed mechanisms for analysis of specific aspects of each subsystem (e.g. the 'needs' aspect of a person). Instead, it provides a framework for an overall assessment of a client in their own unique context.	Good identification of the limitations of this theory.
A further approach that could be used in this case is relational theory (Cait, 2016). It is common for a sibling to over-identify with an ill sibling or to feel guilt about their sibling being ill. They may even believe that their behaviour can affect their sibling's illness (Murray, 2000). In particular, this theory can be applied to Louella's case as it seems that her emotional state is set in relation to her brother. This theory addresses critical ecological systems theory's lack of detailed mechanism in the person subsystem, addressing the needs, resources and responses of the person in detail.	Good linking to a further approach to bridge the gap of using critical ecological systems theory.

Example: A weak case study analysis

Ben has been diagnosed with a brain tumour. Judy is distraught and blames herself for not seeking medical advice sooner. She is worried about Ben's younger sister, Louella. Judy's husband is not coping with the many hospital visits required for Ben's treatment. They do not have any family support.	The case description has been taken directly from the case study. There is no interpretation of the case.
The main problem in this case is Ben's medical issue and that his mother is unable to care for him adequately. Judy waited too long before she took Ben to the doctor, and now she feels guilty that he has become so sick.	Incorrect key issues identified. It is not Ben's medical condition that is the key issue, but how the family members are coping with it. Judgement is evident in the language used: e.g. 'problem' rather than 'issue', 'Judy waited too long' indicates blame. The suggestion that Judy not seeking immediate medical help caused a deterioration of Ben's illness is unfounded.
Critical ecological systems theory can be used to understand this case.	Appropriate theory used for the case, but there is no justification for why.
Judy and Louella are both emotional because of Ben's brain tumour. Critical ecological systems theory explains that the causes of issues can often directly relate to each other in a cyclical way. Ben is sick, which makes his sister sad, and this makes her mother feel guilty.	Inadequate application of the theory to the case. There is no direct indication of a cyclical cause, and the explanations are limited. There is also no discussion of other parts of the theory.

One solution is for Judy to quit her job so that she can spend more time caring for Ben. A mother's job is to care for her children, and according to attachment theory this is beneficial for the mother–child relationship (Payne, 2014).	This approach to the case does not take the holistic context into account: Quitting a job and losing one household income is unrealistic for most families and will likely add financial pressure to an already stressful situation. This statement that the caregiver role is a mother's responsibility displays judgement. Attachment theory has been inaccurately used in order to make the writer's point.
Ben's father's hospital phobia can be treated using cognitive behavioural therapy. If successful, he could be desensitised to his fear of hospitals and would be able to visit his son again.	This approach would require the consent of Michael, Ben's father. He would need to agree that this is a goal for him and understand that cognitive behavioural therapy is more than just desensitisation. The other aspects of cognitive behavioural therapy could also be used to reduce Michael's discomfort with the hospital setting.
Judy can be asked to draw on her friends more for help, and using humanistic theory, she can learn to be more empathic to her friends.	Humanistic theory posits that the client–therapist relationship can be healing in and of itself. To use humanistic theory to address Judy's reluctance to ask her friends for more help will require her to value herself more. The ability to receive and accept help is not easy, and the relationship with the social worker can facilitate an increased sense of worthiness that can promote help-seeking behaviour.

Language Focus: Modal verbs

When writing about a potential course of action (as in a case study analysis), the following modal verbs can be used:

Will	Intention, future, pre-arranged plan	This assignment *will* discuss...
Would	Possible, future	Ecological systems theory *would* be relevant to this case...
Can	Possible, future, ability	A social worker *can* contribute by...
Could	Possible, past, present, future	The social worker *could* clarify the requirements of...
May	Possible, future, real	The social worker *may* want to provide...
Might	Possible, future, unreal	The client has expressed that he *might* be interested in...

| Must | Obligation, necessary | A patient *must* be assessed within 2 hours of... |
| Should | Obligation, advice, opinion, suggestion, recommendation, proposal | The social worker *should* consider a range of... |

When writing a case study analysis, you should avoid repeating any colloquialisms that are used in the wording of the case study. For example, a case may describe the client's children as 'kids' based on the way the client is said to have spoken about their children. You should always choose the more formal (academic) term despite the language used in the case study.

It is important to remember that:

There is no one correct approach to analysing a case study. Rather, what makes a strong analysis is your ability to make sense of the situation and to make your own interpretation of the case clear. It is important to discuss the reasons for taking into account various aspects of the case, and this requires that you reference EBP. It is worthwhile to keep in mind those aspects of the case that are particularly relevant to social work practice. One way to demonstrate this is to link your analysis to theoretical concepts in social work relevant to the case.

Social work is a contextual practice driven by particular ethical concerns that are outlined by both international and country-specific social worker associations. For this reason, the approach that you take to analysing a case will require that you adopt a certain ethical position. It is important that you acknowledge both the discrepancy between the life choices and values of the client as outlined or implied in the case study, and that you weigh these against the relevant country-specific social worker association's code of ethics.

Key points from this chapter
- Ensure you take a contextual perspective on case studies and their key relevant issues
- Explicitly demonstrate how theories can be applied to relevant aspects of the case study, including the intervention
- Apply a range of theories in a complementary way to address the various issues in the case study
- Differentiate between possible relationships between events and implying causation when analysing the information given about the case
- Avoid judgement or bias when describing and analysing a case

Suggested solutions

ACTIVITY 9.1

Identifying the level of engagement

Micro: Strained communication between Antonia and Stavros. Stavros's changes in sleep patterns.

Meso: Stavros not attending school regularly. Stavros' attention to Facebook and his communication with friends via social media rather than face-to-face communication.

Macro: Changes in family relationships and the role of parental authority. Gendered relations in society, communities and families.

Chrono: Availability of personal computers and digital devices. People's engagement and possible addictions to internet interactions.

ACTIVITY 9.2

Identifying the key issues of a case

Is Stavros' school refusing? Is he fearful and anxious or rebellious?

What are the internet patterns of teenagers, and how does this inform your thinking about Stavros? Is he showing signs of internet addiction?

What are some of the issues in post-separation parenting and how (if at all) do these apply to Stavros' aggression towards his mother?

ACTIVITY 9.3

Identifying relevant theories

Theory	Description	Levels of engagement
Critical ecological systems theory	A holistic, person-in-environment approach	Micro, meso, macro, chrono, multi-level: Focus is on the interaction between systems.
Attachment theory	Early caregiving relationships help children meet their emotional needs for comfort, security and protection. This early bonding assists individuals with personal development throughout life.	Micro: Focus is on the relationship between the caregiver(s) and child.

Theory	Description	Levels of engagement
Client-centred theory	People's growth and development are achieved through a relationship with the social worker, who offers genuine acceptance, empathy and congruence.	Micro: Focus is on the interpersonal relationship between the client and social worker.
Narrative therapies	A collaborative, non-pathologising and non-blaming approach to enable clients to separate the problem from their person.	Micro: Focus is on the re-authoring of the client's story to enable a new and better story.
Cognitive behavioural therapy	An approach to changing people's thoughts, beliefs and attitudes to assist them to develop coping mechanisms and improve emotional regulation.	Micro: Focus is on psycho-social interventions with clients to promote their mental health.
Solution-focused therapy	Clients' strengths are amplified to support their capacities to make desired changes in their own lives.	Micro: Focus is on the client achieving their goals and solutions.

ACTIVITY 9.4

Identifying bias and judgement in writing

Underlined statements reflect the author's judgement or bias.

1. The client seems unwilling to take responsibility for their care.
2. The health support staff has raised concerns with the client's family several times about the client's lack of adherence to their care plan.
3. The client's living conditions suggest limited interest in maintaining a clean and tidy apartment.
4. The client has no interest in maintaining her rental property.
5. The client reports being too tired to do housework. She prioritises activities other than housework in order to keep attending her workplace regularly.
6. The client seems uninterested in taking care of her apartment.
7. The client seems overwhelmed by the prospect of cleaning up her dishes.
8. The client appears to struggle with the simplest tasks.

ACTIVITY 9.5

Describing a relationship vs. causation

Stavros withdraws from his extended family and school friends...	... coincided with his father leaving the family home.	Possible connection
	... because his father left the family home.	Causative connection
Stavros increasingly ignores his mother...	... because he is now the oldest male in the household.	Causative connection
	... and this coincides with his increasing use of his computer and social media.	Possible connection
Stavros' sleeping patterns are changing...	... because he is now a teenager and all teenagers change their sleeping patterns.	Causative connection
	... and this coincides with his increasing use of his computer at night before bedtime.	Possible connection
The panic attack that Chloe, Stavros' sister, had...	... coincided with her running up the stairs on a hot day.	Possible connection
	... was caused by her father leaving the family home a few weeks earlier.	Causative connection

Further reading

Chenoweth, L. & McAuliffe, D. (2018). *The road to social work and human service practice*. South Melbourne: Cengage Learning.

Coady, N. & Lehmann, P. (eds.) (2016). *Theoretical perspectives for direct social work practice: A generalist-eclectic approach*. 3rd edition. New York: Springer Publishing Company.

Geldard, D., Geldard, K. & Foo, R. Y. (2017). *Basic personal counselling: A training manual for counsellors*. 8th edition. Sydney: Cengage Learning.

Harms, L. (2010). *Understanding human development: A multidimensional approach*. 2nd edition. South Melbourne: Oxford University Press.

Healy, K. (2014). *Social work theories in context: Creating frameworks for practice*. 2nd edition. London: Red Globe Press.

Jordan, R. R. (2003). *Academic writing course: Study skills in English*. Harlow: Pearson Education.

Maidment, J. & Egan, R. (eds.) (2016). *Practice skills in social work & welfare: More than just common sense*. 3rd edition. Sydney: Allen & Unwin.

Milner, J., Myers, S. & O'Byrne, P. (2015). *Assessment in social work*. 4th edition. London: Red Globe Press.

O'Hara, A. & Pockett, R. (2011). *Skills for human service practice: Working with individuals, groups and communities*. 2nd edition. South Melbourne: Oxford University Press.

Payne, M. (2014). *Modern social work theory*. 4th edition. London: Red Globe Press.

Writing a Literature Review

In this chapter you will learn:

- What a literature review is (and is not)
- The purpose of a literature review
- Where a literature review 'fits' within an evidence-based practice (EBP) model
- The steps in conducting a literature review:
  - Identifying your topic and core concepts
  - Identifying, locating and deciding on appropriate literature
  - Evaluating the literature
  - Organising and writing the review

What is a literature review?

A literature review is an examination of a set of written materials on a specific topic. It is completed so as to better inform that topic, either by answering a question or identifying gaps in knowledge (Talbot and Verrinder 2008: 52). Broadly speaking, there are two types of literature review:

1. Standalone literature reviews, which are conducted to answer a specific question. For example, students may be asked to survey the literature – in response to a set question – and to formulate conclusions based on this.
2. Foundational literature reviews, which are the foundation of further work, and which seek to identify patterns, gaps and importantly a focus for research. Students may complete such reviews as part of writing a research proposal, and/ or establishing the groundwork for a study they need to complete.

Here is a summary and comparison of these two types of literature reviews:

Foundational

The aim is to scope and assess existing knowledge to highlight knowledge and gaps (or areas which need further investigation)

This type of review seeks to develop a research question (as the foundation for ongoing research)

At the end of the review, there should be a clear justification presented for a proposed research question and study

Standalone

The aim is to assess (summarise, synthesise and evaluate) a very specific body of knowledge

This type of review seeks to answer a research question

At the end of the review, there should be clear conclusions drawn, and an answer to the question posed

What does a literature review look like?

The following is an annotated example of a literature review:

Example: Literature review: Undiagnosed mental illness in young people who have experienced parental imprisonment in Australia

Excerpt	Annotation
Granger (2019) sought to investigate and map undiagnosed mental health problems in young people in New Zealand who had experienced the imprisonment of a family member.	The study aim and context are described clearly. This enables the reader to see the connection to the topic. This is in the study focus, related study population and comparable geographical setting.
75 young people aged 15–25 years participated via an anonymous online questionnaire.	This brief description of methods shows the boundaries of the study. This allows for a more meaningful analysis of the findings to be presented later in the text.
This compares favourably with the sample sizes of research conducted in Australia, the setting of interest, for example Potter and Weasley (2017), who specifically examined the impact of parental imprisonment on children's mental health.	Here the writer is evaluating by comparing the study with other similar research (and importantly giving the specific reference as evidence), and presenting a conclusion.

Excerpt	Annotation
The study findings indicate high levels of distress, but poor access to mental health services, and limited formal diagnosis, particularly for young men. While these findings reiterate those presented by Potter and Weasley (2017), they are in contrast to the trends indicated in McGonagle's (2015) work. That longitudinal study in the UK indicated that mental health literacy for this group of young people and access to services had improved over the past decade.	The evaluation of Granger's (2019) research is clear here, and compares their findings with those of other studies, highlighting how they are similar but also differ. Note the inclusion of brief, contextual information about McGonagle's (2015) study, which allows those findings to be more clearly understood and critiqued.
This is likely to have been influenced, however, by the targeted public health campaign that occurred during that period by a national not-for-profit organisation.	The findings of the related materials, which seem to be in contrast to the study being discussed (Granger 2019), are evaluated by considering the geographical and historical context in which that study was conducted.
Overall, the anonymous nature of Granger's (2019) data collection suggests that the findings are likely to be quite accurate, although of course, they do not capture the views of students who do not have easy or reliable access to technology.	Considering Granger's (2019) methods here allows for a more nuanced evaluation and conclusion to be drawn about the findings, as well as the potential gaps.
Previous related research shows that this is likely to include those from lower socio-economic areas.	This builds on the earlier evaluation of potential gaps resulting from the study's methods, by being more specific, and linking to past research. Note, however, that no substantiating evidence is presented; that would strengthen the argument.
Overall, Granger's (2019) findings, read in conjunction with related research, suggest that undiagnosed and untreated mental illness is likely to be a problem for young men in Australia who experience parental imprisonment. It is possible, however, that the online methods used may serve to exclude those who are perhaps more likely to be suffering, thereby underestimating the extent of the problem.	Here the writer synthesises their evaluation of a range of sources to draw conclusions, and present new ideas.

Evidence-based practice

One of the key features of social work is the use of a range of knowledge, or evidence, to engage in problem solving around human wellbeing. Using such resources requires skills to critically read and evaluate information, and to ensure decision-making and interventions are based on well-considered and relevant knowledge. The reading required of this process of inquiry and discovery involves you becoming the author of your own understanding (Kurland 2000). It is this understanding of the evidence, when combined with your practice knowledge and clients' views and values, that forms the basis of evidence-based practice.

The basic steps in the EBP process involve locating the best evidence in relation to a specific concern and appraising its quality and applicability, before integrating this into practice (Rubin and Parrish 2007). One common way of identifying evidence and examining it is through a literature review. A literature review has a core role in EBP (Aveyard 2019: 9), as bringing together and examining a wide body of materials on a topic provides practitioners with a stronger, more informed basis for their practice.

In many ways, a literature review is a standard form of assessment, though there is also a lot of variation in how literature reviews are described. Because of this, literature reviews are sometimes poorly understood and explained.

ACTIVITY 10.1

Reflecting on previous literature review examples

Stop for a moment and either find a textbook or look at a writing task you have previously been set as an assignment. How is a literature review defined?

What is 'literature'?

What is deemed to be 'literature' will vary depending on the topic area you are working in and the purpose of your review. One approach identifies four distinct types of literature that may be included in a review (Aveyard 2019: 44–46, citing Wallace and Wray 2016). The following table outlines where you may find these types of literature. See also Chapter 3 for more details on locating key source materials.

LOCATING APPROPRIATE LITERATURE

Literature type	What this provides	Where this can be located
Research literature	Reports findings from systematic investigations (i.e. they have an aim, methods, findings and conclusions) to answer a specific question.	• Journal articles • Book chapters • Academic textbooks
Practice literature	Typically written by practitioners and may include their expert opinion or a reflection on a topic. May provide a description of an intervention (as an example of good practice). May contribute to debates on a topical issue, etc.	• Journals (often those that are more practice or practitioner oriented) • Organisational reports • Conference proceedings • Discussion papers

Literature type	What this provides	Where this can be located
Theoretical literature	Provides a model of how things are expected to happen (e.g. the strain theory of criminology would expect that some people commit offences because they are under pressure [strain] to achieve certain socially desirable goals, without having the means to do so).	• Textbooks
Policy literature	Provides guidelines for organisations or practitioners which are used to make decisions and determine a course of action.	• Government websites • NGO websites • Professional associations' websites • Political party websites

In the majority of instances, however, literature reviews rely mostly on research evidence (Aveyard 2019). When selecting research literature, consideration must be given to using that which is most robust. In this context, the term 'robust' means research – and findings – which are strong. This means the findings:

- Are an accurate account of what the study intended to measure (Are there other factors which could explain the findings?)
- Can be replicated by others (Is there enough detail for others to repeat this study; are they likely to produce similar findings?)
- Can be applied more generally to other situations (not just to your study sample)

Social workers need to use the strongest evidence available in order to base decision-making and actions on relevant and good-quality information. To help make decisions about quality, some scholars subscribe to the idea of a 'hierarchy of evidence'. Such models place studies such as systematic reviews at the top of the hierarchy, and sources such as anecdotal opinion at the bottom (Sackett et al. 1996, cited in Aveyard 2019: 66). (Key terms are described later in this chapter on page Describing a relationship vs. causation.)

Hierarchies of evidence have been formulated to determine effectiveness in health and social care, however, this is not the purpose of many literature reviews (Aveyard 2019). It is therefore important that your study guides what literature you need, and this will depend on your area of research and its purpose. You need to make informed decisions about what literature is available and if it is of good quality.

In regard to social work specifically, knowledge is often located outside of traditional, peer-reviewed publications. For this reason, it is important to consult other sources, notably, *grey literature* (unpublished work or that which is published outside of journals or books) such as government reports, organisational research, practice guidelines, narratives by users and carers, or policy documents (D'Cruz and Jones 2013).

It is generally good practice to seek out the range of available evidence related to your topic and focus on the most rigorous. However, it is also important to ask yourself other questions when deciding on what literature or evidence to include or exclude from your review. (These ideas were introduced in Chapter 3, with practice provided in Activity: Identifying evidence relevant to social work.)

ACTIVITY 10.2

Using big picture skills to read for an assessment task (Example on p. 174)

Think of a topic that you are starting to investigate for an assessment task (it will help if you have done some reading and have a sense of the scope of material available). Taking a 'bigger picture' view, what other reasons, apart from study rigour, can you see for including specific materials in your review? Refer back to Chapter 3 where you were encouraged to think about how your topic has been defined and examined, whose views are absent and the implications for knowledge and practice.

You may want to ask yourself questions about the research, including:

- Does the research offer a particularly new or not previously considered perspective?
- Does the research offer a different way of considering the issue (e.g. perhaps using a new methodology or method)?
- Does the material allow you to understand the research more fully?

A literature review vs. an annotated bibliography

Before we go too much further, it is important to be clear about what a literature review is **not**. One related term/type of assignment is the annotated bibliography; it is not uncommon for students to confuse these. An annotated bibliography is an alphabetical list of citations (this may be journal articles, book chapters, books, etc.) accompanied by a brief account of each source (Jesson et al. 2011).

It is generally accepted that an annotated bibliography may be purely descriptive (citation and summary) or include some evaluation (citation, summary, resource strengths and limitations, along with the relevance to your topic). For this reason, if you are asked to create an annotated bibliography, it is important to pay attention to your lecturer's instructions. Tasks such as these can be useful in helping to define and refine your focus, identify and become familiar with the scope of research in your topic area, and to begin to map and assess these (Monks 2017). This can also help you to prepare for a larger research project, such as a literature review.

The key differences between these two types of writing task are summarised in the following table:

	An annotated bibliography	A literature review
Aim	To provide an overview of individual studies related to a specific topic area.	To analyse and synthesise studies related to a specific topic area.
Structure	A brief statement or outline of the topic, followed by an alphabetical list of individual studies, which includes for each: the citation and a summary of the study (and perhaps some evaluation).	A common structure involves an introduction to the topic (and information on how the studies were identified); integrated discussion and analysis of the studies (see discussion later in this chapter with regard to structuring of this section of the review); and a conclusion.
Evaluation	Some are purely descriptive. For those where there is evaluation, this is focused on the quality and contribution of each individual study.	Analyses and synthesises a body of work relating to a particular topic. Although there is some focus on individual studies, the main focus is on assessing the combined works: evident patterns, strengths, weaknesses, gaps in knowledge, and needs.
Conclusion	A conclusion is not required.	A clear conclusion needs to be drawn, either noting the new insights about the topic – if doing a standalone review; or highlighting the gaps and an area for future research – if the review is foundational.

(Inspired by Monks 2017)

Developing a literature review

A good literature review involves engaging with the work of others (see Chapter 3) and being able to describe and summarise this work. More importantly though, you need to be able to evaluate individual pieces and to compare, contrast and synthesise these in order to form your own conclusions (i.e. your own understandings). These conclusions will either be new insights into the topic, if you are doing a standalone literature review, or will highlight gaps and areas for further research, if doing a foundational review.

To assist with this process, we recommend thinking about this as a stepped process, beginning with identifying your specific topic. This is rarely a simple, linear process, as you will see as we move through this discussion.

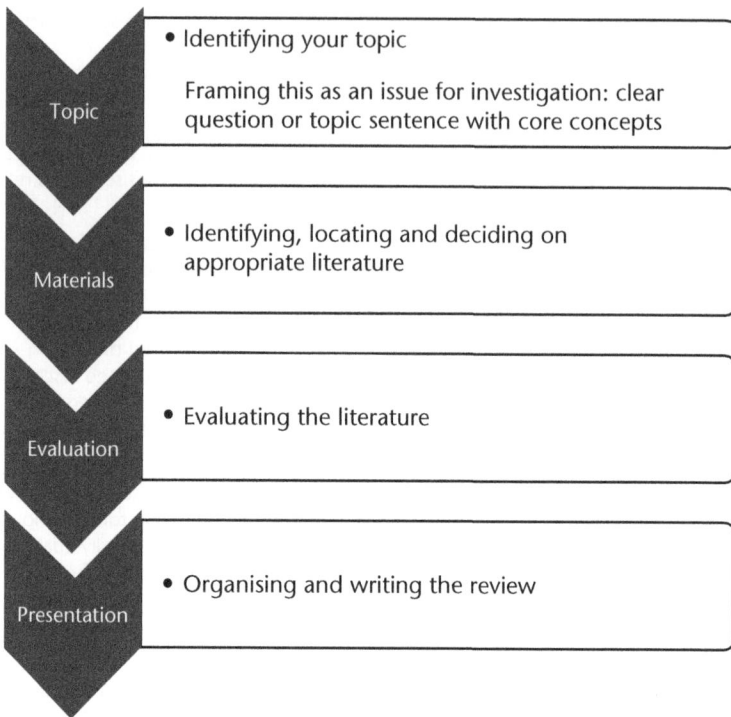

Identifying a topic and core concepts

When starting a literature review, you need to begin by clarifying your topic. To do this, focus on your main concern. Identify whether, for example, your focus is on the needs and experiences of a service user group. Try to be as specific as you can. For example, if you are concerned about women exiting prison, identify the particular aspect that is the focus, such as housing or homelessness.

When making these decisions, you should also ask yourself whether you have chosen a practical and useful area to devote attention to, and to further consider whether this area can and should be researched. Your area of interest may not be a service user group, but may be a specific intervention (for example, a particular parenting programme for fathers in prison) or an issue, such as drug addiction. Again, it is important to be specific. For example, you will need to identify what sort of drugs you mean, or who the user is.

It is also relevant at this time to give some thought to what other disciplines or professions may have produced research, policy or practice guidelines in your topic area. They may present some different perspectives or ways of thinking about the topic. For example, a range of practitioners have contributed to the topic of women leaving prison. These practitioners include those writing in the social advocacy space, as well as researchers from social work, criminology, law, gender studies and public health. If you are working on an assignment now, make a note of what other disciplines may have produced knowledge in your area, as this will help you locate relevant materials.

Language Focus: Offender, inmate, prisoner or criminal?

When working and researching in the area 70.8 of offending and prisons, there is a range of terminology used for those who are involved with the justice system.

In the community: the term *offender* is the commonly used and accepted term across a range of countries to refer to someone who has committed offences.

In prison: The terms *inmate* or *prisoner* are most common, though terms such as *incarcerated person* are also used.

In the community, you may hear people use the term *criminals* or *'crims'*. These are pejorative terms and are not used in academic writing to refer to people, although you will see the term used as a descriptor in areas such as criminal justice, criminal law and criminal behaviour.

The general term *justice-involved* refers to anyone who has been involved with the criminal justice system as a defendant. While this is currently most used in the USA, it is becoming more popular elsewhere, mostly as it seeks to identify, but not label, groups of people.

Terminology matters, as there are likely to be geographical, disciplinary, professional and organisational differences. With regard to the latter, differences are evident across the various statutory and other systems with which *justice-involved* people interact. For example, a woman exiting prison may have been referred to as 'the accused' by the police who arrested her, 'the defendant' by the court which sentenced her, an 'inmate' by the prison, a 'client' by the housing service she is referred to after prison and a 'patient' by the health service she also needs to access. This is relevant when you are conducting a literature review as these variations may also reflect the different terms being used in research articles, depending on what discipline–profession is doing the research, and the key issues on which they are focusing. It certainly helps at the start of this process to think widely about your topic and the range of perspectives, then to focus on your specific area.

ACTIVITY 10.3

Clarifying understanding and communicating clearly (Suggested solutions on p. 174)

Consider one of the examples below or choose an assignment you are working on now. Think about how you could explain, simply, this topic to someone from outside the field of social work. Try to write this down in a single sentence. This will help you to check and refine your own understanding of the topic. It will also help you to clearly identify the core components of your topic.

1. The impact of maternal incarceration on adolescent children
2. The effect of participating in health-focused post-release programmes for women exiting prison

Having established your topic, the next key step is to refine and specify the core concepts. This will ensure you are very clear about your topic, including its boundaries and limitations. In the example above about women leaving prison, it would need to be evident that we meant only adult women (18 years of age and older) leaving prison after serving a period of detention for offences in a specific location (state or country perhaps). Secondly, if you are compiling a foundational literature review as the basis for a study you are planning to conduct, being specific about concepts is invaluable when it comes to deciding where to collect data (who is the sample) and how specific issues will be 'measured'. For example, if you are interested in understanding homelessness, you will need to clarify whether this will be captured by the number of housing moves, or via the types of housing women live in, for example, paying attention to safety, stability, etc.

TIPS: MAINTAINING YOUR FOCUS

Now that you have clarified your topic and the core concepts, it is a good idea to develop a working title or a simple question for your project to keep you focused on the central issues. Here are some things to remember as you do this:

1. At this stage, how specific this title or question needs to be will be influenced by if you are doing a *standalone review* – where you need to have a very specific question – or a *foundational review* – which can be framed more loosely.
2. It is common to revise your initial focus and the key words, either broadening or reducing, depending on how much material you generate initially.

ACTIVITY 10.4

Critiquing a topic statement (Suggested solutions on p. 175)

Ben is planning a standalone literature review, and has posed the following question that he wants to answer: 'What are the experiences of people leaving prison?'

1. What are your initial thoughts on this?
2. What do you think might happen when Ben attempts to search for literature?
3. If Ben is doing a standalone review, do you think his topic/question is specific enough? Why (not)?
4. Are the core concepts clear? (This is important as they tell us what the investigation is focused on.)
5. How might Ben improve on this initial idea?

Identifying, locating and deciding on appropriate literature

Think about the task you are completing, and what you are being asked to do, as a starting point. Is it likely that you will need to engage with any of the other forms of literature highlighted previously on page pp. 160–161? If so, what? Importantly, why?

Rose was an undergraduate honours student whose project title was: 'Examining how Victorian schools respond to students with incarcerated caregivers'. Her research was later written up as an article and published – see McCrickard and Flynn (2015) below.

While the core of the literature review focused on research which investigated the effects of parental imprisonment on children in a school setting, to fully understand this research, the review also needed to examine the role of schools in children's lives. Therefore, the review incorporated an overview of the theory and ideology about the changing role of schools, and the subsequent policies governing practice. It also included an examination of any existing policies with specific regard to the schooling of children who experience parental imprisonment, and research on any impact of such policies and responses.

If you are a student, you will have access to a wide range of databases from which you can source and access peer-reviewed research.

If you are not a current student, there is a range of other accessible sources (sometimes called 'open-access' sources) as follows:

- Directory of Open Access Journals (DOAJ)
  - An independent, community-curated list of open-access, peer-reviewed journals
- The Education Resources Information Center (ERIC)
  - A US-based, online digital library of education research, publications and information
- Google Scholar
  - A free search engine for both peer-reviewed and non-peer-reviewed academic literature
- PubMed: www.ncbi.nlm.nih.gov
  - A free US-based search engine for peer-reviewed academic life sciences and biomedical literature
- ResearchGate.net
  - A commercial, European-based website for academics to create profiles, upload and share research work and publications (both peer reviewed and non-peer reviewed)
- Academia.edu
  - A commercial, US-based website for academics to create profiles, upload and share research work and publications (both peer reviewed and non-peer reviewed)

Whatever sources you access, it is wise to search widely and use multiple strategies, as social work is a discipline that has interests which intersect with many others. Whatever method/s and sources you choose to search, this should be methodical and documented, so that it can be replicated by someone else. You can keep your own records or use online/library tools. Refer back to Chapter 3 for our tips on searching for literature.

Deciding what to include involves quality control as well as some reading and evaluation. As discussed above, the literature you use is shaped by the task you are asked to complete, and it is your task to provide a rationale for the inclusion of your sources. Some assignments require you to be very specific about your approach and choices and may ask you to provide a justification.

For example, in relation to systematic reviews, some approaches have very specific rules about what is included and excluded. Strict systematic reviews will typically only include randomised controlled trials (RCTs), with minimum sample sizes. This type of research is less common in many areas of social work. When doing a literature review in social work, it is therefore more common that you, as the author, need to decide on the boundaries, and what is included and excluded. To help in that process, the following table provides a series of questions to consider; these focus on the applicability, relevance and quality of the work being examined.

QUESTIONS TO CONSIDER AS YOU DECIDE ON WHAT LITERATURE TO INCLUDE		
	Considerations	**Questions and implications**
Applicability	Geographical context	To what extent is the geographical context in which this study was done similar to my setting? (Similarity may be considered in terms of issues such as ethnic groupings and history, such as colonisation, as well as social structures. It is not just prison and justice systems that vary widely across countries; so too do health and mental health systems, child welfare and protection services, responses to family and intimate partner violence, and education systems, to name a few that relate to social work.) Is that environment sufficiently similar for me to be able to claim that the findings are applicable in my context?
	Study population	To what extent is the study population sufficiently similar to likely groups in my population? In what ways are they similar or different? What are the limitations of application in my setting?
	The framing of the issue	How has the issue been framed and investigated? For example, are women leaving prison seen as people in need of practical and emotional support (health issue) or as people who need to be controlled and monitored (law and order issue)? This will have an effect on the types of research done, and the findings presented.
	Overall, in asking yourself these questions and making decisions about applicability, it is very likely that you will need to do some additional reading and investigation – to better understand the context of studies you are reading	

	Considerations	Questions and implications
Relevance	Relationship to my topic	How does the material specifically connect to my topic? Does it focus on the same key concepts? If not, does it address at least two of these concepts? If not, you may need to ask 'is it relevant?' What is the specific connection to my topic? For example, does it examine the same intervention, or investigate the needs of the same or a similar service user group, etc.?
	Recency and impact	When was the source material published? Does it reflect the most up-to-date knowledge? In the social sciences more generally, the past decade is the typically accepted standard. Is the work 'seminal'? This type of source presents ground-breaking work that influences later developments. In these instances, being recent is then obviously less of an issue. You can identify these works as they are often commonly referred to in the more recent publications.
Quality	How has quality been addressed?	Has the paper been peer reviewed? This is a common standard applied when thinking about quality in journal articles. Peer review means that the work has been subject to a 'blind' (anonymous) review by qualified academics and assessed to offer useful knowledge. Ulrichsweb is a database which identifies which journals are peer reviewed or not. You can access this via your library if you are a current student. Many social work journals are peer reviewed, for example, *The British Journal of Social Work* or *International Social Work*. An example of a non-peer-reviewed resource is *The New Social Worker*, which is a magazine-style publication. The peer review process ensures that all work is looked over by an independent, expert assessor, though you cannot rely solely on this as your quality check (Jesson et al. 2011). Reasons for this include potential for publication bias, as reviewers are often selected for their expertise in a particular area. This may also mean that reviewers have much vested in their 'position' and may find it difficult to see alternative, or competing, viewpoints. You still need to ask the critical questions discussed on p. 37.

Evaluating the literature

A very helpful way to start is with an annotated bibliography, discussed above. This can help you to scope out the existing materials and what they contribute to your specific topic, how the findings were generated, what the findings indicate, as well as the limitations. A helpful strategy for gaining an overview is to combine the information on each study into a table using the following headings:

- The article reference
- Study details – aim, methods, sample, data collection and ethical issues
- Findings and conclusions
- The implications for your study

Using a table will allow you to see the patterns across what you have read more easily. Patterns might be simple things such as the location of studies (e.g. most studies have been conducted in the USA, but you are located in the UK), or may relate to the findings, or the methods used to conduct the studies. This allows you to describe, evaluate and compare the materials (Thomas 2000), take a systematic approach to your analysis and begin your synthesis – making connections between the key areas identified in your analysis of each article.

Organising and writing the review

It is important to remember that there is not one correct way to write and present a literature review. The patterns that you identify across the material you read will help you to determine a useful way to organise and structure this writing. See p. 45 for common patterns for organising a range of writing tasks. These approaches include chronological, topical–thematic, and problem and solution. The following table shows some common organising principles and examples.

STRATEGIES FOR STRUCTURING A LITERATURE REVIEW

Literature review organising principles	Example
Type of literature (e.g. policy, practice papers, theory, etc.)	See Rose's example on p. 167 about how Victorian schools respond to students with incarcerated caregivers, where she presented theory, policy and empirical research.
Topic or theme	In this approach, literature is organised by the themes identified in the findings presented in the literature.
Location (e.g. geography, practice setting)	This approach groups literature by the setting in which it is conducted. This can be useful if there are distinct trends in different settings, which can be compared with and contrasted to inform knowledge in your setting.

Literature review organising principles	Example
Chronological	This presents the literature review as developing over time. This can be useful if knowledge in your topic area has developed in quite a sequential and progressive way. A word of caution though – it can be the type of approach that can slip back into an annotated bibliography (i.e. listing and describing the studies and their findings).
Research approaches (e.g. methods or participant groups)	For example, research into social work interventions is often undertaken from worker or service user perspectives; you could structure a review around these differing perspectives.
The 'wheel'	This approach draws together research from different but related strands; it is used when the primary topic has not been subject to any specific research.

(Inspired by Flynn & McDermott 2016; Talbot & Verrinder 2008; Thomson 2016)

ACTIVITY 10.5

Identifying the structure in a literature review (Suggested solutions on p. 175)

Find an article you have recently read or use the example below.

McCrickard, R & Flynn, C 2015, 'Responding to children of prisoners: The views of education professionals in Victoria' *Children Australia*, vol. 41, no. 1, pp. 39–48, doi: 10.1017/cha.2015.15

- Locate the literature review section (sometimes called the Literature review, Background or even just Introduction).
- Can you identify the structure the author has used?

Using reporting verbs to describe and evaluate the work of others

When writing a literature review, you will be describing and evaluating other people's research. To do this, you will need to use the right vocabulary – in this case, reporting verbs. The words you choose can also show your attitude to, and evaluation of, someone's work as illustrated in the table below. See p. 65–66 for more on reporting verbs and p. 103–104 on hedging and boosting language.

Language Focus: Examples of reporting verbs in social work literature reviews

The following reporting verbs are listed in order of the most tentative at the top to most strongly worded at the bottom, with neutral in the middle. Examples from social work literature are provided.

Appear: Authors use this when they are presenting a more tentative conclusion, based on evidence (might be new knowledge or a more limited evidence base)

Further, it **appears** that not only do these children do less well, but they are also more likely to disengage from school, which possibly adds to their poorer outcomes. (McCrickard & Flynn 2015, p. 41)

Suggest: This is often used a bit like 'appear' – so more tentative conclusions based on the evidence

These findings **suggest** that independent skilled visas are being issued to some migrants from the Middle East who require further support on arrival so as to be able to integrate and participate more fully in the community. (Rynderman & Flynn 2014, p. 281)

The most recent estimate in Victoria was made some 15 years ago, when it **was suggested** that around 3,000 children resided in households affected by parental imprisonment (Tudball, 2000). (McCrickard & Flynn 2015, p. 2)

Describe: Used by authors to provide details of what they have read (often useful for understanding their conclusions)

Al Idani (personal communication, 16 July 2009) ... **describes** how expected behaviour in some Middle Eastern countries could be seen to be at odds with what is expected in a job interview in Australia. (Rynderman & Flynn 2014, p. 271)

Find: Used to present specific findings or data (it should be clear here that this is separate from the conclusions authors form on this basis)

Roberts (2012) **found** that a specific fear of stigmatisation in the school environment is one of the greatest concerns for families in Scotland. (McCrickard & Flynn 2015, p. 40)

Indicate: Used to show the link between evidence and a conclusion

The literature clearly **indicates** that the arrest and imprisonment of a parent has profound, long-lasting and detrimental impacts on children (Jones et al. 2013; Murray et al. 2012). (McCrickard & Flynn 2015, p. 40)

Her study **indicates** negative ethnic stereotyping of those from the Middle East as being 'underhand devious and cunning' (Hawthorne, 1997: 41). (Rynderman & Flynn 2014, p. 270)

Note: This is an interesting one, which people use differently. Some use it when it is a minor comment or side note, while some use for an additional point.

Salvaris (1995) also **notes** that more extreme costs of smaller government and managerialism include loss of democratic principles, civil rights and the independence of public servants. (Alston & McKinnon 2005, p. 9)

Stigma is seen to have further effects; Braman (2004) and Nesmith and Ruhland (2011) both **noted** that affected families and carers struggled with the negative stereotypes accompanying imprisonment, which often results in this being kept a secret from others. (McCrickard & Flynn 2015, p. 2)

Recognise: Used mostly to highlight and acknowledge an issue perhaps previously overlooked

Having a parent involved in the criminal justice system **had been recognised** by the Victorian Child and Adolescent Monitoring System (VCAMS) to be an indicator of concern, although it was also acknowledged that little had been done to assess or address outcomes for these children. (McCrickard & Flynn 2015, p. 2)

Report: Used to present findings

He **reports** that in the Middle East, during interviews for jobs, the discussion typically focuses on qualifications and possibly experience; no personal matters such as family, hobbies, interests and philosophies are discussed. (Rynderman & Flynn 2014, p. 271)

Show: Used to present findings

In both countries 2001 census data **show** migrants from Iraq as having the poorest work access. (Rynderman & Flynn 2014, p. 270)

Conclude: Used to sum up evidence and make a key point

He **concludes** that Middle Eastern job applicants in Australia therefore may have no experience of formal interviews for employment in which there is discussion of personal interests and ideas, and that this may cause significant anxiety and likely poorer interview performance. (Rynderman & Flynn 2014, p. 271)

Argue: Used by authors to present their own position or case

Bottrell and Goodwin (2011) **argued** that, because of their existing relationships with families, staff members should provide information and support that enables families to access other agencies. (McCrickard & Flynn 2015, p. 41)

While some **argue** that social work has always been international in character (McDonald 2006; Midgley 2001), others **would argue** that there are key debates to be addressed and resolved about globalisation versus localisation, Westernisation versus indigenisation, multiculturalism versus universalism and universal versus local standards (Gray and Fook 2004). (Brydon et al. 2014, p. 592)

> **Key points from this chapter**
> - The term 'literature review' can mean a lot of things – make sure you clearly understand the task set
> - There is a range of ways of conducting and writing a literature review depending on your aim and focus
> - Literature reviews are versatile: they can act as a foundation for, or response to, a research question
> - Conducting a literature review requires you to have a specific topic or focus, and to critically read and evaluate literature

Suggested solutions

ACTIVITY 10.2

Using big picture skills to read for an assessment task

When Catherine was developing a literature review on the impact of maternal imprisonment on adolescents (also discussed below in relation to terminology) in Australia, she identified a lack of in-depth material from the perspective of adolescents about their experiences. She located two studies that she included. Although these were (1) published by not-for-profit, advocacy and support services (i.e. were 'grey literature' and not subject to rigorous peer review); (2) conducted in the UK; and (3) looked at imprisonment of family members, not just mothers, these studies were assessed as valuable as they offered a very specific adolescent viewpoint, gathered via in-depth methods, outlining detailed experiences.

ACTIVITY 10.3

Clarifying understanding and communicating clearly

1. The impact of maternal incarceration on adolescent children
   This review seeks to understand the emotional and behavioural consequences for young people when their mother is in prison.
2. The effect of participating in health-focused post-release programmes for women exiting prison
   This review seeks to understand women's health service access and their overall health and wellbeing after participating in programmes to support them as they leave prison.

ACTIVITY 10.4

Critiquing a topic statement

Suggested ideas

1. At the moment, Ben's question, and the core concepts are framed very generally and it is difficult to identify his primary concern.
2. Being so general will also make finding relevant materials very difficult.
3. As Ben is writing a standalone review, i.e. one that seeks to answer a question, he will need to develop this idea and focus it more specifically. This can be done by clarifying the core ideas in the question: What are the <u>experiences</u> of <u>people leaving prison</u>?
4. The core concepts are not clear. What specific types of *experiences* does Ben want to focus on? Here is where preparatory reading can help hone in on a topic, by first identifying what the range of issues are for people leaving prison. Research shows a number of challenges, including the risk of drug overdose, housing or obtaining employment. Focus on one element. Who does Ben mean by *people*? (i.e. who is the study population of interest?). Again, a little background reading would show a range of differences between groups of people in prison, from gender differences, to age, as well as the types of crimes people have committed; these all have implications for their release and reintegration in the community. Focus on a specific group. Although not absolutely necessary, depending on the experience Ben focuses on, it may be helpful to be more specific about the timeframe involved with *leaving prison*, as some experiences are more evident in specific periods (e.g. the risk of drug overdose and death being very high in the first 6 weeks post-release).
5. Taking all of this into consideration, Ben might refocus his question as follows (Please note, this is only one of many options): 'How do men aged over 50, who have been recently released from prison, describe their experiences of job seeking?' Once Ben starts to search, he may find there is not enough material on this topic. He may need to widen his focus a little to include other perspectives, e.g. How are the job-seeking experiences of men aged over 50 and recently released from prison, described by men and community corrections staff?

ACTIVITY 10.5

Identifying the structure in a literature review

This review by McCrickard and Flynn (2015) of the school experiences of children with incarcerated parents, uses *themes* as the organising principle; it presents the following themes:

1. The population – children of prisoners

2. The effects of parental imprisonment on children in a school setting

- Stigma
- Behavioural issues
- Academic engagement and performance

3. School responses to children of prisoners

Further reading

Aveyard, H. (2019). *Doing a literature review in health and social care: A practical guide.* 4th edition. Maidenhead: Open University Press.

Becker S., Bryman, A. & Ferguson, H. (2012). *Understanding research for social policy and practice: Themes, methods and approaches.* 2nd edition. Bristol: Policy Press.

D'Cruz, H. & Jones, M. (2013). *Social work research in practice: Ethical and political contexts.* London: Sage.

Healy, K. & Mulholland, J. (2019). *Writing skills for social workers.* London: Sage.

Kiteley, R. & Stogdon, C. (2014). *Literature reviews in social work.* London: Sage.

Writing Case Notes on Placement

In this chapter you will learn:

- What case notes look like
- The language features specific to case notes
- Key considerations for writing case notes
- How case notes assess the person in situation through different levels: relational, social, structural, cultural and time
- How to develop and describe risk assessments and goal and intervention plans

What are case notes?

Case notes document a service user's case and generally comprise three components:

1. An assessment of the situation
2. A risk assessment
3. A goal plan

This documentation is an integral responsibility for social workers and indeed all health professionals. The way that health professionals listen to and write about service users plays an important role in service users' experiences. Accurate and detailed record-keeping can enhance outcomes for service-users, while poor record-keeping can result in poorer outcomes (see Cumming et al. 2007; Preston-Shoot 2003).

Decisions that social workers make are based on a complex matrix of practice experience and observations, ethical considerations, consumer wishes and values and collateral information from carers and other service providers. Encompassing all of these perspectives in case notes, in a concise way, is challenging but crucial to capture the fuller picture of the service user's experience.

Service user and carer perspectives are important to incorporate into social work practice. Apart from tokenistic references, service user and carer views have historically been voiceless in record keeping, but this is no longer considered acceptable. This is because omissions in case notes can result in harm (emotionally and physically), and social workers have a duty of care to avoid this occurring. As such, case notes need to anticipate risks for service users and provide action plans that will prevent them from getting hurt (Australian Government Department of Health 2004; BASW 2014).

What is the purpose of writing case notes?

In brief, there are four main reasons for taking case notes:

1. To keep a history of the person's case
2. To make referrals to other agencies
3. Accountability
4. Legal responsibility

Case notes are an integral responsibility within all of the health and mental health professions. They provide transparency and a chronological record of interactions, observations and actions.

Writing case notes after a critical incident can be clarifying and cathartic for social workers. This process encourages the social worker to reflect on and identify their own strengths, in addition to the service user's problem-solving skills in difficult situations. It also offers an opportunity to review the treatment plan in the context of historical information on file, reflecting on what has or has not worked in the past.

Most health and human services use electronic record systems for case note writing, making integrated care more achievable. Teams can access one another's notes, which encourages continuity of care and prevents individuals and departments from working in silos. Having electronic notes also prevents service users' support from being disrupted when social workers go on leave or get a new job.

Case notes can have medicolegal implications. At times you may be required to describe your support provision in the lead up to a critical incident. You may have to write a statement to the coroner, police or family court, and your notes could be subpoenaed as evidence. When you are working with a service user who is facing court, it is important to raise this at the beginning of a session.

Consider how you would like to be represented in case notes. Service users can access their files through Freedom of Information requests. For this reason, ensure your notes are true and respectful representations of the service user.

Consider your discipline-specific obligations relating to mandatory reporting, ethics outlined by the Association of Social Workers for your country, your workplace's organisational values and relevant policies and legislation (e.g. the Mental Health Act 2014 or the Children Youth and Families Act 2005 in the Australian context).

Key considerations when taking case notes

- Ensure case notes are clear, concise, accurate, reliable, relevant to request and presented appropriately (Australian Government Department of Health 2004)
- Use plain language and avoid professional jargon
- Record case notes as soon as possible to avoid forgetting details
- Include your name and role, the date and the service user's details

What do case notes look like?

Look at this example showing the language and structure used for a clinical case note in a community mental health setting. Time constraints and organisational expectations will determine the brevity of these notes. Note that they are generally not only brief but also direct, omit main verbs and use abbreviations. Often, a new line is started for a new topic.

Example: A case note

Date of contact
13/9/2019

Time of contact
15:30

Type of contact (telephone, in person, other)
In person

Participants
Social worker
Service user, Jessica Jones

Purpose of contact
Planned home visit to review mental state, following concerns raised by family around Jessica's emotional dysregulation.

Contact
Jessica greeted social worker at the door. Happy to have discussion in the living room. Parents weren't present for the review.
Jessica expressed concern about her relationship with her parents. She says her parents are giving her curfews at night and she's feeling 'boxed in'*. She wants to go out at night to meet up with her new friends from TAFE. Doesn't want to be left out/ left behind socially.
She reports sleep and appetite are adequate. Nightmares have dissipated.

Mental state examination
Immediately built rapport. Warm and engaging.
Jessica was wearing clothing appropriate for the weather. Adequate personal hygiene.

Good eye contact.

Affect: reactive.

Mood: euthymic. Jessica describes feeling 'in the middle'.

Nil irritability despite difficult conversation today.

Speech: slightly faster pace. Tone and volume normal.

Thought form: circumstantial at times, however always able to return to the conversation topic with some prompting from social worker. Goal-directed, particularly when speaking about TAFE.

Jessica says she hasn't experienced auditory hallucinations for 2 months.

Cognition: alert. Memory and concentration seemed intact but not formally assessed. Orientated to time, place, person.

Nil psychomotor agitation.

Insight and judgement: Jessica's understanding of her mental health is good, and she's able to articulate early warning signs and coping mechanisms (medication and sensory modulation). She is asking for help to negotiate with family as she recognises the current struggle. This is a significant strength/protective factor.

Risk assessment

No acute concerns re mental state, however there is potential for further fracture within the family unit, and this may have implications for Jessica's support network and housing situation in the future.

Overall impression

No overt deterioration in mental state. Jessica's explanatory model attributes her family's increased concern with her recent surge in independence and personal growth. This is in the context of her family experiencing significant carer burnout and vicarious trauma, having witnessed Jessica self-harm and needing treatment under the Mental Health Act on multiple occasions.

Management plan

Jessica is seeking support from the treating team to communicate with family around her needs/wants.

Family meeting required.

Offer referral to carer support team.

Consider referral to the Bouverie Centre if family work isn't effective.

Next anticipated contact

Schedule family meeting at the clinic for 17/10/19 at 15:00.

Social worker name and designation

Cara White SW3

Notes

* Use the person's words rather than paraphrase if possible.

Language features of case notes

Headings provide structure for the information about the service user's case. Use these headings to ensure that all of the necessary information is included. Case notes should be written using brief and succinct language. Sentences may be incomplete (e.g. main verbs lacking such as in 'Family meeting required'), and articles may be dropped (e.g. 'the/a'). Abbreviations are commonly used for brevity, and special vocabulary (e.g. nil) and contracted forms are used (e.g. isn't).

It is important to be clear who is being referred to at all times. Occasionally, the use of pronouns can cause confusion, so it is sometimes better to repeat who or what is being referred to for the sake of clarity. Remember that case notes will be used by other professionals and may be used for legal purposes. Be mindful of the tenses you use in case notes. If you include direct quotes from the service user, it is important to do this as accurately as possible. This means using the same words as well as the same tense.

Avoid bias and judgemental language when writing assessment notes. As a social worker, you need to write factually and avoid making assumptions. See pp. 215–216 for more on this. Case notes should be written respectfully and avoid stigma as outlined below (p. 196).

See pp. 215–216 for more on this.

ACTIVITY

Identifying typical features of case notes (Suggested solutions on pp. 196–197)

Read the case notes above and underline the features that are particular to case notes.

Identify instances of:

- Brevity
- Abbreviations or acronyms
- Assumed knowledge or expertise
- Assumed specific audience – perhaps writing to certain disciplines and levels of experience/expertise
- Use of service user's words

Writing respectfully

Writing respectfully generally requires more words on the page and takes more time until the writer gets used to the change in approach. The team too will need to get used to how to 'read' more respectful prose. This is needed to fully represent a person, what they tell you about themselves, and their situation.

An example of a respectfully written text from pp. 179–180 is:

Overall impression

No overt deterioration in mental state. Jessica's explanatory model attributes her family's increased concern with her recent surge in independence and personal growth. This is in the context of her family experiencing significant carer burnout and vicarious trauma, having witnessed Jessica self-harm and needing treatment under the Mental Health Act on multiple occasions.

While this could be written in shorthand, much information that is important would be lost. For example, this could be documented as:

Jessica's self-harm is a burden to her family.

There is a risk, however, that longer texts may not be read as carefully as shorter texts by other professionals, so there is a need to juggle competing demands.
Here is another example of a short but less ideal text:

Patient Richards presenting with schiz. episode triggered by AoD abuse.

More patient-centred, recovery-oriented and respectful language might be:

Mr Bradley Richards is a 34-year-old male who has a lived experience of severe and persistent mental health challenges. He is a proud father of daughter Claire who is 6 years old.

He has previously worked as a labourer. Recent downturns in the building industry have limited contract work available for non-tertiary-educated staff. Mr Richards finished schooling in year 11 due to the initial onset of his mental health challenges and associated symptoms of poor self-care, low motivation and challenges in concentration.

Recent loss of work has placed financial challenges on Mr Richards, and therefore his relationship with Claire's mother – with whom Claire lives – is more strained. At times of stress Mr Richards increases alcohol consumption, which at other times would be well described as social drinking. The heavier alcohol consumption appears to have had a negative impact on Mr Richards in worsening his mental health, including symptoms of psychosis.

Stigma is perpetuated through dehumanising language used by service providers. The most common example is the use of 'my client'. Such language has been referred to as micro aggressions: invisible, patronising phrases with a condescending tone of voice (Nemec et al. 2015). The underlying message is that the service user is too vulnerable to try new things without being cradled by the service provider. This is problematic, because we know that growth and significant learnings come from thoughtful risk-taking (Nemec et al. 2015) and interfering with this process may, in fact, hinder or slow down someone's recovery.

What to consider before you start writing

Before you start writing your case notes, you need to consider several factors: Do you have any constraints such as time? What is your role with the service user? Are there any limitations such as legal ones – mandated reporting linked to your role, and/or is the service user receiving involuntary treatment? You will need to consider the importance of listening to and communicating with the service user, and identify the best approach to gathering appropriate information. Here are some points to consider:

- Review collateral information (e.g. information provided by family, friends or the GP).
- Review what has and has not worked in the past, as documented in the file.
- Review notes from last visit.
- Check your electronic records system for contacts with triage after hours.
- Ask yourself the following questions: What is noteworthy in this instance? Who is your audience? How is this information going to be used? If I have to take unplanned leave next week, have I included enough information for another social worker to pick up where I left off?
- Plan the structure of your notes – e.g. if you identify a risk in your notes, classify how immediate and/or in crisis the risk is; demonstrate how you are going to address the risk and in what timeframe.
- Gather all the information the service user has on their own health, by viewing the person themselves as the primary resource for information you respect and utilise.

A description and annotated example of a weak set of case notes follows. This illustrates the sort of things to avoid. Following this is an annotated example of a strong set of case notes, including the language that you will be expected to produce.

Example: A weak set of case notes

Ana is a 45yo woman. Dx of Schizophrenia and a recipient of the DSP. Hx of homelessness but currently living in an OOH property in Oakleigh with her two sons who are in their early 20s. Her estranged husband lives in Melton. She has no other family supports and no known friendships.	This description does not tell us anything about Ana's human side. While progress notes have been described as '…dry lists of dates, payments and skeletal factual accounts that only tenuously refer to the rich complexity and subtlety of the encounter' (Swartz 2006), this should be avoided. Instead, social workers should aim to embody the richness of the person and their strengths in their notes. Note use of abbreviations: Dx (diagnosis), DSP (Disability Support Pension), Hx (history), OOH (Office Of Housing).

Ana was BIBA to Monash hospital on 23/1/19 after her sons reported <u>bizarre</u> behaviour. She was reportedly walking outside in the middle of the night talking to the power lines in the street. She wrapped foil around the whitegoods and radio in the kitchen and wouldn't let anyone use them.	Be cautious of the stigma perpetuated by certain words. The etymology of 'bizarre' is explored in a historical essay on psychiatric vocabulary (Gilman 1983). In the twentieth century, the term referred to language production, delusions that are multiple and fragmented, affective changes and the general behaviour of people with schizophrenia. However, the roots of the word 'bizarre' are embedded in a label used to describe a 'frightening' 'inarticulate' 'madman'. Note use of abbreviations: BIBA (brought in by ambulance).
Once admitted she was given a full medical workup, including MRI and CT scans. Ana <u>seemed drug affected</u> at the time of admission, so the doctors ordered a UDS. It came back negative.	Clinical records should be non-judgemental. Words that may lessen the objectivity of a statement include 'appeared' and 'seemed' (Cameron & Turtlesong 2002). Allow the reader to draw their own conclusions from your observations. For example, instead of describing someone as 'drunk' you could talk about their slurred speech or an unsteady gait. Note use of abbreviations: UDS (urine drug screen). Acronyms that are commonly understood need not be spelled out – e.g. MRI and CT scans.
While on the ward, Ana <u>sabotaged</u> her treatment by <u>refusing</u> to take medication. She <u>went AWOL</u> twice, and her sons had to return her to the hospital on both occasions. On return to the ward, Ana <u>denied</u> illicit substance use.	Language should be impartial and free from unfounded speculations and stigmatising language. Avoid using words such as 'uncooperative', 'manipulative', 'abusive', 'obnoxious', 'normal', 'spoiled', 'dysfunctional', 'functional' and 'drunk' because they have negative connotations and are open to personal interpretation and judgement (Cameron & Turtlesong 2002). Use of the word 'denies' casts doubt on the validity of the history provided by the service user. This word is particularly used in health, in the context of deviant behaviours (Anspach 1988). Note use of abbreviations: AWOL (absent without leave).
Ana was referred to <u>me</u> in the lead up to discharge to Ax her living conditions. <u>During my H/V, Ana's rental was malodorous, and she'd obviously been hoarding for some time. Her sons don't work, they just play computers all day and they are not qualified to be her carers.</u> There were piles of unpaid bills on Ana's kitchen table, including an eviction notice. When I spoke to Ana she <u>lacked insight</u> into the problem. She insists that she wants to return home.	Using the terms 'me', 'my' and 'I' can dilute the objectivity of a progress note. Consider using 'social worker', 'writer' or 'author' instead. Also, weigh up who needs to be heard in the progress note, remembering that there can be an uneven access to voice in clinical documentation (Swartz 2006). This paragraph is immersed in unfounded speculations and assumptions. Counsellors should avoid labels, personal judgements, value-laden language or opinionated statements (Cameron & Turtlesong 2002). Note use of abbreviations: Ax (assessment), H/V (home visit).

Follow up: Ana's living environment is a fire hazard. Given Ana's poor judgement, the <u>TT</u> will need to contact the <u>OPA</u> and possibly apply for <u>EPOA</u> to make decisions around her living environment. Consider CATT support on <u>D/C</u> and refer to the <u>MST</u>. Aim to discharge on 1/2/19.	Use plain English. There has been documented evidence of medical jargon creating a top-down power dynamic between medical professionals and service users (Phillips 1996). Additionally, abbreviations and acronyms can cause ambiguity around the meanings and lead to misinterpretations and subsequent safety issues (Kuhn 2007). Note use of abbreviations: TT (treating team), OPA (Office of the Public Advocate), EPOA (Enduring Power of Attorney), CATT (Crisis Assessment and Treatment Team), D/C (discharge), MST (Mobile Support Team).
It is highly likely that this <u>admission will fail</u> due to Ana's <u>poor compliance with treatment</u>, lack of social supports and other <u>self-defeating behaviours.</u>	Progress notes are often written as a form of handover to other health professionals, so it's important that they instil optimism and confidence in the reader. Notes that focus on the hopelessness of the situation may have negative consequences for service users and health professionals alike. Research into job burnout of mental health professionals found that poor employee wellbeing (variables being stress, fatigue and perceptions around working with demanding service users) was associated with poorer outcomes for service users (Scanlan & Still 2013).

Example: A strong set of case notes

Ana is a 45yo El Salvadorian woman currently living in Oakleigh. Ana is a former hairdresser, stamp collector and mother of two. Ana has a <u>Diagnosis of Schizophrenia</u> and is currently receiving the Disability Support Pension.	It is important to reflect on what information is noteworthy and should be included in case notes. Factors to consider include audience, organisational values, policies, expectations and the social worker's own bias. Social workers do not diagnose, so, for example, in the field of mental health, there is some contention as to whether they should use the psychiatric perspective of the Diagnostic Statistical Manual (DSM) in their progress notes. DSM diagnoses have been found to: (1) help service users make sense of their experiences, (2) facilitate reimbursement by third-party payers, (3) assist in decision-making around medication, communication, continuity of care and psycho-education, (4) validate a person's suffering and (5) formulate realistic hopes (Probst 2013).

Ana was brought in by ambulance to Monash hospital on 23/1/19 after her sons reported concerns around her mental health. They disclosed that she had been walking outside in the middle of the night, talking to the power lines in the street. They added that she wrapped foil around the whitegoods and radio in the kitchen and wouldn't let anyone use them. Once admitted, Ana was given a full medical workup, including <u>MRI and CT scans</u> to rule out any neurological concerns. She was also given a urine drug screening. All tests came back negative.	It is acceptable to use acronyms in situations where the short form would be more easily identified than the whole term (e.g. HIV, a.m./p.m.) (Mathioudakis et al. 2016).
While on the ward, Ana struggled to participate in decision-making around her treatment as all discussions were held in English. She couldn't articulate her concerns around side effects and consequently self-ceased her medication. Once an interpreter was brought in, Ana was able to collaborate with the doctors around her treatment and she agreed to restart her medication regime, with a few modifications to the plan.	Progress notes should reflect the whole picture. A dynamic perspective that accounts for human motivation (e.g. desires, wishes, impulses) and the external world (e.g. structures, rules, demands) is an ethical and honest way to write about others (Rasmussen 2015). By highlighting the service user's narrative, the reader gets a clearer representation of the service user's sense of agency in the moment.
On two occasions, Ana left the ward and went home without approval from her treating team. Her sons supported her to return to the ward each time without issue. After the second occurrence of unplanned leave, Ana revealed that she felt unsafe sharing a room with a stranger. The treating team moved her to a single room.	Everyone should be represented in progress notes through a compassionate lens. This can be achieved by attending to the service user's subjective sense of safety and trust (Rasmussen 2015).
Ana was referred to social worker in the lead up to discharge. Social worker and Ana visited her home and collaboratively identified several tasks that needed follow up. Social worker had concerns around the wellbeing of Ana's cats, which had been toileting inside the house since she'd been in hospital. Ana didn't agree that this was an issue however she did acknowledge that she was struggling to care for them. Ana collected piles of boxes of stamps which were obstructing doorways and posed a trip hazard. Ana highlighted that these were very precious to her however she was happy to explore alternative storage options and have Post-Acute Care (PAC) do a clean-up.	At times, social workers are confronted with the tension between recognition of people's rights to self-determination, decision making, informed risk taking (DHHS 2011) and the mental health system's caution around medicolegal issues and perceived danger. The oscillation between the two areas should be included in progress notes to demonstrate the decision-making journey. Social workers should aim to identify the idiosyncratic aspects of the service user's presentation, including personal strengths, as this ensures a deeper understanding of the service user and a more personalised treatment approach (Macneil et al. 2012).

Ana's sons were present during the home visit. They raised concerns around Ana's unpaid bills and social isolation (she has no contact with her ex-husband nor any other extended family or friends). <u>They are experiencing carer burden</u> and are seeking help.	In this example, the social worker has made a statement based on their clinical experience and personal observation. As objective as we would like to be, we can never be completely unbiased in our social work assessments. A psychodynamic perspective proposes that every social worker has a unique identity, personality, life history and social location (Rasmussen 2015). Given that social work assessments are entirely relational activities, the social worker's bias will impact the interpretation and formulation of the assessment information. It is, therefore, imperative that social workers have a deep understanding of their sense of self when working with clients.
Follow-up: Social worker will explore these issues with Ana 1:1 and offer a family meeting to discuss options including carer support networks, financial counselling or financial administration (if Ana's risk of homelessness escalates and all other options have been exhausted). Ana has a lived experience of homelessness and has developed strong survival skills and resilience. Given this, her contribution to the decision-making process should be given precedence. Referrals to an animal welfare organisation and PAC could also be arranged with Ana's consent.	Explain the decision-making process and the service user's involvement in this journey. Giving primacy to the service user's expert knowledge may have positive implications for their personal recovery and agency (Courtney & Moulding 2014).
Ana is in the early stages of recovery, and her distress tolerance will remain low for some time. However, addressing Ana's housing, financial and social stressors will greatly reduce the pressure on her mental health. She also has two powerful protective factors – <u>she wants to recover, and her sons are supportive of her</u>.	Use hopeful recovery-oriented language in all interactions and documentation (DHHS 2011). Hope has been found to be a key factor in facilitating recovery; It is sometimes also called the 'placebo' effect. There are always opportunities to identify strengths or supports that mitigate the impact of the mental illness (Macneil et al. 2012).

The following is an example of record-keeping negligence. Because of the case manager's poor note-taking and lack of transparency and attention to continuity of care, the service user did not receive the help he needed. This activity tests your ability to identify poor practice in case note taking.

ACTIVITY

Identifying negligence in the process of taking case notes (Suggested solutions on pp. 197–198)

Read the case below and identify what mistakes or omissions were made in the case notes that contributed to the poor outcomes for Terry's care.

Terry's case

Terry presented to the emergency department seeking help for his increasing agitation and feelings of suicidality. The assessment team searched Terry's history on their medical records and found that he is case managed within the hospital's outreach programme. There is mention of Terry's mother's death; however, it is not timestamped, so the recency of this significant event/risk factor is not highlighted. Additionally, the case manager's mental state examinations have been clearly copied from previous weeks, leaving out important clinical observations of Terry's changing and deteriorating mood, affect, behaviour and speech. Moreover, Terry's case manager did not write an interservice management plan explaining Terry's support needs if/when he presents in crisis.

Terry doesn't feel comfortable talking about his grief with a stranger because in the past he hasn't been believed and that's why he doesn't mention it to the assessment team. However, he does tell them that he has been using methamphetamines on and off for the past three weeks to cope with stress.

Without context, Terry is wrongly assessed as a drug seeker and denied an admission to the psychiatric inpatient unit. He is sent home on his own for follow up by his case manager. His medication is not reviewed and referrals for grief/loss counselling and the crisis assessment team are not submitted.

Language Focus: Client, consumer, patient, service user or expert by experience?

The language and labels that we use in both mental health and health matter because they define the power dynamic between the person delivering the service and the person receiving it.

The term 'patient' stems from the Latin verb 'pati', which translates as 'to suffer' (Goldstein & Bowers 2015). The word 'consumer' emerged in mental health care much more recently – indeed commonly used over just these last 20 years – a derivation of the Latin 'consumere', which means 'to use' (Goldstein & Bowers 2015). This phrase, and the discourse surrounding it, opposed the pre-existing paternalism within the mental health sector by highlighting a person's active role in their own treatment and their right to have a choice. It also, however, emphasised market language as health-care has become a commodity in post-industrial and more affluent nations.

In the UK, concerns have been raised around the use of the word 'client' (McLaughlin 2009). This is because the word assumes a hierarchical power position in which the social worker helps the passive client, who does not have the capacity to help themselves.

The current use of the term 'service user' emerged from the consumerist move-ment of the 1990s and the democratic tradition of encouraging people to have a say in their own treatment decisions. Critics have raised a number of issues around this language. The word 'users' has negative connotations as globally it has associations with people who are addicted to illicit substances. There is also concern around the flawed homogenisation of this group of people, assuming that they all have one voice and one identity and that they all use the same service (McLaughlin 2009).

One alternative option is to use the term 'expert by experience' or a person with a 'lived experience'. It has been suggested that this label reclassifies the service user as someone who has specialist knowledge, and because of this, it encourages mutual sharing and respect for skills between the social worker and service user (McLaughlin 2009). These terms also reflect the evolution of consumer involvement in mental health policy and practice.

Given the nuanced nature of these labels and their ability to act as a signifier of social control, it is problematic to champion one term over another. Instead, it is best to ask each individual how they would like to be referred to (McLaughlin 2009).

Generally, the term 'service user' is used everywhere in the world except Australia, where the term 'consumer' is commonly used.

For a history and context around some of this language, see Goldstein and Bowers (2015).

Organising case notes

Case notes may be organised according to chronology and/or themes. Over time, case notes will build on previous case notes as they record the progress of a service user. It is likely that case notes will refer to previous events or observations involving the service user, and provide details and outcomes of interventions or referrals, therefore providing details of a service user across a period of time.

The way you organise case notes is often dictated by the funding body of the organisation you are working in. Other times, it may be that the organisation's staff has determined how to order case notes to ensure urgent matters are mentioned first to be dealt with, with lesser details covered later. Alternatively, it may be that staff has determined a need to know about financial and legal issues early to make plans with people within what is affordable for them and in keeping with any legal obligations or requirements impacting their care.

Case notes in different contexts

The way case notes are written will differ considerably between organisations, fields of practice, countries and even practitioners within the same organisation, and may vary somewhat in the details they focus on. Depending on the work context and the objective of a social worker's work with a service user, case notes can be very specific with a narrow focus, or be quite broad and vary over time. The text below provides an example of the differences found in case notes within three sub-settings located in the mental health context.

Case notes in a mental health setting

Acute settings:

In these settings, case notes are still primarily handwritten on wards and then scanned into electronic records once the service user has been discharged. As a result, your notes need to be legible, structured, succinct and task focused. The social worker role within psychiatric in-patient units is heavily weighted on discharge planning, and that's what your colleagues (registrars, nurses and consultants) will be scanning your notes for. Ideally, your case note should be one to two paragraphs long (unless something significant happened), including a sentence for each of the following points:

- Your interaction/engagement with the person
- Observations around their affect or mood (but not necessarily a full mental state examination)
- Describe your intervention
- What was achieved
- What needs to happen next, within what timeline

As your notes need to make sense to all relevant disciplines such as nursing, medical and occupational therapy, using social work jargon and acronyms is unhelpful.

Non-acute or community treatment settings:

In community teams, notes are more narrative because social workers are seeing service users within their environment. This means exposure to all elements of the person – family, friends, football team affiliations, illicit substance use, grief and loss, pets and physical health issues.

The role of the community social worker intermittently involves treatment under the relevant Mental Health Act. (If a Community Treatment Order is varied to an In-patient Order, the treating team needs to demonstrate that it has exhausted less restrictive interventions first. This will need to be proved via a paper trail. The Mental Health Tribunal and the Office of the Chief Psychiatrist monitor this.)

Social workers in community teams have responsibility for the wellbeing of service users after hours and on weekends, so case notes should include contingency plans that account for a 24-hour clock. Triage, crisis assessment and treatment teams, and police, ambulance and clinical early response teams do not have time to scroll through long-winded stories; they just need the key details. Given this, it is helpful to use sub-headings and bullet points.

Sub-acute settings:

The readership in this area is different from those outlined above because these units (called Prevention and Recovery Care) are run in partnership with non-clinical services. Non-clinical services support service users on their recovery journey and maximise their opportunities for participation in the community. They recruit from a broader pool of staff (in terms of discipline and experience) than clinical services. For this reason, case notes need to be accessible to a diverse audience.

Because of the partnership, social workers need to be mindful that their notes are free from medical jargon and acronyms. They also need to be aware of using clinical words such as 'relapse' or 'symptom' and how this might be interpreted outside the area of mental health services.

Assessment at different levels: relational, social, structural, cultural, time

In conducting an assessment, social workers assess intrapsychic factors in the person's thinking and feelings, beliefs and cognitions. The worker also assesses their interpersonal factors and relationships, social factors and interactions, the impact of policies and institutions in society, and also of society itself, including its norms and values. These different levels of analysis should be reflected in case notes produced by social workers, as social work aims to see the person in situation and work at different levels. These levels are outlined below.

Individual and relational (the micro level): The micro level explores factors such as a service user's understanding of the situation, individual strengths and available resources, physical factors (e.g. health), wellbeing, addiction, psychological factors (e.g. grief and loss) and experiences of violence, abuse and neglect.

Social (the meso level): The meso level includes factors such as a service user's family, significant others, social support, membership of groups and associations, strengths within the family or friendship context, relationships with people who work for organisations involved in a service user's care, health, education, income, housing and employment.

Structural (the exo level): The exo level includes factors relating to organisational systems that are beyond the direct input or control of the service user. This might include the organisations (larger structures) involved in a service user's care, including health services, educational institutions, income or social security providers, housing services and supported employment providers or vocational rehabilitation services.

Cultural (the macro level): The macro level focuses on the following broader societal factors: legislative and policy requirements relevant to a service user's situation, ethical factors, discrimination, culture, dominant discourses (e.g. the sick role under the medical model), relevant environmental factors (e.g. access to affordable childcare, respite, disability services, etc.), community demographics (e.g. an ageing suburb, a predominantly low socioeconomic group area, or a suburb with very high migration from a particular ethnic group or cultural country of origin) and strengths in the community cohort.

Time (the chrono level): The chrono level focuses on whether the above factors are static or changeable over time in a person's day or week, over time in a person's month or year, over time in a person's life story and experiences, and over time depending on services involved and policies and cultural understanding.

ACTIVITY

Identifying issues and describing them respectfully (Suggested solutions on p. 199)

Read the case description below and identify whether the following five sentences from Emily's case notes are clear, concise, accurate, reliable, relevant to request and presented appropriately.

Case description:

Social worker, Emily, has been referred to work with Sarah, who was admitted to hospital two weeks ago. Emily tries using miracle and Socratic questions (techniques from narrative therapy and solution-focused brief therapy) to find out how Sarah would like her life to look after hospital. Sarah's immediate reaction is apprehension and hostility because the conversation has triggered feelings of abandonment and rejection. Sarah sees Emily's questioning as evidence that she is going to be discharged imminently, without any support. Sarah believes that Emily does not understand the turmoil she is currently experiencing.

1. Sarah has difficulty trusting health professionals due to past negative experiences.
2. My client seems uncooperative and difficult to work with.
3. Sarah needs to clarify some goals for when she is discharged from hospital.
4. Goal planning was not possible due to the service user's hostile reaction to the SW.
5. Sarah demonstrates limited insight.

Risk assessment

Case notes should include a psychosocial assessment that takes into account physical, psychological and social aspects of people's lives and is primarily informed by the ecological, systems and life-course theories. Because of the holistic nature of this model, and its acknowledgement of both individual and social factors, it is a helpful framework to use for general assessments (AASW 2015a).

Social workers are well placed to be responsive to coexisting conditions and complex needs as they acknowledge the interface between the individual and the environment (AASW 2015a) and recognise that a personal issue often cannot be addressed without addressing the systemic factors surrounding it.

Social workers are not expected to be specialists in every area of health and human services. However, they are expected to screen for various issues that could be areas for intervention. This requires an awareness of static factors and a dynamic risk assessment approach as shown in the following table (Balaratnasingam 2011).

Risk Assessment: Risk factors for suicide

Static	Dynamic
Previous self-harm	Active suicidal ideation
Diagnosis of mental disorder (especially depression)	Guilt
Substance abuse (especially alcohol)	Hopelessness
Family history of suicide	Current substance use
Recent stressor or loss	Psychosocial stressors
Age, gender, marital status (older age, male, divorced)	Problem-solving deficits

To address risk, this approach adopts co-produced safety plans, which account for multiple narratives from the service user, their carer and/or family and social workers. This provides a deeper understanding of the threat at hand because families and/or carers add important contextual information (Felton et al. 2017). Additionally, service users often identify a broad range of risks, for example, medication side-effects, adding a rich evaluation of the situation (Felton et al. 2017). Co-produced risk assessments can result in a shared responsibility for safety (Adshead et al. 2018), which has positive long-term implications in the prevention of compassion fatigue and carer burnout.

In working with Sarah from the activity above, for example, Emily might become concerned about the risk of suicidality and might ask questions to explore this further. The following table illustrates how her risk assessment might read using the risk factors in the table above.

Example: Risk assessment

Sarah has been diagnosed with a mental disorder and has a past history of family conflict and losses. She presents today (25 Feb 2020) with a moderate current level of suicide risk, due to mild but ambivalent expressed suicidal ideation, moderate sense of guilt, high sense of hopelessness, the psychosocial stressor of imminent discharge to living alone with limited financial and coping resources, and a lack of confidence in her problem-solving abilities. Sarah stated: "I am scared and don't know how I will cope by myself." She said: "I don't feel like life is worth living at the moment." She has noted: "I don't have any friends or family to help me."

Goal planning towards interventions in practice

An intervention plan is what the social worker intends to do; a service will expect a social worker to complete this. This contrasts somewhat with a goal plan, which addresses what the service user would like to achieve or do. A skilled social worker will achieve both in a single goal planning exercise and document.

Before starting goal planning, a social worker will need to establish whether the service user is ready to talk about the future. For some, bringing this up prematurely may be confronting, terrifying and an indication that the social worker does not understand where the service user is at in their recovery. Social workers need to be sensitive and creative in approaching goal planning, and sometimes this involves taking a side step.

Before goal planning begins, it is helpful to explore values. This is an important step in the process as values are the beliefs that define what is important to us. People are more likely to follow through with goals when they are congruent with their values. The International Federation of Social Workers' global definition of the profession's core mandates acknowledges the need to work *with*, rather than *for* people (IFSW 2014). Social workers need to tune in to and develop an understanding of the service users' unique cultural values, beliefs and traditions. The definition encourages an interactive and dialogic process and highlights that every person has their own values and way of knowing.

With this in mind, ensure the goal planning process is entirely collaborative and that you are going at the service user's pace. Discuss the non-linear process of recovery, normalising the oscillations of motivation and mood. Also, when discussing goals with the service user, make sure you are using language that they are comfortable with. The words 'goal' and 'plan' can cause a lot of apprehension, particularly for those who have experienced long periods of institutionalisation. For example, the mental health system has at times been preoccupied with goal planning for the purpose of reaching key performance indicators, rather than recovery, and service users are acutely aware of this.

A goal plan should answer the question of what the service user wants to achieve or do. The following questions should be considered when developing a goal plan.

- Do the goals address the problem(s) as stated?
- Are the stated goals attainable during the timeframe for treatment or work together?
- Will the service user be able to understand the goals as written, so they are accurate?
- Will both the service user and the programme or service find these goals acceptable/achievable?
- Has the service user's stage of readiness to change been considered in the goals as stated?

An example of a goal plan for the service user Sarah is provided in the table below. Note the collaborative approach taken by the social worker and the service user which informs this goal plan.

Example: Goal planning

Sarah has reported that she would like to be and feel safe on her return home after discharge. Her goal is to regain confidence and autonomy in decision making in her life.

To achieve this transition to confidence and autonomy, Sarah would like to be visited by the service. Emily has negotiated this will be with the crisis team twice a week for the first two weeks, and then for a fortnightly meeting with the case worker from the community mental health service for two months while Sarah regains her confidence. After this time, they will reassess frequency of contact and nature of contact, including whether Sarah can then come in for reviews at the mental health clinic.

Sarah plans not to engage in self-harm during this time. If she feels at risk of doing so, she will use the 24-hour phone number she has been provided with.

After the initial two weeks, Sarah has expressed the goal to start to re-establish links with friends and family, first by telephone and then in person for a coffee or lunch. By meeting in the daytime she will not be frightened of travelling in the dark at night alone, and she is less likely to be exposed to drinking – an issue since Sarah reports that alcohol reduces her feeling of being safe and in control.

Sarah will start to think about a return to work or study, as later goals, and will have a discussion about this with her social worker Emily. That discussion will be put on hold for the first month, however, so as to avoid adding stress by trying to achieve too much too soon.

It is a good idea to ensure the planned goals are in line with SMART goals. These state that goals are: specific, measurable, attainable, realistic and time-limited/timely.

- Specific – Are there specific activities included in the plan? Will the service user understand what is expected if and when you share the goals as stated?
- Measurable – Can any change or progress toward meeting the goals and objectives be documented and evaluated over time?
- Attainable – Will the service user be able to move toward meeting the objectives?
- Realistic – Can the service user meet the goals given their current situation?
- Time-limited/timely – Is the timeframe specified for the goals and objectives?

ACTIVITY

SMART goal planning (Suggested solutions on p. 200)

Evaluate how SMART Sarah's goal plan outlined above is.

While goal planning can be very stressful for service users, it may also create significant angst for social workers. High caseloads, unrealistic expectations from executive management and time constraints around episodes of care contribute to the mounting pressure that may be experienced by some social workers. Parallel processes describe the psychoanalytic concept of transference. Social workers can displace their chronic frustration and anger with the system into their interactions with service users. Social workers become hopeless about their capacity to make a difference and simultaneously lose faith in the service user's ability to move forward in life (Bloom 2010). Without the energy and motivation for planning, the work becomes reactive and crisis-oriented and service providers resort to more coercive measures (Bloom 2010). This is something that all social workers should keep in mind throughout their careers.

Key points from this chapter

- Writing case notes is an integral part of social work practice
- Case notes should include an assessment of the situation, a risk assessment and a goal plan
- Your role and work context may shape the substance and structure of your notes
- Social work assessments should focus on different levels: relational, social, structural, cultural, time
- Case notes are underpinned by social work ethics and values, with an emphasis on respect
- Focus on the service user's own perception of their situation and what is important

---

Suggested solutions

ACTIVITY

Identifying typical features of case notes

Brevity
> Jessica greeted social worker at the door. Happy to have discussion in the living room.
> Immediately built rapport. Warm and engaging
> Adequate personal hygiene
> Family meeting required

Abbreviations or acronyms
> Nil
> re
> SW3

Assumed knowledge or expertise
> Mood: euthymic
> Nil psychomotor agitation

Assumed specific audience
> Jessica's explanatory model attributes her family's increased concern with her recent surge in independence and personal growth.

Use of service user's words
> 'boxed in'
> 'in the middle'

Identifying negligence in the process of taking case notes

Read the case below and identify what mistakes or omissions were made in the case notes that contributed to the poor outcomes for Terry's care.

Terry's case

Terry presented to the emergency department seeking help for his increasing elevation and suicidality. The assessment team searched Terry's history on their medical records and found that he is case managed within the hospital's outreach programme. There is mention of Terry's mother's death; however, it is not times-tamped (1) so the recency of this significant event/risk factor is not highlighted. Additionally, the case manager's mental state examinations have been clearly copied from previous weeks, leaving out important clinical observations (2) of Terry's changing and deteriorating mood, affect, behaviour and speech. Moreover, Terry's case manager did not write an interservice management plan (3) explaining Terry's support needs if/when he presents in crisis.

Terry doesn't feel comfortable talking about his grief with a stranger because in the past he hasn't been believed (4) and that's why he doesn't mention it to the assessment team. However, he does tell them that he has been using methamphetamines on and off for the past three weeks to cope with stress.

Without context (and illicit substance use in the background) Terry is wrongly assessed as a drug seeker and denied an admission to the psychiatric inpatient unit. He is sent home on his own for follow up by his case manager. His medication is not reviewed and referrals for grief/loss counselling, and the crisis assessment team are not submitted.

1. Information about the timeframe is missing. This information is important as reference points help to prioritise risk factors and provide causal explanations for others. For example, the loss of an immediate family member may have been given more weight than illicit substance use had the assessing social worker known that it had just occurred. Elevation and suicidality may have been viewed through a lens of grief/loss, rather than illicit substance, had the reader known the context.
2. The documentation of up-to-date clinical observations is lacking. This is important as psychiatry cannot rely on measures used in other areas of medicine, such as blood tests and body temperature. As such, clinical observations of subtle changes in mental state are crucial. They provide significant information about a person's physiological presentation and elements of their consciousness and unconsciousness. Understanding the timelapse in which a change in mental state occurs is important in the development of psychological formulations. For example, the frequency and duration of cycles of hypomania and depression may indicate certain subtypes of bipolar disorder, allowing more individualised treatment.

3. <u>The case does not have an interservice management plan.</u> This functions as an evidence-based method of mapping and planning appropriate supports. These plans prevent teams from working in silos because they connect health services, increase continuity of care and result in people getting assistance at the right time. Interservice plans are designed for use after-hours and therefore need to be clear (for visual clarity use sub-headings), succinct and written in a language that multiple disciplines can understand. When writing a plan, it is helpful to visualise a busy and stressful environment, such as an emergency department. Your notes will possibly be skimmed over by an overwhelmed junior psychiatry registrar who knows nothing about the person you are working with. The plan needs to provide the registrar with context, instruction and enough confidence to follow through on the interventions suggested. The registrar should not feel that they are holding the bulk of the responsibility for safety planning as this can lead to reactive responses. As with all measures mentioned in this chapter, the service user should be the main driver of the plan, given that they have to follow through on it.

4. <u>The service user has previously not been believed and therefore is reluctant to discuss his grief.</u> This can impact on the service user's willingness to discuss important details or seek help from social workers. People with mental health difficulties frequently face social stigma and discrimination. Within mental health services, different diagnoses attract different perceptions and varying levels of compassion, care and, at times, neglect. Being vulnerable with a complete stranger is challenging in normal conditions; however, if a person has not been listened to or believed for decades (because of the effects of stigma), there may be significant shame and reluctance when it comes to asking for help. Accurate case notes that keep the service user at the forefront, can give the service user a voice in their treatment, even when they are not ready to articulate it.

ACTIVITY

Identifying issues and describing them respectfully

1. <u>Sarah has difficulty trusting health professionals due to past negative experiences.</u>
This statement is clear, concise, relevant and accurate, but unreliable, too concise and inappropriately presented.

This is a fairly typical presentation of a brief case note. It is clear and relevant because it will dictate the amount of time that needs to be allocated to the engagement phase. It is accurate to say that historical experiences impact service users' trust in the health sector. It is too concise, however, as it would be helpful to know more about the nature of those past negative experiences as this will shape service provision. For example, when allocating a worker to support a woman who has experienced sexual violence, ideally she should be offered a choice around the gender of the social worker.

Without essential information about Sarah's past, this statement lacks reliability and is therefore inappropriate.

2. <u>My client seems uncooperative and difficult to work with.</u>
This statement is concise, but irrelevant, inappropriately presented, lacks clarity and is inaccurate and unreliable.

The wording is concise; however, it is neither reliable nor accurate because, as mentioned earlier in this chapter, 'my client' elicits patronising images of the service provider holding ultimate knowledge and power over the service user. Instead, use the person's name, i.e. 'Sarah', to avoid using a label where possible.

The statement 'uncooperative and difficult to work with' is a judgement call and therefore inappropriate; however, describing the underlying barriers to engagement is relevant. For example, differing cultural definitions and perceptions of mental illness or compulsory treatment can undermine service users' autonomy.

Moreover, Emily's definitions of 'uncooperative' and 'difficult' need clarification as this has implications for treatment planning. Perhaps Sarah does not have the vocabulary to describe what she is feeling? Perhaps she is nervous and compensating by expressing outward reticence? The onus should be on the social worker to find creative ways to engage the service user, even when this may be challenging. However, by labelling Sarah as 'uncooperative' and 'difficult', this statement places the blame on Sarah for poor engagement.

3. <u>Sarah needs to clarify some goals for when she is discharged from hospital.</u>

This statement is relevant, but inappropriately presented and lacks clarity. It is too concise, and the accuracy and reliability is questionable.

The statement needs clarification regarding who the audience is and what the motives are behind the statement. Discussing goals is relevant to discharge planning; however, this statement has undertones of pressure and it is unclear where the pressure emanates from. Are these systemic expectations or Sarah's aspirations?

The statement is inappropriate because it shifts responsibility for the goal planning process onto Sarah. Shared accountability has therapeutic value because service users who have buy-in are more likely to follow through on goals. Having said this, it is also important that, when relinquishing responsibility to the service user, this does not then result in blaming them when the goals are not met.

Without further information, we cannot know if the statement is accurate or reliable.

4. <u>Goal planning was not possible due to the service user's hostile reaction to the</u>
<u>social worker.</u>

This statement is concise and relevant; however, it is not presented appropriately and needs more clarity to assess its accuracy and reliability.

The word 'hostile' is relevant as it is used in mental state examinations to describe a person's observable expression of their feelings.

It is concise; however, it does not include a description of how Sarah talks, looks and acts in Emily's presence. It is therefore difficult to evaluate whether Emily's assessment of the situation is accurate or reliable.

The statement is not presented appropriately, as more context is needed.

5. <u>Sarah demonstrates limited insight.</u>

This statement is relevant, but too concise and inappropriately presented. More clarity is needed to measure its accuracy and reliability.

It is relevant to comment on insight as this has implications for discharge planning, treatment adherence and good treatment outcomes. However, insight is multidimensional by nature; therefore, it is too simplistic and inappropriate to write that it is 'limited'. Non-specific adjectives such as 'poor', 'fair' and 'limited' are used in case notes due to time constraints, brevity and the lack of attention given to the assessment of insight (Casher & Bess 2012). It is good to be concise but not at the expense of the integrity of a case note.

Emily needs to be specific about what she is referring to by 'insight'. For example, does this refer to Sarah's insight into the need for treatment, her expectations around her ability to live independently or her understanding of the parallels between drug use and deterioration in her overall wellbeing?

Without context, we cannot know if it is accurate or reliable.

ACTIVITY

SMART goal planning

S) The goals may initially seem abstract; however, they are broken down into more specific tasks. For example, the need for safety, confidence and autonomy results in twice-weekly home visits from the mental health team. Social isolation is addressed via gradual re-exposure to friends and family via phone and face-to-face meetings. The risk of relapse into alcohol use is mitigated by Sarah avoiding definitive trigger points (going out at night). It is good to avoid being too general.

M) More detail is needed for these to be measurable goals. Ask Sarah how she will know if she has achieved her goals and how the mental health team will be able to identify the changes. What will it look like? Sometimes, depending on the person's temperament, level of motivation and stage of recovery, it is helpful to be concrete. For example, "in three months I will have made contact with two friends via phone and had one face-to-face meeting with family". This can generate a sense of achievement when the goal is met.

A) Sarah is the expert on herself so she will be the best judge as to whether these goals are attainable. Having said this, it is the social worker's role to provide oversight to ensure Sarah is not setting herself up to fail. For example, aiming to avoid self-harm for six weeks post discharge creates a considerable amount of pressure and could exacerbate Sarah's pre-existing feelings of self-loathing if she then hurts herself. The goal could be broken down into smaller wellness goals. For example, "Every time I feel unsafe I will cover myself with a weighted blanket, listen to white noise using my noise cancelling headphones and squeeze a stress ball".

R) The period immediately after discharge from hospital is the most risky; therefore, Sarah will likely need more than just a 24-hour phone line to prevent her from self-harming – especially given that she has already identified two significant risk factors (relapse into alcohol use and social isolation). Realistically, she may need more scaffolding around this goal in order for her to achieve it. For example, Sarah could practise sensory modulation and distress tolerance skills and be provided with a sensory kit on discharge.

T) The goals have been given a timeframe, and they can be achieved in a reasonable amount of time. It is sensible for Sarah to postpone her commitment to study and work as she may be overwhelmed simply trying to keep herself safe after leaving hospital. Additionally, Sarah has set herself several small goals instead of one grand life goal. Smaller timeframes are within reach and visible, making it easier for Sarah to keep motivated.

Further reading

Chenoweth, L. & McAuliffe, D. (2017). *The road to social work & human service practice*. 5th edition. South Melbourne: Cengage Learning.

Healy, K. & Mulholland, J. (2019). *Writing skills for social workers*. London: Sage.

Hoyle, V., Shepherd, E., Flinn, A. & Lomas, E. (2018). Child social-care recording and the information rights of care-experienced people: A recordkeeping perspective. *British Journal of Social Work*, *49*, 1856–1874. https://doi.org/10.1093/bjsw/bcy115

Maylea, C. (2019). *Social work and the law: A guide for ethical practice*. London: Red Globe Press.

Milner, J., Myers, S. & O'Byrne, P. (2015). *Assessment in social work*. London: Red Globe Press.

Rice, S., Day, A. & Briskman, L. (eds.) (2018). *Social work in the shadow of the law*. 5th edition. Leichardt: The Federation Press.

Wilson, J. Z. & Golding, F. (2016). Latent scrutiny: Personal archives as perpetual mementos of the official gaze. *Archival Science*, *16*(1), 93–109. https://doi.org/10.1007/s10502-015-9255-3

Writing a Placement Report

In this chapter you will learn:

- About the purpose of a placement report
- About the components and structure of a placement report
- How to write learning goals using appropriate language
- How to document placement experiences and use various learning tools such as process records to achieve learning goals
- About the use of direct, succinct and factual language to write a placement report

---

What is a placement report?

A placement report maps, structures and documents the teaching and learning requirements of a placement. Typically, a placement report identifies a range of activities that occur throughout a placement and reports on how these have been addressed and achieved. Students will have varying starting points, learning styles, needs and personalities, and so there will be a range of tasks required to achieve the required placement outcomes. These outcomes are incorporated into a negotiated individualised learning and teaching framework that supervisors and students can use to plan, review and analyse the progress of the placement (Cleak and Wilson 2018).

The placement report should be the result of the combined efforts of the student and the supervisor and take into account the academic requirements of the university as well as agency requirements.

There are generally three components of a placement report:

1. The learning plan (educational agreement or contract)
2. The mid-placement report (progress review)
3. The final report

At each stage, the student is required to submit relevant information and evidence to the supervisor, who also contributes to the report and provides feedback. Feedback takes the form of detailed notes as well as a rating of the student's performance (e.g. 'capable', 'beginning capability', 'not capable').

The placement report is a dynamic tool and should be revised as the placement progresses. It is common for the liaison staff member to review and suggest changes to the placement report at the beginning and midpoint of the placement. The supervisor and student also use the document as the basis for assessing the progress of the learning goals and to ensure that the learning plan is still relevant to the student's needs.

Defining the terminology

Each course, each state and each country will have their own version of a placement report. Although the content and the requirements are very similar, they may use different terminology. For instance, one programme in New Zealand calls the placement report a Collaborative Assessment Form, and in the United Kingdom, it is called the Practice Learning Agreement.

For the purposes of this chapter, we use the term 'placement report'.

What is the purpose of a placement report?

Student learning on placement is negotiated through the placement report, which helps to:

- Define the structure and detail of a range of the learning goals to be undertaken on placement
- Describe the methods to be used to complete the tasks
- Outline when activities will be undertaken to achieve these goals
- Outline how the learning outcomes will be achieved and how these will be assessed by the supervisors and the university
- Document the achievement of the tasks, including student reflections
- Provide the supervisor's assessment of how the planned tasks have been achieved

There are many stakeholders that write in the placement report, read it and use it as evidence that sufficient social work activities have been achieved. In addition to students, these include supervisors, liaison staff members and the university, who will ultimately use this documentation to assess and grade a student's performance and learning on placement.

Conducting an audit of what you bring to a placement

The first step in developing a learning plan for a placement report is to conduct an audit of the things that you bring to the placement (Cleak and Wilson 2018). This comprises the skills, knowledge and experience that you have gained throughout your life and includes the following:

- *Education history* – including specialisations such as politics, women's studies, criminology and mental health. Education provides useful background knowledge in most placements. The learning achievements of a previous placement would also be relevant.

- *Work history* – including paid and voluntary work in welfare-oriented or other fields. Previous work experience of any type gives you important knowledge and skills.
- *Personal history* – including any significant life events, such as being a parent, suffering the death of a significant person, having a disability, migrating from another country, travelling, or other experiences that have shaped your thinking and maturity.
- *Specific skills or abilities* – such as knowing another language, specific IT skills or research skills.
- *Future career ambitions* – it is reasonable to consider what passions and specific areas of social work practice brought you to social work and in what you would like to work once you graduate.

ACTIVITY

Using the audit to develop learning goals (Suggested solutions on p. 218)

Use the audit tool to reflect on your personal background, situation, interests, skills and professional goals and answer the questions below. Based on these, or on the example provided below, develop sample learning goals.

What I know and want to know

I work part time in retail, and my first placement gave me some experience with basic interviewing. I feel I am able to engage with clients generally but want to build my confidence in engaging and gathering information with clients who are hard to reach or who have complex problems.

I have worked as a disability support person in my past, so I would like to work at the organisational level rather than in direct work with clients.

My last placement did not have a social worker on site, so I would like to be placed in a large organisation where I can be part of a social work team and observe their practice.

I came to social work because I wanted to work with young people. I can engage with them well but would like to get a better understanding of what services are available to them.

What should a learning plan include?

The learning plan should include (Cleak and Wilson 2018):

- Goals: what learning is to happen
- Tasks: how it is to happen
- Timeframe: when it is to happen
- Learning outcomes and method of evaluation: how you know that it has happened

Although there is no common model for documenting these learning goals and learning outcomes for a social work placement, they all show remarkable similarities in what needs to be covered. This is the case because, internationally, the field education component of all professional programmes reflects some universal principles. The International Federation of Social Work (2012) provides some overarching standards that students need to achieve. They include:

> *Clear plans for the organisation, implementation and evaluation of the theory and field education components of the programme.*
> *Field education should be sufficient in duration and complexity of tasks and learning opportunities to ensure that students are prepared for professional practice.*
> *Ensuring that the curricula help social work students to develop skills of critical thinking and scholarly attitudes of reasoning, openness to new experiences and paradigms, and commitment to life-long learning.*

So, wherever you are studying in the world, the learning framework will be similar, and you will be evaluated on a range of generic knowledge and skills. Your job is to articulate how these generic goals can become part of your own learning goals and what you specifically want to learn.

Structuring and organising a social work learning plan

The following excerpt of a student learning plan includes the points outlined above and illustrates how the structure of this agreement might look. Note that the language used must be clear and direct and sentences should be succinct.

Example: Excerpt of a student learning plan

Learning area	Goals	Tasks	Timeframe	Learning outcome & evaluation
Policy: an understanding of the legislation and social policies that influence the field of practice.	To understand how policies and procedures inform my casework with child protection clients.	I will research statutory, legal and procedural requirements relevant to child protection practice I will keep a summary of the major points in a document.	I will need to have this knowledge in order to apply to a case, so by week 4, I will have completed this task. My knowledge will improve as I work with different cases.	I will have a completed document of the major requirements relevant to child protection. This will be presented to my supervisor, who will review my summary document and provide feedback.

As indicated above, the student's learning plan should reflect their personal and professional learning goals and how they can achieve them. However, the context of each social work programme requires that the learning plan is also guided by:

1. The formal requirements outlined by the professional accreditation guidelines in each country

In Australia, the professional accreditation body for social workers is the Australian Association of Social Workers (AASW 2012). In New Zealand, it is the Social Workers Registration Board (SWRB), and in the United Kingdom, the regulatory body is Social Work England and the Professional Standards Guidance documents (2019). These include some of the formal requirements such as the length of placement (number of hours required), the supervision requirements and some of the essential content, such as child protection and mental health knowledge and practice, cultural safety and working with Aboriginal and Torres Strait Islander peoples with Māori. As such, the process and content of this agreement is largely set.

2. The AASW Code of Ethics (2010a), the ANZASW Code of Ethics (2019) and the BASW Code of Ethics (2014)

3. The specific requirements of the university's social work programme

These might include the particular pedagogical approaches or methods taught in a university's courses. For instance, a school may subscribe to a critical reflection approach and would want students to use this framework in their practice. Another school may teach community development and would require this approach to be applied in placements.

4. The learning needs of the student

Students come with a variety of personal and professional experiences, working histories, interests and ambitions, and although students may have had limited choice of placements in recent years, there may be opportunities for a particular learning goal to be met. For example, a student with a background in psychological practice may benefit from having a goal of applying a psychological framework to counselling clients. Additionally, final-year students will be more likely to have specific learning goals to supplement the ones obtained in their first placement.

5. The specific placement agency

Some placement agencies, by the nature of their service, have very clear learning opportunities and/or limitations about what they can provide students on placement. For example, an advocacy service may not have any access to service users, or a crisis service may not be able to offer longer-term work such as case management.

Structuring and organising a placement report

As already discussed, each programme has its own placement report requirements, though due to accreditation guidelines, there may be remarkable similarities in the basic learning elements that students need to achieve.

In the State of Victoria, Australia, for example, The Victorian Combined Schools of Social Work have used a common template based on the AASW National Practice Standards (2003) and the AASW Code of Ethics (2010a) for students since 2011. The learning goals and written assessments were integrated into this template to better enable tracking of students' learning tasks, methods and capabilities as the placement progressed. The terminology contained in placement reports from overseas social work programmes may sometimes be different, but the intention of each learning area will be very similar. This single document is added to at mid placement and again for the final report (Cleak et al. 2015). The nine learning areas are illustrated in the following table.

Learning area	Task	Example of a learning outcome
Values, ethics and professional practice	Awareness of contextually relevant ethics in accordance with the AASW Code of Ethics	Maintaining an open and respectful perspective towards the values, views and opinions of others, while demonstrating a commitment to enhancing the self-determination of individuals, social units, communities and cultures
Organisational and community context	An understanding of the organisation's legal and political context within the human services field	Demonstrating an appreciation of the connection between legislative frameworks and organisational structure and functioning, and their impact on practice
Policy	An understanding of the legislation and social policies that influence the field of practice	Demonstrating an ability to perceive, analyse and communicate in relation to social and political issues and contexts
Use of knowledge in practice	An understanding of theories and methodologies relevant to practice and an ability to reflect critically upon their use and application	The ability to apply relevant theory to practice settings, including relevant theories of societal functioning and human behaviour
Effective interpersonal and communication skills	Demonstrates skills required to communicate and work effectively with others	Suggested inclusions are: • Interpersonal skills • Teamwork • Report-writing • Referral and consultation
Self-learning and critical reflection	The ability to take responsibility for one's own learning and development, and to perform at a level of competence appropriate to a beginning social work practitioner, including the skills to manage one's future career and the transition from university to professional practice	For example, the ability to participate proactively in negotiating and developing the supervisory relationship and to critically reflect on practice

Assessment and intervention skills	Applying knowledge of assessment, intervention and referral skills to practice	The ability to undertake multidimensional assessments in a collaborative manner with individuals, families, groups and communities across a diverse range of circumstances
Research	Recognition of research as an integral part of social work practice; demonstrating knowledge and understanding of different types of social research	Demonstrates an understanding of how research knowledge informs practice – through locating and critically analysing current literature, research and practice knowledge relevant to the placement setting
Culturally sensitive practice	Develop understanding and knowledge of cultural diversity in order to work in a culturally responsive and inclusive way	Critically reflects on own subjectivity, personal values, social locations, cultures/racial identifications and beliefs and how these impact on interactions with service users, supervisors, community members and colleagues; and on organisational policies and practices

Gathering evidence of your learning on placement

Your ability to describe, document and offer evidence of your own learning on placement will largely determine how successful you are on placement. Your university and the agency where you are undertaking your placement will prescribe a number of learning goals that you will need to achieve. That said, the onus is still on you to contribute to these and to provide evidence of this learning to ensure that you pass the placement and demonstrate your suitability for the profession. This means that you need to consider the necessary documentation to collect, and how, to provide evidence of your learning goals.

> *Too often students who have a real talent in terms of their social work*
> *practice on placement do not always evidence their skills and knowledge*
> *in a way which demonstrates their full potential. This leaves your practice*
> *and effort sold short and does not do justice to you, your practice educa-*
> *tor and all the other people who helped you learn and develop.*
> (Edmondson 2013: 89)

Placement report checklist

- Make yourself familiar with all the university assessment documents.

  This will ensure you know their requirements, including due dates, who to send them to and who needs to sign them. A placement is a university subject like all of your other classroom subjects, so it will have learning outcomes and assessment criteria. It is not uncommon for students' progress on placement to be compromised because of documentation errors.

- Revisit the audit you developed in the initial stage of developing your learning plan.

  This should give you some ideas of what you already know and what you want to know. For example, if you have an educational background in feminist studies, you might be interested in exploring these concepts in a family violence setting. Or alternatively, because you already have this knowledge, you might be more interested in extending your theories by applying a psychological framework when placed in a family violence setting.

- Clarify what you want to learn and what the agency can offer you before you begin your placement.

  You have probably already had a pre-placement meeting with the agency and hopefully your supervisor, so you will have some knowledge of their mission, their service users and the likely tasks for placement. Remember that your placement agency will have their own requirements and sometimes limitations on what a student can do. This may compromise the attainment of your own learning goals, e.g. because clients must be interviewed with the supervisor present, students are not invited to staff meetings or the completion of their own research agenda.

- Have a clear sense of what evidence you will need to produce in order to pass your placement.

  The university documentation requirements, as well as the agency's expectations, will help you begin to map out your work on placement, how you will collect and collate your evidence and then report on this.

- Start collecting evidence of your performance from the beginning of your placement, rather than just before you are required to submit a piece of work to your supervisor.

  This will become very important when you are discussing your learning achievements with your supervisor and your liaison staff member, for both the mid-placement report and the final assessment. It is not uncommon for there to be a disagreement between the student and/or the supervisor or the university about your progress on placement, so it will be in your interest to have examples of your work to verify the attainment of learning. Do not just rely on what you can remember.

- Keep a reflective journal, diary or log.

    All social work placements require students to demonstrate how they understand and apply reflection and critical reflection to their practice. Reflective logs, diaries or journals are useful ways to record your daily tasks and reflections as you progress during placement rather than relying on memory. Remember, placements will typically get busier and you will almost certainly forget things that occurred several weeks ago (Edmondson 2013). See Chapter 8 for more guidance on reflective writing.

- Set goals for your placement in collaboration with your field educator using the learning plan as a guide.

    This will ensure these tasks will be made available. If related opportunities arise, you can amend the agreement to reflect this. This process means that you can increase your ability to be flexible and open to learning in areas that may not be your core interests or reflect on assumptions that informed your original learning goals. Negotiating this is helpful in determining how to document and discuss them during supervision and include them in the final assessment.

Documenting your practice

Whether you are asked formally or informally by your supervisor to summarise your work as part of your review of learning, being able to prepare, present and evaluate your work will be very helpful. The following sources are ways that you can outline concisely and clearly what you have done. They include:

- Process recordings
- Critical incident analysis
- Writing a case summary, a case study or a psychosocial assessment
- Observing and shadowing others
- Direct observation of your practice by your supervisor or team members
- Meetings, presentations, clinical meetings and other team events
- Case presentation
- Reflective practice summaries or journal

    The key to successfully documenting your practice is to consistently document your experiences and develop a learning portfolio of evidence of your professional development throughout your placement rather than waiting until the middle or end, when you may have forgotten many of the details.

    This section now briefly summarises a couple of these learning tools and offers examples.

Process recordings

Process records are highly detailed written accounts of practice after it has happened, and include some analysis and reflective interpretation of the content, both factual and emotional (Cleak and Wilson 2018). Most process records use a verbatim description of what happened or as much as can be remembered and offers students the opportunity to critically reflect on their practice. They are generally used to record interactions with individual clients but can also be used to record family interviews, meetings and interventions with community groups. The following is an example of a process record, but the headings could vary, depending on the purpose of the exercise; for instance, you might want to work on responding appropriately to an angry client or exploring your feelings when working with a recently bereaved client or service user.

Example: Process record

Content	Client: "I am not sure why you are here as I am managing just fine" Student: "That's great to hear that you feel you are managing, but I know that you have recently been hospitalised after a fall so I was also here to see if there is anything else that you might need."
Student response	My role is to assess the client's capacity to manage at home on their own but I need to engage with him first if I want him to continue talking with me.
Client response	The client is probably concerned about losing his independence and having to leave his home. He could also be angry about being asked about his capacity.
Knowledge/ skills used	I should use the Code of Ethics re client autonomy and self-determination. There is also the professional and agency responsibility of ensuring duty of care to ensure client safety. I need to explain my role and what resources the agency may be able to offer.
Reflection	I think I came across as a bit patronising and paternalistic – I could have worded my introduction better. On reflection, the client may also be feeling powerless as I may be seen as the one in authority (younger, educated, employed, etc.). Perhaps I should reassure the client of my respect for his wishes and rights. It would be beneficial to do some more reading on aspects of social divisions and forms of oppression such as gender, age, disability and language.

Critical incident analysis

This learning tool is another opportunity to analyse, reflect on and document an event that occurs on placement. The incident can be either a difficult or a challenging event, or a positive experience that highlights your growing professional awareness and achievement of learning. Like a process record, a critical incident analysis is completed after the event has occurred and encourages you to process what is happening. It also encourages you to consider the available choices and the consequences of each choice, and provides you with an opportunity to gain more personal insight and awareness.

Consider the following example of a critical incident that occurred on placement. The student response reflects on why it happened and why it was critical (adapted from Cleak and Wilson 2018). Note that it includes the details of the event, the student's feelings, interpretations, insights and learnings. (See also pp. 123–124 on reflecting on a placement experience.)

Example: Critical incident analysis

Question	Student response
What images do you recall? E.g. sounds, smells, surroundings, etc.	My image of the home visit with my supervisor is very powerful. I recall the depressive nature of the house. It was rundown, dirty, cluttered and yet the child's bedroom was colourful, full of toys and well decorated – such a contrast!
Which people, comments or actions stand out in your mind? What did you feel about this?	I recall that there were a number of people in the house of varying ages and all eager to talk to us. I thought that was reassuring as I was expecting the family to be hostile because we were coming from a government agency.
What do you think they were feeling?	I thought that the parents may be worried because they were informed that we were coming to assess the home situation of their new baby; yet I noticed that they seemed relaxed and friendly so maybe they felt confident about their parental ability and rights.
What have you learned from this incident? What skills and knowledge do you need to develop further as a result of your reflection?	The experience was somewhat confusing. It reminded me that, when one has conflicting feelings and impressions, it is important to not make assumptions and to explore them further. It made me very aware of not making assumptions about peoples' capacity and that everyone is unique. I definitely need more experience interacting with a range of service users to feel more confident in undertaking home visits.

TIP: USING NOTES IN YOUR PLACEMENT REPORT

The language you use in your notes or journals may be informal, but it is important that you ensure that the language you use in a placement report is formal and adheres to academic language standards.

Writing a mid-placement and final report

Placements have a beginning, middle and end, and until now, the chapter has concentrated on describing how to set up the placement report to reflect the learning goals that need to be achieved and how they will be completed and evaluated.

At the mid placement, the student and supervisor are required to demonstrate what learning has been attained, what still needs to be done to reach these goals by the end of the placement and any changes that need to be noted. That might include goals that have changed, been modified or are no longer achievable.

The final report is an important component of the placement report and is used to document the student's overall progress in the placement. Details of the achievement of a student's learning goals need to be clear and objective and written to support decisions about the student's level of performance. The final report has a number of functions apart from outlining the student's capabilities and skills achieved on placement. It usually forms the basis of planning the next placement, or students may use the report to gain credit in further studies. It can also be used for career planning.

It is important that what is written uses clear language, that critical and positive comments are made on the basis of specific examples and that the limitations of the agency with respect to the student's learning are noted.

The following example uses one of the learning goals described in the earlier example and shows how a mid-placement and final report could be completed:

Social work learning area	Goals	Tasks	Timeframe	Evaluation
Assessment and intervention skills	Task 1. Develop a range of intervention options for addressing client issues using a range of theoretical frameworks. Task 2. Gain confidence and skills in doing intake interviews. Task 3. Make appointments with the relevant agencies and particularly focus on differing roles and the way to collaborate effectively for better service delivery.	Articulate your rationale for choosing particular interventions in specific situations. By shadowing workers doing intake interviews, and add to my own knowledge of social work intake interviews. Keep records of the agency's visits in my reflection journal and discuss what I learned.	Cases will be allocated from week 4 and continue throughout placement	Supervision sessions and feedback. Completion of three process recordings. Learning journal. Direct observations. Discussion feedback from team/other professionals. Agency visits and records of them to be shared with supervisor.

Example: A mid-placement report

Student:

Task 1) I have been working with four patients so far and used regular discussions with the supervisor before developing intervention plans with the patients and working them through. Feedback from my supervisor indicated that they were appropriate and helpful and based on frameworks such as systems approaches.

Task 2) I observed my supervisor's and colleagues' questioning skills while they were working on the intake roster. I have been assigned to suggest follow-up referrals for some of the intake cases, although I have not yet had an opportunity to undertake an intake interview on my own.

Task 3) Agencies visited included the palliative care unit, the mental health inpatient unit, CASA (Centre Against Sexual Assault), inpatient rehabilitation, Hospital in the Home service, and two aged care facilities. Ongoing arrangement to visit more agencies, and I have discussed what I learned and takeaways in the supervision every week.

Supervisor:

Example: A final report

Student:

Task 1) I have been very lucky to achieve my goal of working with ten patients from a range of inpatient and outpatient clinics. These were mainly patients with chronic illnesses, and many were in need of alternative residential care. It was also great learning for me to work with different social workers and see the different approaches and frameworks they use. Reading case notes and assessments in different departments also gave me insights and learnings about a variety of theoretical approaches.

Task 2) Unfortunately, I did not have many opportunities to undertake any intake cases on my own as, on many of the days I was rostered on with my supervisor, there were no appropriate cases to assess. However, I was exposed to many learning opportunities to observe social workers demonstrating their crisis intervention approaches rather than the slower-paced work in the wards. I would like to ensure that my final placement exposes me to more crisis work, such as in an emergency housing service.

Task 3) During the latter half of the placement, I visited oncology social work, respite care services, paediatric outpatient services, a NDIS coordinator, Aboriginal social work and clinical psychology. It was very good learning to see how they worked differently from the inpatient teams, which have stricter time constraints and are more focused on discharge planning from the early stages of the intervention. Oncology social work and palliative care social workers were more frequently exposed to mortality on a daily basis. Attending case conferences in some of these units helped me develop an understanding about how they work as a team. After each visit, I recorded the key learnings and some reflections in my discussion with my supervisor and talked about how social work interfaces with these different services.

Language characteristics of a placement report

A placement report must be written using formal, factual and objective language, as the document is intended for academic and professional training purposes (see Chapter 3 on distinguishing between fact and opinion).

Further, the language you use needs to be succinct, with brief (though not vague, unclear or non-specific) descriptions that do not include superfluous information. You will also be required to identify key points and record details such as timeframes, names or numbers where relevant.

The following example illustrates what such language looks like:

Example: Placement report writing

Task 1) Professional code of behaviour, standards and values are in line with AASW Code of Ethics. I believe maintaining professional integrity means ensuring not only appropriate professional conduct but also appropriate personal conduct and relationship with the clients.

Task 2) I identified and discussed many ethical dilemmas in the practices, between the patients, in the system, and gaps between the policy/services and the situation surrounding the patients. Further discussion was made regarding the tension between organisational expectation, patient/sw's goal/risk management/available resources.

Task 3) Have visited neuropsychologist and speech therapist. I made a question to a neuropsychologist as to how they determine the decision-making capacity of the patient, and the discussion with her was highly insightful. I also found that organisational policy, funding and resource allocation policy are related to this issue. Meeting with oncologist has already been arranged.

Placement reports require objective and factual language. For this reason, students need to be aware of the distinction between observation vs. opinion or judgement when writing their placement report (see Activity: Identifying judgement, bias and personal opinion in Chapter 9). The following activity tests your ability to identify objective and factual language.

ACTIVITY

Identifying formal, factual and objective language (Suggested solutions on p. 219)

Identify which of the sentences below use formal, factual and objective language. For those sentences that do not, explain what the issue is and why.

1. The service user stated with a raised voice "I don't want to be here and you can't make me stay".
2. It seemed as though the patient was eager to talk to the social worker.

3. When I first met the service user, she was recovering from an injury inflicted by her partner.
4. The patient had been drinking heavily.
5. The patient arrived in the emergency department after he was found asleep in the park. He smelt of alcohol, and he had an empty bottle of vodka in his bag.
6. The patient was friendly and open and will benefit from counselling.
7. The patient responded positively to my questions and showed good insight into the reasons why she was feeling depressed, which are good indicators that counselling will be beneficial for her.

The style of a placement report must align with good academic writing principles. For example, you need to use clear language, complete sentences and appropriate vocabulary. See also Chapter 6 on using appropriate vocabulary.

Writing learning goals: Identifying appropriate language

Goal	Comment
Supervisor to review my client contact sheets.	The sentence is direct and succinct; however, it is incomplete as it lacks a main verb.
My supervisor will give me feedback on my presentation to the team.	The language is clear and direct, but could be more formal.
Discuss in supervision sessions.	The language is direct; however, it is vague as it lacks adequate detail. This sentence is incomplete as it lacks a main verb.
I want to be able to identify a range of social work theories during placement.	Although this is a short, clear and direct statement, the goals are vague and unclear. (A single placement would not normally be able to offer a full range of theoretical learning opportunities. This can result in the student not achieving the appropriate learning in even one theory.) Inappropriate vocabulary choice of 'want to'.

ACTIVITY

Using appropriate language for learning goals

Rephrase the sentences from the above table using the comments provided.

- Supervisor to review my client contact sheets.
- My supervisor will give me feedback on my presentation to the team.
- Discuss in supervision sessions.
- I want to be able to identify a range of social work theories during placement.

The following activity tests your ability to identify appropriate language for a placement report.

ACTIVITY

Appropriate writing for a placement report (Suggested solutions on p. 220)

Identify whether the groups of statements below that would be typically found in a placement report are appropriate or not. Explain why. Comment on the language used.

Learning plan

- I want to work with hospital patients...
- I want to undertake social work tasks in the hospital...
- I would like to interview and write up my contacts with hospital patients...
- I would like to develop my understanding of...
- I would like to become familiar with...
- I will prepare a report...
- I will apply a person-centred approach to my interaction with...
- I aim to conduct at least two family meetings to demonstrate the role of social work within the multidisciplinary team, especially a person-centred approach to our care plan.
- The group facilitator will attend a group session with me and give feedback on my group-work skills in writing that I can share with my supervisor.
- Successful completion of my part of the ethics application within the suggested timeframe.
- An evaluation form will be completed by the self-help gardening group participants, which will include feedback about my facilitating role.

Mid-placement report

- I identified and discussed many ethical dilemmas when I observed my supervisor.
- I identified and discussed many ethical dilemmas in the interviews I observed with patients. It showed me how there is a discrepancy between patients' needs and expectations and organisational expectations and available resources. This seems to drive the emphasis on discharge planning in aged care particularly, which seems to limit patients' choices about discharge options.

Final placement report

- As I have a refugee background, it was important for me to understand how the hospital interfaces with other services and how they connect with the patients who are discharged home. From undertaking agency visits and looking at websites, I was able to learn this and could demonstrate my knowledge by making appropriate referrals to these services.

Key points from this chapter

- A placement report consists of three components:
    - A learning plan
    - A mid-placement report
    - A final report
- A placement report requires careful documentation prior to and throughout a placement and should include the following four components:
    - Goals: what learning is to happen
    - Tasks: how it is to happen
    - Timeframe: when it is to happen
    - Outcomes: how you know that it has happened
- The requirements, structure and organisation of a placement report will depend on:
    - The placement agency
    - The formal requirements outlined by the professional accreditation guidelines in each country
    - The university's social work programme
    - The student's learning needs
- You will need to clearly and factually document and describe your experiences and learning on placement
- Language must be formal, factual, objective and succinct

Suggested solutions

ACTIVITY

Using the audit to develop learning goals

Sample learning goals

Be able to conduct an interview with clients who have a number of issues, such as a homeless person or a client with mental health issues.

To undertake a project in the agency I am placed in. It could be a quality assurance exercise or an evaluation of a service.

To be placed in a team to observe how social workers discuss a case collaboratively and input ideas about the assessment and intervention plans.

To have the opportunity to work with young clients to understand their service needs and to be able to refer them to appropriate community agencies.

Identifying formal, factual and objective language

1. Formal, factual and objective. The statement shows the exact words used by the service user and describes how they were uttered. The language choice is appropriate for academic writing.
2. Inappropriate. Without further context provided, the reader does not know what this statement is based on. Use of 'seemed' needs to be clarified.
3. Objective and factual details provided regarding the first meeting with the client and the reason why she was admitted to hospital. Formal language is used.
4. Inappropriate. This statement has no detail to explain how the writer knows this. The language is appropriate for academic writing.
5. Formal, factual and objective. The writer was able to provide detailed information about the patient's behaviour that substantiated the assessment. Language appropriate for academic writing is used.
6. Inappropriate. The writer does not offer any information to qualify why the patient was friendly and no evidence to support the assumption that the patient would benefit from counselling. The language choice is appropriate for academic writing.
7. Formal, factual and objective. This statement offers useful information to substantiate the assessment of the patient's characteristics. The language choice is appropriate for academic writing, though the sentence is too long.

Using appropriate language for learning goals

My supervisor is to review my client contact sheets.
My supervisor will provide me with feedback on my presentation to the team.
'I would like to discuss [topic] in supervision sessions.'
I would like to be able to identify a range of social work theories during placement.

Appropriate writing for a placement report

Learning plan	
• I want to work with hospital patients... • I want to undertake social work tasks in the hospital... • I would like to interview and write up my contacts with hospital patients...	Inappropriate. The learning plan should be directed at balancing a number of elements required for practice in the human services (Rogers & Langevin 2000): • Being: Refers to qualities and attributes of the learners and how they construct and make meaning of their experiences • Doing: Refers to the acquisition of skills and behaviours • Thinking: Refers to the ability to analyse, reason and conceptualise • Knowing: Refers to theories, concepts and knowledge In this example, the student only talks about the element of *doing*. The sentences are short and direct, though lacking in detail. Issues with some vocabulary choices. More academic appropriate language needed: • 'want to' > 'would like to' • 'write up' > 'document'
• I would like to develop my understanding of... • I would like to become familiar with... • I will prepare a report... • I will apply a person-centred approach to my interaction with...	Appropriate. This student has used a range of learning activities that balances *doing*, *thinking* and *knowing*. The beginnings of these sentences are clear and direct. Appropriate academic language used.
• I aim to conduct at least two family meetings to demonstrate the role of social work within the multidisciplinary team, especially a person-centred approach to our care plan.	Appropriate. This statement suggests a specific and achievable learning goal and is clear about what approach the student wants to practise. This would then make it much easier to assess the learning. The first half of this sentence is clear and direct, though the second is unclearly worded. This could be stated in a second sentence for clarity: • 'I aim to conduct at least two family meetings to demonstrate the role of social work within the multidisciplinary team. I would especially like to integrate a person-centred approach to our care plan.'

• The group facilitator will attend a group session with me and give feedback on my group-work skills in writing that I can share with my supervisor. • Successful completion of my part of the ethics application within the suggested timeframe. • An evaluation form will be completed by the self-help gardening group participants, which will include feedback about my facilitating role.	Appropriate. The student has listed a range of different types of evidence of learning, including different people and clear, objective activities. Clear and direct sentences are used with appropriate academic language. The second sentence is incomplete as a main verb is lacking: 'I aim to successfully complete my part of the ethics application within the suggested timeframe.'

Mid-placement report

• I identified and discussed many ethical dilemmas when I observed my supervisor.	Inappropriate. This statement does not give any clear evidence of specific learning around ethical issues. A direct sentence, though lacking in detail. Appropriate language is used.
• I identified and discussed many ethical dilemmas in the interviews I observed with patients. It showed me how there is a discrepancy between patients' needs and expectations and organisational expectations and available resources. This seems to drive the emphasis on discharge planning in aged care particularly, which seems to limit patients' choices about discharge options.	Appropriate. The student was able to link a specific issue that she experienced with an ethical issue pertinent to social work, namely self-determination. The language uses short direct sentences and is appropriate for academic writing.

Final placement report

• As I have a refugee background, it was important for me to understand how the hospital interfaces with other services and how they connect with the patients who are discharged home. From undertaking agency visits and looking at websites, I was able to learn this and could demonstrate my knowledge by making appropriate referrals to these services.	Appropriate. The student has made a personal and professional connection between her learning needs and why she wanted to learn it and then demonstrated how she was able to use that knowledge in her developing practice. Good use of clear and direct sentences. Academic language used.

Further reading

Cleak, H. (2009). *Assessment and report writing in the human services*. Southbank: Cengage Learning.

Cleak, H. & Wilson, J. (2018). *Making the most of field placement*. 4th edition. Southbank: Cengage Learning.

Edmondson, D. (2013). *Social work practice learning*. London: Sage.

Healy, K. & Mulholland, J. (2019). *Writing skills for social workers*. London: Sage.

References

Adshead, G., Crepaz-Keay, D., Deshpande, M., Fulford, K.B. & Richards, V. (2018). Montgomery and shared decision-making: Implications for good psychiatric practice. *The British Journal of Psychiatry*, *213*(5), 630–632.

Allen, J., Briskman, L. & Pease, B. (2009). *Reconstructing social work practices in critical social work: Theories and practices for a socially just world*, 2nd edn, Allen & Unwin, Crows Nest.

Alston, M. & Bowles, W. (2003). *Research for social workers: An introduction to methods*, 2nd edn, Allen & Unwin, Crows Nest.

Alston, M. & McKinnon, J. (eds.). (2005). *Social work: Fields of practice*, Oxford University Press, Oxford.

Anspach, R.R. (1988). Notes on the sociology of medical discourse: The language of case presentation. *Journal of health and social behavior*, 357–375.

Aotearoa New Zealand Association of Social Workers (ANZASW). (2019). *Code of ethics*. https://anzasw.nz/wp-content/uploads/Code-of-Ethics-Adopted-30-Aug-2019.pdf

Askeland, G.A. & Fook, J. (2009). Critical reflection in social work. *European Journal of Social Work, 12*(3), 287–292. https://doi.org/10.1080/13691450903100851

AASW. (2003). *Practice standards for social workers*. https://www.aasw.asn.au/document/item/16

Australian Association of Social Workers. (2010a). *Code of ethics*, AASW, Canberra. https://www.aasw.asn.au/practitioner-resources/code-of-ethics

Australian Association of Social Workers. (2010b). Australian Association of Social Workers. https://www.aasw.asn.au/news-media/2010

AASW. (2012). Australian Social Work Education and Accreditation Standards (ASWEAS) 2012 V1.4. https://www.aasw.asn.au/document/item/3550

Australian Association of Social Workers. (2013). *Practice standards*. https://www.aasw.asn.au/document/item/4551

Australian Association of Social Workers. (2015a). *Scope of social work practice psychosocial assessment*. https://www.aasw.asn.au/document/item/8312

Australian Association of Social Workers. (2015b). *Submission to the standing committee on health: Inquiry into chronic disease prevention and management in primary health care*. https://www.aasw.asn.au/document/item/7786

Australian Association of Social Workers. (2020). *Australian Social Work Education and Accreditation Standards (ASWEAS)*, AASW, Canberra, pp. 1–37.

Australian Commission on Safety and Quality in Health Care (ACSQHC). (2018). Australian Charter of Health Care Rights. Retrieved from https://www.safetyandquality.gov.au/wp-content/uploads/2012/01/Charter-PDf.pdf

Australian Government Department of Health. (2004). *Writing case notes*. https://www1.health.gov.au/internet/publications/publishing.nsf/Content/drugtreat-pubs-front11-fa-toc~drugtreat-pubs-front11-fa-secb~drugtreat-pubs-front11-fa-secb-5~drugtreat-pubs-front11-fa-secb-5-2

Australian Government Department of Health and Human Services. (2011). *Framework for recovery-oriented practice*. https://www2.health.vic.gov.au/getfile/?sc_itemid=%7b47D26EAC-5A2C-44FA-A52A-

2F387F3C4612%7d&title=Framework%20for%20Recovery-oriented%20 Practice

Aveyard, H. (2019). *Doing a literature review in health and social care: A practical guide*, Open University Press, McGraw-Hill Education, London.

Balaratnasingam, S. (2011). Mental health risk assessment – A guide for GPs. *Australian Family Physician, 40*(6), June 2011.

Bartels, L. (2010). *Emerging issues in domestic/family violence research*. https://aic.gov. au/publications/rip/rip10

Bartlett, T.S. (2018). Supporting incarcerated fathers: An exploration of research and practice in Victoria, Australia. *Probation Journal, 66*(2), 201–218. https://doi. org/10.1177/0264550518820115

Battaglia, L., Flynn, C. & Brown, G. (2018). International students engaged in Australian social work study: An exploratory study. *Advances in Social Work and Welfare Education, 20*(2), 47–62.

Bay, U. (2014). *Social work practice: A conceptual framework*, Palgrave Macmillan, London.

Bay, U. & Macfarlane, S. (2011). Teaching critical reflection: A tool for transformative learning in social work? *Social Work Education, 30*(7), 745–758.

Berkman, B., Maramaldi, P., Breon, E. & Howe, J.L. (2003). Social work gerontological assessment revisited. *Journal of Gerontological Social Work, 40*(1–2), 1–14.

Berkman, B., Gardner, D., Zodikoff, B. & Harootyan, L. (2006). Social work and aging in the emerging health care world. *Journal of Gerontological Social Work, 41*(1–2), 203–217.

Bielefeld, S. (2016). Neoliberalism and the return of the guardian state: Micromanaging Indigenous peoples in a new chapter of colonial governance, in W. Sanders (ed.), *Engaging Indigenous economy: Debating diverse approaches*, ANU Press, Canberra, pp. 155–169.

Bloom, S. (2010). Organisational stress and trauma-informed services, in B. Levin & M. Becker (eds.), *A public mental health perspective of women's mental health*, 1st edn, Springer Science and Business Media, pp. 295–311.

Bowell, T. & Kemp, G. (2005). *Critical thinking: A concise guide*, Routledge, Abingdon.

Braddy, L. & Erhardt-Rumpe, M. (2018). Aged care: Health, assessments, in-home care and residential care, in M. Petrakis (ed.), *Social work practice in health: An introduction to contexts, theories and skills*, Allen & Unwin, Crows Nest, pp. 200–218.

Brechin, A., Brown, H. & Eby, M.A. (2000). *Critical practice in health and social care*, Sage, London.

Brydon, K., Kamasua, J., Flynn, C., Mason, R., Au, R., Ayius, D. & Hampson, R. (2014). Developing an international social work education collaboration: A partnership approach between Monash University, Australia and University of Papua New Guinea. *International Social Work, 57*(6), 590–604. https://doi. org/10.1177/0020872812444939

Byrne, L., Happell, B. & Reid-Searl, K. (2017). Risky business: Lived experience mental health practice, nurses as potential allies. *International Journal of Mental Health Nursing, 26*(3), 285–292.

Cait, C. (2016). Relational theory, in N. Coady & P. Lehmann (eds.), *Theoretical perspectives for direct social work practice: A generalist-eclectic approach*, 3rd edn, Springer Publishing Company, New York, pp. 179–202.

Cameron, R.S. & Das, R.K. (2019). Empowering residential carers of looked after young people: The impact of the emotional warmth model of professional child-care. *British Journal of Social Work*.

Cameron, S. & Turtle-Song, I. (2002). Learning to write case notes using the SOAP format. *Journal of Counseling & Development, 80*(3), 286–292.

Casher, M.I. & Bess, J.D. (2012). Determination and documentation of insight in psychiatric inpatients. *Psychiatry Times*.

Certo, N., Mautz, D., Pumpian, I., Sax, C., Smalley, K., Wade, H.A., Noyes, D., Luecking, R., Wechsler, J. & Batterman, N. (2003). Review and discussion of a model for seamless transition to adulthood. *Education and Training in Developmental Disabilities, 38*(1), 3–17.

Chatfield, T. (2017). *Critical Thinking*, Sage, London.

Citizens Advice Bureau. (2019). *Domestic violence and abuse.* https://www.citizensadvice.org.uk/family/gender-violence/domestic-violence-and-abuse/

Cleak, H. & Wilson, J. (2018). *Making the most of field placement*, 4th edn, Cengage, Southbank.

Cleak, H., Hawkins, L., Laughton, J. & Williams, J. (2015). Creating a standardised teaching and learning framework for social work field placements. *Australian Social Work, 68*(1), 49–64.

Coady, N. & Lehmann, P. (Eds.). (2016). *Theoretical perspectives for direct social work practice: A generalist-eclectic approach*, Springer Publishing Company, New York.

Coleman, H. & Unrau, Y.A. (2008). Qualitative data analysis. *Social work research and evaluation: Foundations for evidence based practice*, 370–386.

Coles, A. (2018). The art of note writing: Art therapy and clinical notes (L'art de rédiger des notes: l'art-thérapie et les notes cliniques). *Canadian Art Therapy Association Journal, 31*(2), 101–104.

Courtney, M. & Moulding, N.T. (2014). Beyond balancing competing needs: Embedding involuntary treatment within a recovery approach to mental health social work. *Australian Social Work, 67*(2), 214–226.

Crisp, B.R. (2017). The challenges in developing cross-national social work curricula. *International Social Work, 60*(1), 6–18.

Cumming, S., Fitzpatrick, E., McAuliffe, D., McKain, S., Martin, C. & Tonge, A. (2007). Raising the Titanic: Rescuing social work documentation from the sea of ethical risk. *Australian Social Work, 60*(2), 239–257.

D'Cruz, H. & Jones, M. (2004). *Social work research: Ethical and political contexts*, Sage, London.

D'Cruz, H. & Jones, M. (2013). *Social work research in practice: Ethical and political contexts*, Sage, London.

D'Cruz, H., Gillingham, P. & Melendez, S. (2007). Reflexivity, its meanings and relevance for social work: A critical review of the literature. *British Journal of Social Work, 37*, 73–90. https://doi.org/10.1093/bjsw/bcl001

Department of Health and Human Services (DHHS) Victoria. (2016). *Refugee and asylum seeker health and wellbeing*, viewed 10 November 2016. https://www2.health.vic.gov.au/about/populations/refugee-asylum-seeker-health

Duan, G., Chen, J., Zhang, W., Yu, B., Jin, Y., Wang, Y. & Yaoa, W. (2015). Physical maltreatment of children with autism in Henan Province in China: A cross-sectional study. *Child Abuse & Neglect, 48*, 140–147. https://doi.org/10.1542/peds.2016-1817

Duncan, J. (2019). *Reading critically – Handout*, The University of Toronto. https://www.utsc.utoronto.ca/twc/writing-process

Dunk-West, P. (2013). *How to be a social worker. A critical guide for students*, Red Globe Press, London.

Edmondson, D. (2013). *Social work practice learning*, Sage, Los Angeles.

Felton, A., Wright, N. & Stacey, G. (2017). Therapeutic risk-taking: A justifiable choice. *BJPsych Advances, 23*(2), 81–88.

Fischer, J. & Dunn, K. (eds.). (2019). *Stifled progress: International perspectives on social work and social policy in the era of right-wing populism*.

Flynn, C. & McDermott, F. (2016). *Doing research in social work and social care: The journey from student to practitioner researcher*, Sage, London.

Flynn, C., Alston, M. & Mason, R.A. (2014). Trafficking in women for sexual exploitation: Building Australian knowledge. *International Social Work, 57* (1), 27–38.

Fook, J. (2007). Reflective practice and critical reflection, in J. Lishman (ed.), *Handbook for practice learning in social work and social care: Knowledge and theory*, 2nd edn, Jessica Kingsley, London, pp. 363–375.

Forrest, A. (2014). *The Forrest Review: Creating parity.* https://www.pmc.gov.au/sites/default/files/publications/Forrest-Review.pdf

Geldard, K. & Geldard, D. (2012). *Personal counseling skills: An integrative approach*, Charles C Thomas Publisher, Springfield.

Geneva Convention Relating to the Status of Refugees 1951 and Protocol 1967. United Nations, New York. United Nations Conference of Plenipotentiaries on the Status of Refugees and Stateless Persons, Geneva.

Gibbs, G. (1988). *Learning by doing. A guide to teaching and learning methods*, Oxford Polytechnic, London.

Gilbert, H., Rose, D. & Slade, M. (2008). The importance of relationships in mental health care: A qualitative study of service users' experiences of psychiatric hospital admission in the UK. *BMC Health Services Research, 8*(1), 92. https://doi.org/10.1186/1472-6963-8-92

Gilman, S.L. (1983). Why is schizophrenia "bizarre": An historical essay in the vocabulary of psychiatry. *Journal of the History of the Behavioral Sciences, 19*(2), 127–135.

Goldstein, M.M. & Bowers, D.G. (2015). The patient as consumer: Empowerment or commodification? Currents in contemporary bioethics. *The Journal of Law, Medicine & Ethics, 43*(1), 162–165.

Grant, M.J. & Booth, A. (2009). A typology of reviews: An analysis of 14 review types and associated methodologies. *Health Information & Libraries Journal, 26*(2), 91–108.

Greetham, B. (2018). *How to write better essays*, 4th edn, Red Globe Press, London.

Greig, A., Lewis, F. & White, K. (2003). *Inequality in Australia*, Cambridge University Press, Port Melbourne.

Harms, L. (2010). *Understanding human development: A multidimensional approach*, 2nd edn, Oxford University Press, South Melbourne.

Healy, K. (2012). Community work, in K. Healy (ed.), *Social work methods and skills: The essential foundations of practice*, Red Globe Press, London, pp. 169–201.

Hughes, M. & Heycox, K. (2010). *Older people, aging and social work: Knowledge for practice*, Allen & Unwin, Crows Nest.

Hutchinson, E. (2011). *Dimensions of human behaviour*, 4th edn, Sage Publications, California.

Ife, J. (2012). *Human rights and social work: Towards rights-based practice*, 3rd edn, Cambridge University Press, Port Melbourne.

Ife, J. (2016a). *Community development in an uncertain world: Vision, analysis and practice*, 2nd edn, Cambridge University Press, Port Melbourne.

Ife, J. (2016b). Human rights and social work: Beyond conservative law. *Journal of Human Rights and Social Work*, *1*(1), 3–8.

Immigration and Asylum Act. (1999). http://www.legislation.gov.uk/ukpga/1999/33/contents

International Federation of Social Workers. (2012). *Global standards*. https://www.ifsw.org/global-standards/

International Federation of Social Workers. (2014). *Global definition of social work*. https://www.ifsw.org/what-is-social-work/global-definition-of-social-work/

Jesson, J.K., Matheson, L. & Lacey, F.M. (2011). *Doing your literature review: Traditional and systematic techniques*, Sage, Thousand Oaks.

Kirkwood, S. (2018). History in the service of politics: Constructing narratives of history during the European refugee 'crisis.' *Political Psychology*, *49*, 1456–1470. https://doi.org/10.1111/pops.12511

Kitchener, B.A., Jorm, A.F. & Kelly, C.M. (2013). *Mental health first aid manual*, 3rd edn, Mental health first aid Australia, Melbourne.

Kolb, D.A. (1984). *Experiential learning: Experience as the source of learning and development*, Prentice Hall, Englewood Cliffs.

Kuhn, I.F. (2007). Abbreviations and acronyms in healthcare: When shorter isn't sweeter. *Pediatric Nursing*, *33*(5).

Kurland, D 2000, 'Critical reading, at its core, plain and simple', criticalreading.com

Kurland, D. (2010). *Reading and writing ideas as well as words*. criticalreading.com

Langton, M. (2017). The cashless debit card is working and it is vital – Here's why. *The Conversation*. https://theconversation.com/the-cashless-debit-card-trial-is-working-and-it-is-vital-heres-why-76951

Lynn, N. & Lea, S. (2003). 'A phantom menace and the new apartheid': The social construction of asylum-seekers in the United Kingdom. *Discourse & Society*, *14*(4), 425–452. https://doi.org/10.1177/0957926503014004002

Maclean, M., Sims, S., Bower, C., Leonard, H., Stanley, F. & O'Donnell, M. (2017). Maltreatment risk among children with disabilities. *Pediatrics*, *139*(4). https://doi.org/10.1542/peds.2016-1817

Macneil, C.A., Hasty, M.K., Conus, P. & Berk, M. (2012). Is diagnosis enough to guide interventions in mental health? Using case formulation in clinical practice. *BMC Medicine*, *10*(1), 111.

Mangen, A., Anda, L.G., Oxborough, G.H. & Brønnick, K. (2015). Handwriting versus keyboard writing: Effect on word recall. *Journal of Writing Research*, *7*(2).

Manthorpe, J. & Simcock, P. (2018). The role of social work in supporting people affected by Creutzfeldt–Jakob Disease (CJD): A scoping review. *The British Journal of Social Work*.

Mathioudakis, A., Rousalova, I., Gagnat, A.A., Saad, N. & Hardavella, G. (2016). How to keep good clinical records. *Breathe*, *12*(4), 369–373.

McCrickard, R. & Flynn, C. (2015). Responding to children of prisoners: The views of education professionals in Victoria. *Children Australia*, *41*(1), 39–48. https://doi.org/10.1017/cha.2015.15

McDonnell, C., Boan, A., Bradley, C., Seay, K., Charles, J. & Carpenter, L. (2018). Child maltreatment in autism spectrum disorder and intellectual disability: Results from a population-based sample. *The Journal of Child Psychology and Psychiatry*, *60*(5), 576–584. https://doi.org/10.1111/jcpp.12993

McInnis-Dittrich, K. (2014). *Social work with older adults: A biopsychosocial approach to assessment and intervention*, Pearson Education, Boston.

McKinnon, J. & Bay, U. (2013). Social work enabling sustainable ecological living. *Australian Social Work*, *66*(2), 153–155. https://doi.org/10.1080/0312407X.2013.795884

McLaughlin, H. (2009). What's in a name: 'Client', 'patient', 'customer', 'consumer', 'expert by experience', 'service user' – What's next? *The British Journal of Social Work, 39*(6), 1101–1117.

McLaughlin, H. (2012). *Understanding social work research*, 2nd edn, Sage, London.

Mehrotra, A. (2015). Refugee health. *InnovAiT, 8*(11), 668–676. https://doi.org/10.1177/1755738015596028

Mendes, P. (2008). Integrating social work and community-development practice in Victoria, Australia. *Asia Pacific Journal of Social Work and Development, 18*(1), 14–25.

Mendes, P. (2015). Compulsory income management: A policy solution looking for a problem? *ABC News,* 18 May 2015, viewed 14 November 2016.

Minderoo Foundation. (2017). Submission to the Senate Community Affairs Legislation Committee, 29 September.

Monks, K. (2017). *Annotated bibliographies: An overview.* Available at https://guides.lib.uw.edu/tacoma/annotated

Morgan, A. & Chadwick, H. (2009). *Key issues in domestic violence,* Summary paper, no. 7. https://aic.gov.au/publications/rip/rip07

Morgan, V.A., Waterrues, A., Jablensky, A., Mackinnon, A., McGrath, J.J. & Carr, V. (2012). People living with psychotic illness in 2010: The second Australian national survey of psychosis. *Australian and New Zealand Journal of Psychiatry, 46*(8), 735–752.

Mueller, P.A. & Oppenheimer, D.M. (2014). The pen is mightier than the keyboard: Advantages of longhand over laptop note taking. *Psychological Science, 25*(6), 1159–1168.

Mully, R. (2002). *Theoretical and conceptual considerations in challenging oppression: A critical social work approach,* Oxford University Press, Don Mills.

Munro, E. & Hardie, J. (2019). Why we should stop talking about objectivity and subjectivity in social work. *The British Journal of Social Work, 49*(2), 411–427.

Murray, J.S. (2000). Attachment theory and adjustment difficulties in siblings of children with cancer. *Issues in Mental Health Nursing, 21,* 149–169.

Myers, K., Kroes, S. & Petrakis, M. (2018). A foundation for dual diagnosis practice: Wisdom, tools and resources, in M. Petrakis (ed.), *Social work practice in health: An Introduction to contexts, theories and skills,* Allen & Unwin, Sydney, pp. 135–152.

Nagy, G. & Falk, D. (2000). Dilemmas in international and cross-cultural social work education. *International Social Work, 43*(1), 49–60.

Ndofor-Tah, C., Strang, A., Phillimore, J., Morrice, L., Michael, L., Wood, P. & Simmons, J. (2019). *Home Office Indicators of Integration Framework 2019.* https://assets.publishing.service.gov.uk/government/uploads/system/uploads/attachment_data/file/835573/home-office-indicators-of-integration-framework-2019-horr109.pdf

Nemec, P.B., Swarbrick, M. & Legere, L. (2015). Prejudice and discrimination from mental health service providers. *Psychiatric Rehabilitation Journal, 38*(2), 203.

Nguyen, T., Embrett, M.G., Barr, N.G., Mulvale, G.M., Vania, D.K., Randall, G.E. & DiRezze, B. (2017). Preventing youth from falling through the cracks between child/adolescent and adult mental health services: A systematic review of models of care. *Community Mental Health Journal, 53*(4), 375–382.

O'Donoghue, K., Nash, M. & Munford, R. (2005). Conclusion: Integrating theory in action, in M. Nash, R. Munford & K. O'Donoghue (eds.), *Social work theories in action,* Jessica Kingsley, London, pp. 251–260.

O'Loughlin, K. & Kendig, H. (2017). Attitudes to aging, in K. O'Loughlin, C. Browning & H. Kendig (eds.), *Ageing in Australia: Challenges and opportunities*, Springer Science + Business Media, New York, pp. 29–45.

Obst, D. & Kuder, M. (2009). Joint and double degree programs in the transatlantic context: A survey report, in D. Obst & M. Kuder (eds), *Joint and double degree programs: An emerging model for transatlantic exchange*, Institute of International Education, New York, pp. 1–17.

Our Watch, Australia's National Research Organisation for Women's Safety (ANROWS) and VicHealth. (2015). *Change the story: A shared framework for the primary prevention of violence against women and their children in Australia*, Our Watch, Melbourne.

Payne, M. (2012). *Citizenship social work with older people*, The Policy Press, Bristol.

Payne, M. (2014). *Modern social work theory*, 4th edn, Macmillan Education, London.

Pentland, J. (2009). A model from practice. *New Community Quarterly, 7*(2), 3–5.

Phillips, D. (1996). Medical professional dominance and client dissatisfaction: A study of doctor-patient interaction and reported dissatisfaction with medical care among female patients at four hospitals in Trinidad and Tobago. *Social Science & Medicine, 42*(10), 1419–1425.

Pincock, S. (2013). Young people's mental illness and substance abuse a 'two-way street'. *The ABC, 27* June. http://www.abc.net.au/health/features/stories/2013/06/27/3790687.htm

Preston-Shoot, M. (2003). A matter of record? *Practice, 15*(3), 31–50.

Prgomet, M., Douglas, H.E., Tariq, A., Georgiou, A., Armour, P. & Westbrook, J.I. (2017). The work of front line community aged care staff and the impact of a changing policy landscape and consumer-directed care. *British Journal of Social Work, 47*(1), 106–124.

Price, J. (2017). *Submission to the Senate Community Affairs Legislation Committee, 29* September.

Probst, B. (2013). 'Walking the tightrope:' Clinical social workers' use of diagnostic and environmental perspectives. *Clinical Social Work Journal, 41*(2), 184–191.

Rasmussen, B. (2015). A psychodynamic perspective on assessment and formulation, in *Critical thinking in clinical assessment and diagnosis*, Springer, Cham, pp. 151–169.

Ray, M., Milne, A., Beech, C., Phillips, J.E., Richards, S., Sullivan, M.P., Tanner, D. & Lloyd, L. (2015). Gerontological social work: Reflections on its role, purpose and value. *British Journal of Social Work, 45*(4), 1296–1312.

Refugee Council. (2018). *Asylum statistics annual trends.* https://www.refugeecouncil.org.uk/wp-content/uploads/2019/03/Asylum_Statistics_May_2018.pdf

Richards, S., Sullivan, M.P., Tanner, D., Beech, C., Milne, A., Ray, M., ... & Lloyd, L. (2014). On the edge of a new frontier: Is gerontological social work in the UK ready to meet twenty-first-century challenges? *The British Journal of Social Work, 44*(8), 2307–2324.

Roberts, J.Q. (2017). *Essentials of essay writing: What markers look for.* Red Globe Press, London.

Rogers, G. & Langevin, P. (2000). Negotiated learning contracts, in L. Cooper & L. Briggs (eds.), *Fieldwork in the human services: Theory and practice for field educators, practice teachers and supervisors*, Allen and Unwin, Sydney, pp. 216–226.

Rolfe, G., Freshwater, D. & Jasper, M. (2001). *Critical reflection in nursing and the helping professions: A user's guide*, Palgrave Macmillan, Basingstoke.

Ross, B., Pechenkina, E., Aeschliman, C. & Chase, A.M. (2017). Print versus digital texts: Understanding the experimental research and challenging the dichotomies. *Research in Learning Technology, 25*. https://doi.org/10.25304/rlt.v25.1976

Ross, B., Ta, B. & Grieve, A. (2019). Placement educators' experiences and perspectives of supervising international social work students in Australia. *Australian Social Work, 72*(2), 188–205. https://doi.org/10.1080/0312407X.2018.1557230

Ross, B., Ta, B. & Oliaro, L. (2020). Institutional responsibilities: Providing placement for international students. *Social Work Education, 39*(5), 665–680. https://doi.org/10.1080/02615479.2019.1703931

Rothery, M. (2016). Critical ecological systems theory, in N. Coady & P. Lehmann (eds.), *Theoretical perspectives for direct social work practice: A generalist-eclectic approach*, 3rd edn, Springer Publishing Company, New York, pp. 81–108.

Rubin, A. & Parrish, D.E. (2007). Challenges to the future of evidence-based practice in social work education. *Journal of Social Work Education, 43*(3), 405–28.

Rynderman, J. & Flynn, C. (2014). 'We didn't bring the treasure of Pharaoh': Skilled migrants' experiences of employment seeking and settling in Australia. *International Social Work, 59*(2), 268–283. https://doi.org/10.1177/0020872813519659

Sackett, D.L., Rosenberg, W.M., Gray, J.M., Haynes, R.B. & Richardson, W.S. (1996). *Evidence based medicine: What it is and what it isn't.*

Scanlan, J.N. & Still, M. (2013). Job satisfaction, burnout and turnover intention in occupational therapists working in mental health. *Australian Occupational Therapy Journal, 60*(5), 310–318.

Schön, D.A. (1991). *The reflective practitioner: How professionals think in action*, Arena, Ashgate Publishing, Farnham.

Scottish Government. (2018). *New Scots Refugee Integration Strategy 2018–2022*. https://www.gov.scot/publications/new-scots-refugee-integration-strategy-2018-2022/

Segal, L., Guy, S. & Furber, G. (2018). What is the current level of mental health service delivery and expenditure on infants, children, adolescents, and young people in Australia? *Australian & New Zealand Journal of Psychiatry, 52*(2), 163–172.

Shier, L.M., Graham, J.R. & Keogh, J.M. (2019). Social work and the emerging opioid epidemic: A literature review. *British Journal of Social Work, 0*, 1–19.

Shlonsky, A., Rose, D., Harris, J., Albers, B., Mildon, R., Wilson, S.J., Norvell, J. & Kissinger, L. (2016). *Literature review of prison-based mothers and children programs: Final report*. The University of Melbourne in partnership with Save the Children Australia and the Peabody Research Institute. https://www.corrections.vic.gov.au/publications-manuals-and-statistics/prison-based-mothers-and-children-programs

Silverstone, B. (2005). Social work with the older people of tomorrow: Restoring the person-in-situation. *Families in Society, 86*(3), 309–319.

Social Work England and the Professional Standards Guidance documents. (2019).

Sturge, G. (2019). *Migration statistics: How many asylum seekers and refugees are there in the UK*. House of Commons library: Research and analysis from impartial experts. House of Commons, London.

Swartz, S. (2006). The third voice: Writing case-notes. *Feminism & Psychology, 16*(4), 427–444.

Sword, H. (2011). *Stylish academic writing*, Harvard University Press, Cambridge, London.

Talbot, L. & Verrinder, G. (2008). Turn a stack of papers into a literature review: Useful tools for beginners. *Focus on Health Professional Education: A Multi-Disciplinary Journal, 10*(1), 51.

Taylor, B. (2017). *Where should we look to find Britain's 'tradition of welcome' of refugees?* Retrieved from https://refugeehistory.org/blog/2017/6/19/where-should-we-look-to-find-britains-tradition-of-welcome-of-refugees

The British Association of Social Workers (BASW). (2014). *The code of ethics for social work: Statement of principles.* https://www.basw.co.uk/system/files/resources/Code%20of%20Ethics%20Aug18.pdf

The Parliamentary Joint Committee on Human Rights (PJCHR), The Australian Government. (2015). https://www.aph.gov.au/joint_humanrights

Thomas, S.A. (2000). *How to write health sciences papers, dissertations and theses,* Churchill Livingstone, Edinburgh.

Thomas, M. & Buckmaster, L. (2010). *Paternalism in social policy: When is it justifiable?* Commonwealth of Australia. https://www.aph.gov.au/About_Parliament/Parliamentary_Departments/Parliamentary_Library/pubs/rp/rp1011/11rp08

Thomson, P. (2016). Five ways to structure a literature review [blog]. https://pat-thomson.net/2016/08/29/five-ways-to-structure-a-literature-review/

UNHCR. (2017). *Global trends.* https://www.unhcr.org/globaltrends2017/

UNHCR. (2020a). *Asylum seeker.* https://www.unhcr.org/en-au/asylum-seekers.html

UNHCR. (2020b). *What is a refugee?* https://www.unhcr.org/en-au/what-is-a-refugee.html

Walker, H. (2008). *Studying for your social work degree,* Learning Matters Ltd., Exeter.

Western, D. (2018). Women and domestic and family violence, in M. Petrakis (ed.), *Social work practice in health: An introduction to contexts, theories and skills,* Allen & Unwin, Crows Nest, pp. 83–99.

White, M. & Morgan, A. (2004). *Narrative therapy with children and their families,* Dulwich Centre Publications, Adelaide.

Wilson, G. & Campbell, A. (2013). Developing social work education: Academic perspectives. *British Journal of Social Work, 43,* 1005–1023.

Wissink, I., van Gurt, E., Moonen, G., Stams, G.J. & Hendriks, J. (2014). Sexual abuse involving children with an intellectual disability (ID): A narrative review. *Research in Development Disabilities, 36,* 20–35. https://doi.org/10.1016/j.ridd.2014.09.007

World Health Organisation. (2012). *Understanding and addressing violence against women – Intimate partner violence.* https://www.who.int/reproductivehealth/topics/violence/vaw_series/en/

World Health Organisation. (2017). *Fact sheet: Violence against women.* https://www.who.int/news-room/fact-sheets/detail/violence-against-women

Wrigley, S. (2017). Avoiding 'de-plagiarism': Exploring the affordances of handwriting in the essay-writing process. *Active Learning in Higher Education.* https://doi.org/10.1177/1469787417735611

Young, A. (1990). *Justice and the politics of difference,* Princeton University Press, Princeton.

Zastrow, C.H. & Kirst-Ashman, K. (2010). *Understanding human behavior and the social environment,* 8th edn, Cengage Learning, Southbank.

Index